# Data Structures and Programming Techniques

# Data Structures and Programming Techniques

**HERMANN A. MAURER**

*University of Karlsruhe*

Translated by
**Camille C. Price**

*Stephen F. Austin State University*

**Prentice-Hall, Inc.,** Englewood Cliffs, N.J.   07632

*Library of Congress Cataloging in Publication Data*

Maurer, Hermann A     1941–
    Data structures and programming techniques.

      Translation of Datenstrukturen und Programmierver-
fahren.
    Bibliography: P.
    Includes index.
    1. Electronic digital computers—Programming.
2. Data structures (Computer science)   I. Title.
QA76.6 M38313      001.6′42      76–22758
ISBN 0–13–197038–0

A translation of Dr. Maurer's
*Datenstrukturen und Programmierverfahren*
© by B. G. Teubner, Stuttgart.
The sole authorized English translation of
the original German edition published in
the series *Leitfäden der Angewandten
Mathematik und Mechanik*, edited by Dr. Gortler.

10   9   8   7   6   5   4   3

Printed in the United States of America

Prentice-Hall International, Inc., *London*
Prentice-Hall of Australia Pty. Limited, *Sydney*
Prentice-Hall of Canada, Ltd., *Toronto*
Prentice-Hall of India Private Limited, *New Delhi*
Prentice-Hall of Japan, Inc., *Tokyo*
Prentice-Hall of Southeast Asia Pte. Ltd., *Singapore*
Whitehall Books Limited, *Wellington, New Zealand*

# Contents

# Preface

This book is a translation from the German of a book which was developed from a course conducted by Professor Dr. H. Maurer at the University of Karlsruhe. The lecture notes of the course were thoroughly revised and expanded, in collaboration with H. W. Six, into the final form which was published as *Datenstrukturen und Programmierverfahren*.

In this book, techniques will be presented which allow data to be organized in ways suited to problem solving using a digital computer. Such techniques can contribute to the design of efficient, well-arranged programs and therefore ought to be thoroughly familiar to every computer scientist.

The book is self-contained and, except for an acquaintance with some programming language, no specific knowledge of mathematics or computer science is presupposed.

A few remarks are in order on the notational conventions followed in the book. The notations introduced in Sections 1.2 and 1.3 and used consistently thereafter permit a uniform and precise description of the subject matter. The presentation is, however, sufficiently straight-forward so that the book can be used by the casual reader without requiring a careful study of the notational scheme.

Program segments are used throughout the book to provide a description of the algorithms and to illustrate the manipulation of data structures. The use of an assembler language would allow immediate access to the individual memory locations, however because of the unavailability of a widely-known standard assembler language, and for reasons of convenience, a high-level language is used instead. A very simple subset of the PL/I language—actually only a small extension of the Fortran language—is used so that a reader who is only slightly familiar with programming languages can easily follow the programs. The author wishes to thank Miss S. Reiniger for testing the PL/I programs.

*Nacogdoches, Texas*                                                    Camille C. Price

# Data Structures and Programming Techniques

# Introduction

The efficiency, clarity, and complexity of a program for the solution of a given problem depends substantially on the organization imposed on the data to be used, i.e., on the selected data structure. It is the purpose of this book to present the most important data structures, to explain under what conditions which data structures can be used most effectively, and to indicate which programming techniques are most desirable for working with a particular data structure.

In the study of data structures, it is necessary not only to define the concept of a data structure itself but also to state how the data structure can be stored and manipulated. With this purpose in mind, several considerations are appropriate. First, using the general definition of the concept of a data structure, a method will be given for representing a data structure graphically. Then a model of computer memory will be introduced, along with a way of graphically representing the memory locations. With this foundation established, methods of storing data structures can be presented. The actual descriptions of algorithms for manipulating data structures stored in a computer are given using PL/I programs in which the memory locations in the computer memory model are realized using declarations of PL/I variables.

The general foundations referred to are the subject of Chapter 1. Chapter 2 is dedicated to common and simple data structures known as *lists*. In Chapter 3 the particularly important tree structures are emphasized, a topic often treated too lightly. Then in Chapter 4 two types of complex data structures are introduced.

# 1 A Model for the Manipulation of Data Structures

## Section 1.1 Mathematical Preliminaries

**Definition 1.1.1** (Sets and Set Operations) If a set M consists of the n elements $a_1, a_2, \ldots, a_n$, where $n \geqslant 0$, then the set is said to be *finite* and is written $M = \{a_1, a_2, \ldots, a_n\}$. If all the elements of the set M have property P, then M may be written as $\{x \mid x$ has property P$\}$. The set containing no elements is called the *empty* set and is denoted by $\varnothing$. A set that is not finite is said to be *infinite*.

If M is a set, and a is an element of M, then we write $a \in M$; if a is not an element of M, we indicate this by $a \notin M$. If M and N are sets, then M is a *subset* of N, written $M \subseteq N$ or $N \supseteq M$, if every element of M is also an element of N. The set M is called a *proper* subset of N, written $M \subset N$ or $N \supset M$, if $M \subseteq N$ and there is at least one element in N that is not an element of M. Two sets M and N are said to be equal, written $M = N$, if $M \subseteq N$ and $N \subseteq M$.

The *union*, *intersection*, and *difference* of two sets M and N, written $M \cup N$, $M \cap N$, and $M - N$, respectively, are defined as follows:

$$M \cup N = \{x \mid x \in M \text{ or } x \in N \text{ or both}\}$$

$$M \cap N = \{x \mid x \in M \text{ and } x \in N\}$$

$$M - N = \{x \mid x \in M \text{ and } x \notin N\}.$$

Two sets are said to be *disjoint* if their intersection is empty. If M is a set, then the sequence $M_1, M_2, \ldots, M_n$ of pairwise disjoint sets is called a *partitioning* of M if $M = M_1 \cup M_2 \cup \cdots \cup M_n$. a) if $x$ is in $m_i$, it is not in $m_j$, $j \neq i$. (disjoint)
b) $m_i$ is a subset of M.

**Definition 1.1.2** (Tuples and Sequences) An n-tuple A of elements $a_1, a_2, \ldots, a_n$, where $n \geqslant 0$, is a sequence of elements of length n and is written either as $A = (a_1, a_2, \ldots, a_n)$ or as $A = a_1, a_2, \ldots, a_n$. Suppose $A = (a_1, a_2, \ldots, a_n)$ is an n-

2

tuple; then if $b = a_i$, we call b the *ith component* of A, where i is the position of b in A. We write this symbolically as $\pi_A b = i$ or simply $\pi b = i$.    *b = i$\underline{th}$ component of n-tuple A.*

The notational conventions for sets are often applied to sequences. In particular, we speak of an empty sequence (a null-tuple) $\varnothing$; we write $a \in A$ or $a \notin A$, depending on whether a is or is not in the sequence A; and we say two sequences A and B are disjoint if $\{x \,|\, x \in A\} \cap \{x \,|\, x \in B\} = \varnothing$. A sequence B is a subsequence of a sequence A if B is formed by the removal of n elements from A, where $n \geqslant 0$. (Thus, 3, 4, 2 is a subsequence of 6, 3, 0, 12, 4, 2, 7 but not of 6, 4, 0, 0, 12, 3, 7, 2). Two sequences A and B are *equal*, written $A = B$, if A is a subsequence of B and vice versa.

**Definition 1.1.3** (Cartesian Products and Relations) The Cartesian product of two sets M and N, written $M \times N$, is defined to be a set of ordered pairs as follows:

$$M \times N = \{(x, y) \,|\, x \in M \text{ and } y \in N\}.$$

If M and N are sets, then every subset of $M \times N$ is called a *relation* on $M \times N$ (or on M if $M = N$).

Let r be a relation on M. If $(a, b) \in r$, then a is called the *predecessor* of b, and b is the *successor* of a, relative to r. To specify that $(a, b) \in r$, we write $a\, r\, b$; and if $(a, b) \notin r$, we write $a\, \not{r}\, b$.

The *domain* and *range* of a relation r are written symbolically domain (r) and range (r) and are defined as:

$$\text{domain (r)} = \{x \,|\, (x, y) \in r\}$$

and

$$\text{range (r)} = \{y \,|\, (x, y) \in r\}.$$

The *inverse* of a relation r, written $r^{-1}$, is defined by

$$r^{-1} = \{(y, x) \,|\, (x, y) \in r\}.$$

| Relation | = | > | < | ≥ | ≤ |
|---|---|---|---|---|---|
| reflexive | ✓ | | | ✓ | ✓ |
| anti-reflexive | | ✓ | ✓ | | |
| symmetric | ✓ | | | | |
| transitive | ✓ | ✓ | ✓ | ✓ | ✓ |

A relation r on M is called ①*reflexive* if, for every $a \subset M$, $(a, a) \in r$. The relation is called ②*antireflexive* if $(a, a) \in r$ does not hold for any $a \in M$. A relation is ③*symmetric* if $(a, b) \in r$ whenever $(b, a) \in r$; a relation is ④*transitive* if $(a, c) \in r$ whenever $(a, b) \in r$ and $(b, c) \in r$.

**Definition 1.1.4** (Basis of a Transitive Relation) Let r be a transitive relation on M, and $b \subseteq r$. The relation b is called a *basis* of r (and r is called the *transitive hull* of b) if the following holds:

$$r = \{(x, y) \,|\, \text{there are elements } x_0, x_1, x_2, \ldots, x_n \text{ in M,}$$
$$\text{where } n \geqslant 1, \text{ such that (a) } x_0 = x, \text{ (b) } x_n = y,$$
$$\text{and (c) } (x_{i-1}, x_i) \in b \text{ for } i = 1, 2, \ldots, n\}.$$

**Definition 1.1.5** (Equivalence Relations and Equivalence Classes) A relation r on M is called an *equivalence relation* if r is reflexive, symmetric, and transitive. If r is an equivalence relation and $(a, b) \in r$, then a and b are said to be *equivalent*.

If M is a set with equivalance relation r, then M is the union of pairwise disjoint sets. These sets are called *equivalence classes*.

**Definition 1.1.6** (Partial Ordering and Topological Sorting) A relation r on M is called a *partial ordering* if r is transitive and antireflexive. If $A = a_1, a_2, \ldots, a_n$ is a sequence of elements of M and if $(a_i, a_j) \in r$ for $i < j$, then A is *topologically sorted relative to r*.

    *Note:* It should be observed that in every finite set with partial ordering r there exists at least one element having no predecessor and at least one element having no successor.

**Definition 1.1.7** (Total Ordering and Sorting) A relation r on M is a *total ordering* if it is transitive and if conditions a and b below are satisfied:

    (a) If $(a, b) \in r$ and $(b, a) \in r$, then $a = b$.
    (b) For any two elements a and b, either $(a, b) \in r$ or $(b, a) \in r$, or both.

A sequence $A = a_1, a_2, \ldots, a_n$ of elements from M is *sorted* or *ordered* (relative to r) if $(a_i, a_{i+1}) \in r$ for $1 \leqslant i \leqslant n - 1$.

**Definition 1.1.8** (Minimum and Maximum) If M is a set of numbers, then if there exists a smallest number in M, it is called the *minimum* of M and is denoted $\min(M)$. Likewise $\max(M)$ denotes the *maximum* of M and $\max(M) = -\min\{-x \mid x \in M\}$.

**Definition 1.1.9** (Function) A relation f on $M \times N$ is called a *function* from M to N, written symbolically $f: M \longrightarrow N$, if for every $a \in M$ there is exactly one $b \in N$ such that $(a, b) \in f$. Instead of $(a, b) \in f$ we often write $f(a) = b$ or simply $fa = b$. A function $f: M \longrightarrow N$ is called *one-to-one* if whenever $a \neq b$, it follows that $f(a) \neq f(b)$.

## Exercises

**1.1.1**  Let r be the relation:

    $r = \{(1, 2), (2, 3), (3, 5), (3, 4), (1, 3), (1, 4), (2, 4), (2, 5), (1, 5)\}$.

(a)  Show that r is transitive.
(b)  Is r an equivalence relation?
(c)  Determine a basis b on r with four elements.

**1.1.2**  Let r be a transitive relation with basis b:

    $b = \{(1, 4), (2, 5), (5, 8), (0, 3), (3, 6), (6, 9), (4, 1), (8, 2), (9, 0)\}$.

(a)  Is r an equivalence relation?
(b)  Determine the range of r.

**1.1.3**   Let r be the relation:

$$r = \{(3, 1), (3, 2), (4, 6), (4, 7), (5, 4), (5, 6), (5, 7), (6, 7)\} \text{ on } M = \{1, 2, 3, 4, 5, 6, 7\}$$

(a)   Show that r is a partial ordering.
(b)   Determine a topologically sorted sequence of elements of M.

## Section 1.2   Data Structures and Ways of Representing Data Structures

Computers are used extensively in the processing of collections of data. A data collection may be thought of as a collection of data *elements* or *nodes* that have n-tuples of character strings as values. The data elements of a data collection can be analyzed and altered in various ways using a computer.

Some typical examples of values of nodes are triples of character strings, representing the name, quantity on hand, and identification number of a part of a piece of machinery; pairs of numbers defining the arguments and corresponding function values of a certain function; 4-tuples of character strings indicating the name, address, bank affiliation, and serial number of a contractor; and so on.

It is often of interest to know how the nodes in a data collection are related to one another. For example, where nodes represent parts of a piece of machinery, it may be meaningful to indicate that one part is a constituent part of another or that all parts with certain part numbers are to be handled together when reordering is done. Where nodes define function values, each node may be associated with the node having the next largest function value. If the nodes represent contractors, it may be useful to indicate that certain ones are working in the same city.

Connections between nodes of a data collection may be indicated by using relations. The combination of nodes and relations is called a *data structure*.

**Definition 1.2.1** (Data Structure) A *data structure* B is a pair B = (K, R), where K is a finite set of nodes and R is a finite set of relations on K. The value[1] of a node $k \in K$ is denoted by $\omega k$ and is an n-tuple, $n \geqslant 0$, of character strings; $\omega_i k$ denotes the ith component of the (value of the) node k. This is expressed symbolically as $\omega k = (\omega_1 k, \omega_2 k, \ldots, \omega_n k) =$ the "value" of the node $k \in K$.

**Definition 1.2.2** (Notational Conventions) Let B = (K, R) be a data structure, with $r \in R$ a relation and k, k′ nodes. If $(k, k') \in r$, then we say that k′ is a successor of k, k is a predecessor of k′, k and k′ are consecutive, and k points to k′ (all relative to r). If there is no node k′ such that $(k, k') \in r$, then k is called an *end node* (relative to r); if there is no node k′ such that $(k', k) \in r$, then k is called a *start node* (relative to r). Otherwise k is an *inner node*. If k is a node and $\omega k = \varnothing$ (i.e., k is a null-tuple), then k is called a *pointer*. A pointer which points to a start node is called a *start pointer*

---

[1] Where no misunderstanding is likely, no distinction will be made between a node and the value of the node.

and one which points to an end node is called an *end pointer*. A data structure B is said to be *manipulated* if the value of a node is determined or changed or if a node is added to or removed from B.

**Definition 1.2.3** (Graphical Representation of Data Structures) Let $B = (K, R)$ be a data structure. A graphical representation of B is obtained as follows. For every node $k \in K$, a figure is drawn: a circle if $\omega k = \varnothing$ and a rectangle containing $\omega k$ otherwise. If a node k points to another node $k'$ (relative to a relation r), then the figures corresponding to k and $k'$ are connected by a directed line segment. For different relations we choose different types of line segments. Sometimes it is useful to assign names to the figures corresponding to the nodes; such names are written outside the figures.

**Example 1.2.1** The data structure $B = (K, R)$ with 10 nodes $K = \{k_1, k_2, \ldots, k_{10}\}$ and two relations $R = \{T, N\}$, where

$\omega k_1 = $ (machine, 40, 612)

$\omega k_2 = $ (motor, 2, 802)

$\omega k_3 = $ (block, 3, 105)

$\omega k_4 = $ (filter, 2, 117)

$\omega k_5 = $ (tank, 10, 118)

$\omega k_6 = $ (brakes, 60, 230)

$\omega k_7 = $ (ignition, 30, 408)

$\omega k_8 = $ (housing, 17, 507)

$\omega k_9 = $ (frame, 40, 230)

$\omega k_{10} = $ (plates, 1, 702)

$T = \{(k_1, k_2), (k_1, k_8), (k_2, k_3), (k_2, k_7), (k_3, k_4), (k_3, k_5), (k_3, k_6),$
$\qquad (k_8, k_9), (k_8, k_{10})\}$

$N = \{(k_{10}, k_4), (k_4, k_2), (k_2, k_3)\}$

is displayed graphically in Fig. 1.2.1. Since, for example, $(k_3, k_5) \in T$ but $(k_3, k_8) \notin T$, there is a line, marked with T, from node $k_3$ to node $k_5$ but no line from $k_3$ to $k_8$.

The given data structure can be thought of as a rough description of a certain *machine*. Each node k corresponds to a particular part: $\omega_1 k$ is understood to be the name, $\omega_2 k$ is the number of parts on hand, and $\omega_3 k$ represents the part identification number. The relation T explains the composition of the piece of equipment, namely that it consists of two main components: the *motor* and the *housing*, the latter consisting of the *frame* and the *plates*, and so on. The relation N applies to the nodes k, where $\omega_2 k \leqslant 3$, that is, the parts with small quantities on hand. Note that $\omega_2 k \leqslant \omega_2 k'$, where k is a predecessor of $k'$ relative to N.

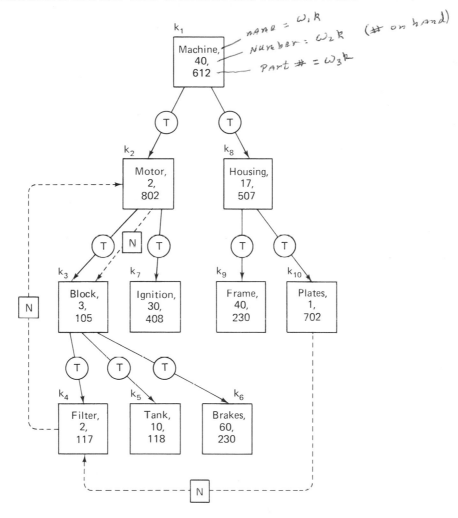

**Figure 1.2.1**

Figure 1.2.2 differs from Fig. 1.2.1 in the addition of a start pointer st (relative to T) and a start pointer sn (relative to N). This data structure describes not only the nodes $k_1, k_2, \ldots, k_{10}$ but also the nodes st and sn, where $\omega st = \omega sn = \varnothing$; in addition to the relations T and N, it also shows the relations $p_T = \{(st, k_1)\}$ and $p_N = \{(sn, k_{10})\}$.

In actual practice, the description of a piece of equipment such as the one just discussed would necessitate a significantly more complicated data structure; not only would the number of nodes be greater and the value of each node consist of more components, but also additional relations to relate, for example, price and terms of a contract, would be of interest. It is sometimes more convenient to describe a situation using several data structures, each having only a few relations, instead of one

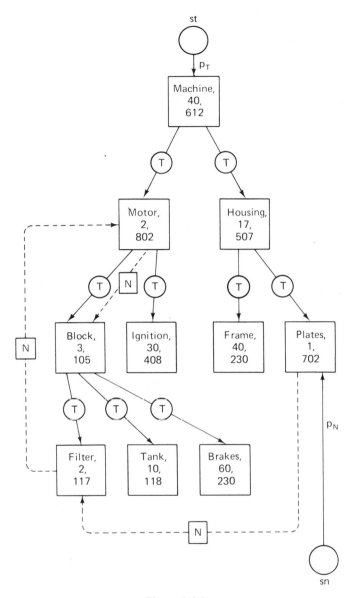

**Figure 1.2.2**

data structure having many relations. With this in mind, our further investigation of data structures will be restricted to those with a small number of relations.

*Remarks*

There is no standard definition for the notion of a *data structure*. The definition given here, using relations, is one of several in which relations play an important role.

## Exercises

**1.2.1**  Graphically represent the data structure $B = (K, R)$ with nine nodes $k_i$ $(1 \leqslant i \leqslant 9)$ and three relations $R = \{N, T, Z\}$, where $\omega k_i = i$.

$$N = \{(k_1, k_3), (k_1, k_9), (k_2, k_3), (k_3, k_1), (k_3, k_2), (k_4, k_5), (k_6, k_8)\}$$

$$T = \{(k_4, k_5), (k_3, k_4), (k_7, k_8), (k_1, k_3), (k_8, k_9), (k_5, k_7)\}$$

$$Z = \{(k_i, k_j) \mid i + j = 7\}.$$

**1.2.2**  Determine all start nodes and end nodes relative to relations N, T, and Z in Exercise 1.2.1.

## Section 1.3  Methods of Storing Data Structures

When considering the actual storage and manipulation of data structures using computers, it is useful to begin by constructing a theoretical model for the storage of the data structure. Each memory location in such a model may be visualized as consisting of two parts, the *data field* and the *pointer field*. The data field serves to store the value of a node k. A pointer field can be used in the realization of a relation r, that is, to indicate the memory addresses of all those locations containing successors of k (relative to r). An *indicator*, which can be either a 0 or a 1, may be associated with every pointer field to give additional information about the data structure.

**Definition 1.3.1**  (Memory) A *memory* consists of a finite number q of *memory locations*, numbered from 1 to q. The location of a memory cell z is called the *address* and is denoted symbolically with $\alpha z$. Conversely, if a memory location with address t is denoted by $\sigma t$, then $\alpha \sigma t = t$ and $\sigma \alpha z = z$. A memory location z consists of a *data field*, whose value is denoted $\delta z$, and $m \geqslant 0$ *pointer fields*. The ith pointer field of a location z defines a *value*, denoted $\rho_i z$, and an indicator, denoted $\tau_i z$. Frequently the indicator is 0 and need not be explicitly expressed.

The value[2] of a pointer field $\rho_i z$ is a t-tuple, $t \geqslant 1$, of whole numbers. The jth component of $\rho_i z$ is denoted by $\rho_{ij} z$. The value of a data field $\delta z$ is an n-tuple, $n \geqslant 0$, of character strings, where the jth component is denoted by $\delta_j z$. Unless otherwise specifically stated, the value of a pointer field $\rho_i z$ consists of only one component, and $\rho_{i1} = \rho_i$. If only one pointer field $\rho_1$ is being considered, then we simply write $\rho$.

**Definition 1.3.2**  (Storing a Data Structure) A data structure $B = (K, R)$ is *stored* by uniquely associating every $k \in K$ with a memory location z, where $\delta z = \omega k$. The memory location z associated with a node k is denoted by $\xi k$, and $\xi k = z$.

**Definition 1.3.3**  (Notational Conventions) Two memory locations z and z' are *consecutive* if $\alpha z' = 1 + \alpha z$. A memory location z is to the left of z' and z' is to the

---

[2]Where no misunderstanding is likely, no distinction will be made between a pointer field and its value or between a pointer component and its value.

right of z if $\alpha z < \alpha z'$. A set M of consecutive memory locations is called a *storage domain*. The *first* location z in a storage domain M, $\alpha z = \min \{\alpha z'' \,|\, z'' \in M\}$, is called the *left end* of the storage domain; the *last* location z' of the storage domain, $\alpha z' = \max \{z'' \,|\, z'' \in M\}$, is the *right end* of the storage domain. A memory location z is said to *point* to a memory location z' (with respect to the ith pointer field or the data field) if the address $\alpha z'$ of z' appears in the ith pointer field or, respectively, the data field of z. If $B = (K, R)$ is a stored data structure and r is a relation, then the nodes K are said to be stored *in* the memory locations $\xi K = \{\xi k \,|\, k \in K\}$, and the terms *node* and *memory location* may be used interchangeably as long as no misunderstanding is possible. For example, the *address* of a node k, symbolically $\alpha k$, is the address of the memory location corresponding to the node k; the value of the ith pointer field of a node k is written symbolically as either $\rho_i k$ or $\rho_i \xi k$. Start locations, end locations, and inner locations (relative to a relation r) correspond to start nodes, end nodes, and inner nodes, respectively.

Definition 1.3.2 is only concerned with storing the values of nodes. We must also consider the realization of the relations; this is done in one of two ways: *sequentially* or *linked*.

**Definition 1.3.4** (Sequential Realization of a Relation) Let $B = (K, R)$ be a stored data structure. A relation r is said to be realized *sequentially* (with step size s) if, for every pair of nodes $(k, k') \in r$, $\alpha k' = \alpha k + s$ holds. In sequential realization with step size s, consecutive nodes are stored in locations whose addresses differ from one another by s. The step size is usually 1 and, in that case, need not be expressed explicitly.

**Definition 1.3.5** (Linked Realization of a Relation) Let $B = (K, R)$ be a stored data structure. A relation r is realized as a *linked* structure (relative to the ith pointer field) if, for every pair of nodes $(k, k') \in r$, $\alpha k' \in \rho_i k$ holds. If $\alpha k' = \rho_i k$ for every pair of nodes $(k, k') \in r$, then the linking is called *linear*. In the linked realization of a relation, the ith pointer field of a node k gives the addresses of all successors of k.

If a relation r is sequentially realized, then we say that the corresponding nodes are sequentially stored. If a relation r is realized as a linked structure, then we say that the corresponding nodes are linked in the memory.

**Definition 1.3.6** (Graphical Representation of Memory Locations) Let Z be a set of memory locations. A graphical representation of Z may be obtained as follows: For every $z \in Z$ with m pointer fields, a rectangle is drawn that is divided from left to right into $m + 2$ segments. The first segment contains $\alpha z$; the second contains $\delta z$; and the remaining m segments contain the values of the pointer fields $\rho_1 z$, $\rho_2 z, \ldots, \rho_m z$. If an indicator $\tau_i z$ is not equal to zero, then a star is attached to the corresponding pointer field. If, in a rectangular segment G of a memory location z, the address $\alpha z'$ of another memory location appears, then G can be connected to the first rectangular segment of memory location z' with a directed line.

For simplification, some of the entries in the rectangular segments corresponding to $\alpha z$, $\delta z$, or $\rho_1 z, \ldots, \rho_m z$ will occasionally be omitted. In some cases, it will be appropriate to supply names to the rectangles or rectangular segments corresponding to the memory locations. These names will be written outside the rectangles or rectangular segments.

**Example 1.3.1** A possible method of storing the data structure $B = (K, R)$ with five nodes $K = \{k_1, k_2, k_3, k_4, k_5\}$ and the relation $r = \{(k_1, k_2), (k_2, k_3), (k_3, k_4), (k_4, k_5)\}$, $\omega k_1 = \text{THAT}$, $\omega k_2 = \text{THE}$, $\omega k_3 = \text{THIS}$, $\omega k_4 = \text{US}$, $\omega k_5 = \text{WE}$, is illustrated in Fig. 1.3.1. The relation r is realized as a linked structure since $\rho k_1 = \alpha k_2$, $\rho k_2 = \alpha k_3$, $\rho k_3 = \alpha k_4$, $\rho k_4 = \alpha k_5$. Note that $\rho k_5$ is not used and is set to 0.

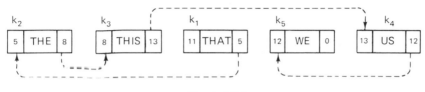

**Figure 1.3.1**

The words $\omega k_1$, $\omega k_2$, $\omega k_3$, $\omega k_4$, $\omega k_5$ are alphabetically ordered, in the sense that each memory location z points to that memory location z' which contains the word which is next in alphabetical order.

**Example 1.3.2** Three possible methods of storing the data structure in Fig. 1.2.1 are presented in Fig. 1.3.2, 1.3.3, and 1.3.4. In the method shown in Fig. 1.3.2, neither of the relations T and N is realized. In Fig. 1.3.3, both relations T and N are shown

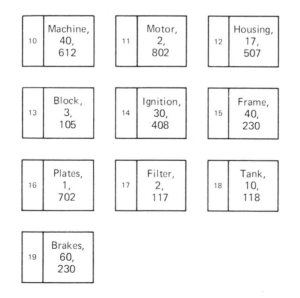

**Figure 1.3.2**

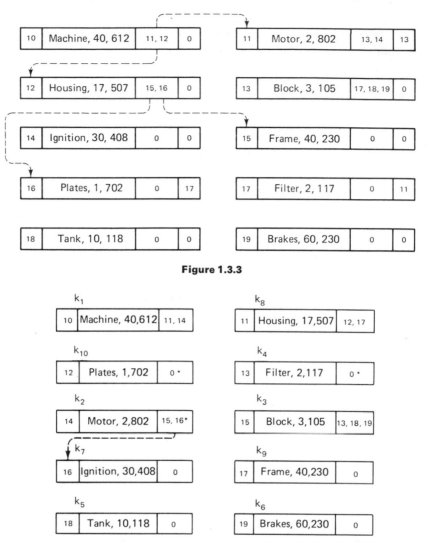

**Figure 1.3.3**

**Figure 1.3.4**

as linked structures, with T as the first pointer field and N as the second. Finally, in the method of Fig. 1.3.4, the relation T is realized as a linked structure and N as a sequential one. Notice that an indicator $\neq 0$ is specified with a star. In this example, a nonzero indicator in the first pointer field of a node k means that k has a successor relative to N. In Fig. 1.3.4, $\alpha k_4 = \alpha k_{10} + 1$ since $(k_{10}, k_4) \in N$; $\alpha k_2 = \alpha k_4 + 1$ since $(k_4, k_2) \in N$; and $\alpha k_3 = \alpha k_2 + 1$ since $(k_2, k_3) \in N$. Since $(k_1, k_8) \in T$, it follows that $\alpha k_8 \in \rho k_1$. The memory location $z = \sigma 14$ points to memory location $z' = \sigma 16$ because the address of $z'$ appears in the pointer field of z. The line from z to $z'$ is then allowed, as specified in Def. 1.3.6. Other lines are similarly allowed.

## Exercises

**1.3.1**   Give a possible method of graphically storing structure B defined in Exercise 1.2.1, in which relation T is realized sequentially and relation N is realized as a linked structure.

**1.3.2**   For the storage method shown in Fig. 1.3.3, determine (a) $\delta\sigma 18$, (b) $\delta_2\sigma\rho_{12}$ $\sigma 13$, (c) $\delta_1\sigma\rho_{12}\sigma\rho_2\sigma 11$.

## Section 1.4   Programming Considerations

The memory model defined in Sec. 1.3 corresponds only in theory to storage in an actual computer. In particular, according to Def. 1.3.1 a memory location may have to contain potentially very extensive data fields (to store arbitrary tuples of arbitrarily long character strings) and arbitrarily many pointer fields having arbitrarily many components. In contrast to this, we must consider the storage capacity of the smallest addressable unit of a computer; such a unit is often called a *computer word* or a *memory word*. In general, computer words are of fixed length and are suitable only for the storage of small data items. One memory cell in the memory model will then usually correspond to a block of computer words in an actual computer.

In the realization of a memory location z having a data field or a pointer field whose value consists of n components, where $n > 1$, it is often appropriate in an actual computer to make use of *indirect allocation* for the data field (or pointer field) in question. Here, roughly speaking, the n values $a_1, a_2, \ldots, a_n$ of a single data field are assigned to n actual memory locations with only one value in the data field. More precisely, let $B = (K, R)$ be a data structure consisting of the n nodes $k_1, k_2, \ldots, k_n$ with values $\omega k_i = a_i$, where $1 \leqslant i \leqslant n$, and a single relation $r \in R$ with

$$r = \{(k_{i-1}, k_i) \mid 2 \leqslant i \leqslant n\}.$$

The data structure B is stored (sequentially or linearly linked) in memory locations $z_1, z_2, \ldots, z_n$ and the value of the data field (or pointer field) of memory location z is replaced by $\alpha z_1$ so that z points to $z_1$, i.e., to that memory location in which the start node of B is stored.

**Example 1.4.1**   Figure 1.4.1(b) illustrates an indirect allocation of the data field of the memory location shown in Fig. 1.4.1(a). Notice that memory location z in (b) points to the first of four consecutive memory locations, in which the four components of the data field of memory location z in (a) are stored. Thus, $\delta_1 z$ with z in (a) is equivalent to $\delta\sigma\delta z$ with z in (b); $\delta_3 z$ with z in (a) is equivalent to $\delta\sigma(\delta z + 2)$ with z in (b). Figure 1.4.2(b) shows an indirect allocation of two of the three pointer fields of the memory location given in Fig. 1.4.2(a). Here $\rho_{12} z$ with z in Fig. 1.4.2(a) is equivalent to $\delta\sigma\rho_1\sigma\rho_1 z$ with z in Fig. 1.4.2(b).

On the basis of the discussion above, it should be clear that our theoretical model of a memory can be realized in an actual computer without difficulty.

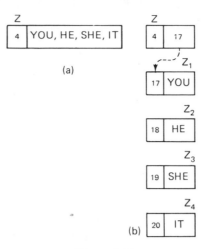

(a)

(b)

**Figure 1.4.1**

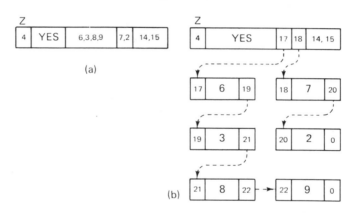

(a)

(b)

**Figure 1.4.2**

Techniques for the storage and manipulation of data structures will be illustrated by programs written in a simple subset of the PL/I programming language. To improve the readability of the PL/I programs, key words will be printed in boldface type.

In addition to the usual built-in functions of PL/I (such as MOD, ABS, FLOOR, LENGTH, etc.) the following three built-in functions are assumed to be available:

NUMBER (X):   Yields *true* if and only if the character expression X is an arithmetic constant.

CONV (X):   Yields the value of the arithmetic constant represented by the character expression X.

ERROR (N):   Prints an error message, with the number N, and causes the calling program to terminate.

A set of similar memory locations numbered from p to q is obtained in PL/I by a declaration of several arrays (in general one array for each component of the data field and each component of every pointer field). The elements of the arrays are numbered from p to q. Unless explicitly agreed otherwise, the meaning of the array names can be inferred from the following list.

D:　　Data field consisting of only one component; corresponds to $\delta$ and $\omega$.
D1:　　First component of the data field; corresponds to $\delta_1$ and $\omega_1$.
D2:　　Second component of the data field; corresponds to $\delta_2$ and $\omega_2$.
.
.
.

R:　　A single pointer field consisting of only one component; corresponds to $p$.
R1:　　First pointer field consisting of only one component; corresponds to $p_1$.
R11:　First component of the first pointer field; corresponds to $p_{11}$.
R12:　Second component of the first pointer field; corresponds to $p_{12}$.
.
.
.

R2:　　Second pointer field consisting of only one component; corresponds to $p_2$.
R21:　First component of the second pointer field; corresponds to $p_{21}$.
.
.
.

Since the data field of memory locations is not used for the storage of pointers, pointers are often treated separately from other nodes in programming. In particular, for pointers with only one pointer field and only one component in the pointer field, a variable is often declared to be of type **FIXED BIN**; the value of the variable gives the value of the pointer field of the pointer.

**Example 1.4.2** The array declarations corresponding to Fig. 1.3.1 are

　　**DCL** R(5 : 13) **FIXED BIN**, D(5 : 13) **CHAR** (4);

The following value assignments would be used to represent the data structure described:

　　D(5) = 'THE'; R(5) = 8; D(8) = 'THIS'; R(8) = 13; D(11) = 'THAT';
　　R(11) = 5; D(12) = 'WE'; R(12) = 0; D(13) = 'US'; R(13) = 12;

The declarations corresponding to Fig. 1.3.2 and 1.3.3 are

　　**DCL** D1(10 : 19) **CHAR** (15) **VARYING**,
　　　　(D2(10 : 19), D3(10 : 19)) **FIXED BIN**,
　　　　(R11(10 : 19), R12(10 : 19), R13(10 : 19), R2(10 : 19)) **FIXED BIN**;

The following are some of the values that are to be assigned:

　　D1(11) = 'MOTOR', D2(11) = 2, D3(11) = 802, R11(11) = 13,
　　R12(11) = 14, R13(11) = 0, and R2(11) = 13.

The declarations corresponding to Fig. 1.3.4 are

> **DCL** D1(10 : 19) **CHAR** (15) **VARYING,**
> (D2(10 : 19), D3(10 : 19), R11(10 : 19), R12(10 : 19),
> R13(10 : 19)) **FIXED BIN;**

The symbol * can be used, for example, to indicate that each address $a$ that appears in a pointer field with a * is stored as $-(a + 1)$. The appropriate value assignments for memory locations with addresses 10 and 14 would then be

> D1(10) = 'MACHINE'; D2(10) = 40; D3(10) = 612; R11(10) = 11;
> R12(10) = 14; R13(10) = 0; D1(14) = 'MOTOR'; D2(14) = 2;
> D3(14) = 802; R11(14) = -16; R12(14) = -17; R13(14) = -1;

### Remarks and References

A complete description and discussion of the PL/I programming language may be found in Neuhold [1][3] and the IBM System/360 PL/I Language Reference Manual.

## Exercises

**1.4.1**   Graphically represent an indirect allocation of the two pointer fields of the memory location

| | EASY | 22, 36, 27, 9, 11 | 4, 3, 17, 27, 8 |
|---|---|---|---|

---

[3][1] and [2] indicate which publication of the author is being referenced (see Bibliography).

# 2 Lists

## Section 2.1   Linear Lists

In dealing with data collections, we often have sets of nodes in which the only connection between the nodes is that every node, with the exception of the last node, has
exactly one successor node. Such a data structure is called a *linear list*.

**Definition 2.1.1** (Linear List)  A *linear list* (of length n) is a data structure $B = (K,$
$R)$, where K consists of n nodes and R consists of exactly one relation N and where
the nodes of K can be ordered so that $N = \{(k_{i-1}, k_i) \mid 2 \leqslant i \leqslant n\}$. Since N defines
a sequence of nodes in a natural way and, conversely, every sequence $k_1, k_2, \ldots, k_n$
of nodes specifies a relation N by $N = \{(k_{i-1}, k_i) \mid 2 \leqslant i \leqslant n\}$, then the terms *linear
list* and *sequence of nodes* are used interchangeably in general. In particular, we often
speak of a linear list with nodes $k_1, k_2, \ldots, k_n$ when we really mean that linear list
whose relation is specified by the sequence $F = k_1, k_2, \ldots, k_n$.

In a linear list B with nodes $k_1, k_2, \ldots, k_n$, $k_i$ is called the *ith node of B*; if $1 < i < n$,
then $k_i$ lies in the *interior* of B. Linear lists appear frequently in application. A table
of function values, a customer file, the list of all the books in a library, the catalog
of all available styles for a shoe manufacturer, the list of members of a club, the
vector of numbers arising from some mathematical problem—all of these are examples
of data collections that can be perceived easily as linear lists, i.e., as sets of nodes with
a first node in which every node but the last has exactly one successor.

The graphical representation of a linear list with nodes $k_1, k_2, \ldots, k_n$ is given
in Fig. 2.1.1.

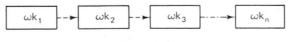

**Figure 2.1.1**

17

The following operations are commonly performed on linear lists:

(1)   To find a node with a given property.
(2)   To determine the ith node in a linear list.
(3)   To introduce an additional node either before or after a given node.
(4)   To delete a certain node from the linear list.
(5)   To arrange the nodes of a linear list in a certain way.

In selecting a method of storing a linear list, it is necessary to consider which of the operations 1 through 5 will be performed and how often, how fast these operations can be executed for the chosen form of storage, and how large the anticipated storage requirements are.

**Definition 2.1.2** (Sequential and Linked Allocation of a Linear List) The method of storing a linear list $B = (K, R)$ with relation $N$ is called a *sequential allocation* if the relation $N$ is realized sequentially in the storage of the list; if $N$ is realized as linked in memory, then the method of storing the linear list is said to be a *linked allocation*. Unless specifically stated otherwise, it is assumed that $\rho k = 0$ for the end node k of a linked allocation. A start pointer or an end pointer or both may also be used in a sequential or linked allocation. Furthermore it is often convenient to use a special memory location whose data field specifies the number of nodes in K, i.e., the *length* of K.

**Example 2.1.1** The data structure B given in Example 1.3.1 is a linear list and Fig. 1.3.1 illustrates a linked allocation of that list. A linked allocation with start pointer a, end pointer e, and length indicator L is shown is Fig. 2.1.2.

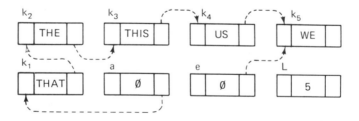

**Figure 2.1.2**

In sequential allocation (using step size s) of a linear list with nodes $k_1, k_2, \ldots, k_n$, access to the ith node is particularly simple since the address of the ith node can be calculated immediately from the address of the first node and the number i by applying the formula

$$\alpha k_i = \alpha k_1 + s(i - 1)$$

Also the storage requirements are small because there is no pointer field. On the other hand, the insertion, deletion, and reordering of nodes require some effort since during these operations many nodes may have to be moved in memory (for example, shifted to the left or right). The following program segments illustrate these practical considerations.

**Example 2.1.2** Suppose there is a sequence of nodes $k_1, k_2, \ldots, k_n$ with integer values stored so that $\alpha k_1 = 1$. There are m memory locations. We shall use a length indicator L that prescribes the number of nodes present. Then we have the declaration

> **DCL** (D(M), L, I, NEW) **FIXED BIN**;

for the m memory locations, the length indicator L, and the auxiliary variables I and NEW.

(a)   The following program segment prints the value of the ith node.

> **IF** (I < 1) | (I > L) **THEN ERROR** (1);
> **PUT LIST** (D(I));

(b)   The following program segment removes the successor of node k, where the address of k is given by the variable I.

> **BEGIN**; **DCL J FIXED BIN**;
>     **IF** I ⩾ L **THEN ERROR** (1); /* IN THIS CASE K HAS NO
>                                                        SUCCESSOR */
>     **DO** J = I + 1 **TO** L − 1; D(J) = D(J + 1); **END**;
>     /* I.E., THE ELEMENTS K(I + 2), K(I + 3), . . . , K(L) ARE
>         MOVED LEFT ONE POSITION ONE BY ONE */
>     L = L − 1;
> **END**;

(c)   The following program segment inserts after node k a new node whose value is given by the variable NEW. Let the address of k be determined by the variable I.

> **BEGIN**; **DCL J FIXED BIN**;
>     **IF** L ⩾ M **THEN ERROR** (1); /* IN THIS CASE ALL MEMORY
>         LOCATIONS ARE ALREADY OCCUPIED AND NO FURTHER
>         ELEMENT CAN BE INSERTED */
>     **IF** I > L **THEN ERROR** (2);
>     **DO** J = L **BY** −1 **TO** I + 1; D(J + 1) = D(J); **END**;
>     /* THE ELEMENTS K(L), K(L − 1), . . . , K(I + 1) ARE MOVED
>         RIGHT ONE POSITION ONE AFTER THE OTHER */
>     D(I + 1) = NEW; L = L + 1;
> **END**;

(d)   The following program segment prints the value of the predecessor and successor of node k, whose address is given by the variable I.

> **IF** (I ⩽ 1) | (I ⩾ L) **THEN ERROR** (1);
> **PUT LIST** (D(I − 1)); **PUT LIST** (D(I + 1));

(e)    The following program segment goes through the nodes $k_1, k_2, \ldots, k_n$ and arranges them in a sequence of nodes $k'_1, k'_2, \ldots, k'_s, k_1, k''_1, k''_2, \ldots, k''_t$ (where $s + t + 1 = n$) such that $\omega k'_i < \omega k_1$ and $\omega k''_j \geqslant \omega k_1$.

```
BEGIN; DCL (I, J, T, AUX) FIXED BIN; T = 1;
    DO I = 2 TO L;
        IF D(I) < D(T) THEN DO; AUX = D(I);
                        DO J = I BY −1 TO 2;
                            D(J) = D(J − 1);
                        END;
            T = T + 1; D(1) = AUX; END;
    END;
END;
```

If we count the execution of one "simple" PL/I instruction as one *step*, then in program segments a and d at most three steps are required, in program segments b and c at most L steps, and in program segment e at most $L^2/2$ steps.

Access to the ith node of a linear list stored as a linked structure is more difficult than it would be if sequential allocation were used. The address of the first node and the number i do not permit a direct determination of the ith node; rather it is necessary to perform, i times, an operation of the type $a = \rho\sigma a$; i.e., it is necessary to go through the chain element by element. Also the storage requirements are greater in a linked allocation because of the use of pointer fields. On the other hand, the insertion, deletion, and reordering of nodes are less difficult than if sequential allocation were used. A comparison of the following program segments with the analogous ones for sequential allocation in Example 2.1.2 shows clearly the advantages and disadvantages of linked allocation.

**Example 2.1.3** Let the sequence of nodes $k_1, k_2, \ldots, k_n$ with integer values be stored as a linked structure using a start pointer A. There are m memory locations available. The required declaration is

```
DCL (D(M), R(0: M), A, I, NEW, FREE) FIXED BIN;
```

(a)    The following program segment prints the value of the ith node.

```
BEGIN; DCL (J, P) FIXED BIN; P = A; R(0) = 0;
    DO J = 1 TO I − 1; P = R(P); END;
    /* NOTE HOW R(0) IS USED TO DETERMINE THE END OF THE
       LIST WITHOUT REQUIRING AN IF WITHIN THE LOOP */
    IF P = 0 THEN ERROR (1) ELSE PUT LIST (D(P));
END;
```

(b)    The following program segment removes the successor of node k, where the address of k is given by the variable I.

```
IF R(I) = 0 THEN ERROR (1) ELSE R(I) = R(R(I));
```

(c) The following program segment inserts after node k a new node whose value is given by the variable NEW. The address of k is determined by the variable I and the variable FREE gives the address of a memory location that has not yet been used.

D(FREE) = NEW; R(FREE) = R(I); R(I) = FREE;

(d) The following program segment prints the value of the predecessor and successor of a node k whose address is given by the variable I.

```
BEGIN; DCL P FIXED BIN;
    IF R(I) = 0 THEN ERROR (1) ELSE PUT LIST (D(R(I)));
    /* THE SUCCESSOR HAS BEEN PRINTED; PRINTING THE
        PREDECESSOR IS MORE DIFFICULT */
    IF I = A THEN ERROR (2); /* SINCE IN THIS CASE NO
                                    PREDECESSOR EXISTS */
    P = A;
    LOOP: IF R(P) = 0 THEN ERROR (3); /* IN THIS CASE NO
        ELEMENT WITH ADDRESS I EXISTS */
        IF R(P) = I THEN PUT LIST (D(P));
            ELSE DO; P = R(P); GOTO LOOP; END;
END;
```

(e) The following program segment goes through the nodes $k_1, k_2, \ldots, k_n$ and arranges them in a sequence of nodes $k'_1, k'_2, \ldots, k'_s, k_1, k''_1, k''_2, \ldots, k''_t$ (where $s + t + 1 = n$) such that $\omega k'_i < \omega k_1$ and $\omega k''_j \geqslant \omega k_1$. The start pointer A finally points to $k'_1$.

```
BEGIN; DCL (T, P, W) FIXED BIN; W = D(A); T = A;
    DO WHILE (R(T) ¬= 0);
        IF D(R(T)) < W THEN DO; P = R(T); R(T) = R(R(T));
                                    R(P) = A; A = P;
                                END;
            ELSE T = R(T);
    END;
END;
```

Work through the program segment above using the structure shown in Fig. 2.1.3. Initially a sequence of six nodes $k_1, k_2, \ldots, k_6$ with start pointer a is given as a linked structure with $\alpha k_i = i + 1$, $\omega k_1 = 5$, $\omega k_2 = 6$, $\omega k_3 = 3$, $\omega k_4 = 7$, $\omega k_5 = 2$, $\omega k_6 = 4$. At the end, we have a new sequence $k'_1, k'_2, k'_3, k_1, k''_1, k''_2$ with

$$\omega k'_1 = \omega k_6 = 4 < \omega k_1, \qquad \omega k'_2 = \omega k_5 = 2 < \omega k_1$$

$$\omega k'_3 = \omega k_3 = 3 < \omega k_1, \qquad \omega k''_1 = \omega k_2 = 6 \geqslant \omega k_1,$$

$$\omega k''_2 = \omega k_4 = 7 \geqslant \omega k_1.$$

In the execution of program segments a, d, and e, a maximum of L steps is required, and in b and c a maximum of three steps is necessary. (L again specifies the number of

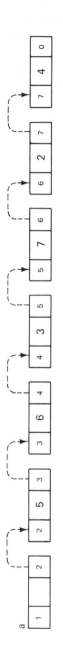
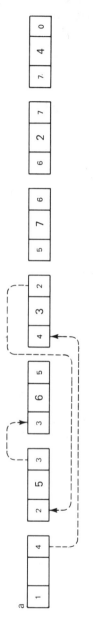
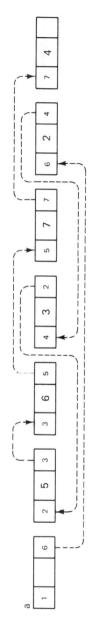
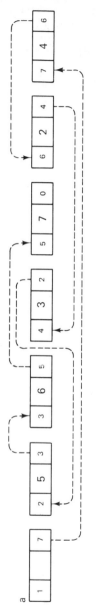

**Figure 2.1.3**

nodes in the linear list.) Thus the step count differs considerably for the two types of storage.

The program segment in Example 2.1.3(d) shows a distinct asymmetry inherent in the linking. It is much more difficult to determine the predecessor of a node k than it is to determine the successor of node k. To eliminate this asymmetry, we introduce *two-way linking*.

**Definition 2.1.3** (Two-Way Linked Allocation of a Linear List) A linear list $B = (K, R)$ with relation N is called a *two-way linked* structure (or a *two-way chain*) if in the storage of the list the relations N and $N^{-1} = \{(k', k) \,|\, (k, k') \in N\}$ are realized in the first and second pointer fields, respectively.

**Definition 2.1.4** (Circular Allocation of a Linear List) A linear list $B = (K, R)$ with relation N and nodes $k_1, k_2, \ldots, k_n$ is said to be *circular* (or *circularly linked*) if the relation N is realized as a linked structure and the end node $k_n$ points to the first node $k_1$, $\rho k_n = \alpha k_1$.

Figure 2.1.4 shows the circular and two-way linked allocation of a linear list with nodes $k_1, k_2, \ldots, k_5$.

It may be helpful at this time to consider an extensive example illustrating the concept of linked allocation.

**Example 2.1.4** A sequence of integers $b_1, b_2, \ldots, b_n$ between 1 and 99999 is given as input. The end of the sequence is marked by an additional number 0. Let $F_i$ (where $1 \leqslant i \leqslant n$) be that sequence obtained by arranging the numbers $\{b_1, b_2, \ldots, b_i\}$ in ascending order.

A program is to be designed that will store the sequence $F_n$ as a linked structure.

In the program given below, at any given time, *one* of the sequences $F_i$ is stored. The next number $b_{i+1}$ is read and then, by "insertion" of $b_{i+1}$ in the proper position of $F_i$, a linked allocation of $F_{i+1}$ is created.

The current "next" number $b_{i+1}$ will be inserted in general into the interior of the already existing linked structure. Three exceptional cases are possible, however.

(a)   There are no elements in the structure (the empty structure).
(b)   The number is to be inserted at the beginning of the structure.
(c)   The number is to be inserted at the end of the structure.

Since cases a, b, and c often occur in linked allocation, it is desirable to design the program so that as little special programming as possible is required for these exceptional cases.

An elegant solution consists of beginning not with an empty structure but rather with a structure of two nodes so that all additional nodes can always be introduced into the interior of the structure.

The following program segment makes use of this idea: Two memory locations z and z', where $\delta z = 0$, $\alpha z = 1$ and $\delta z' = 100000$, $\alpha z' = 2$, serve as boundary loca-

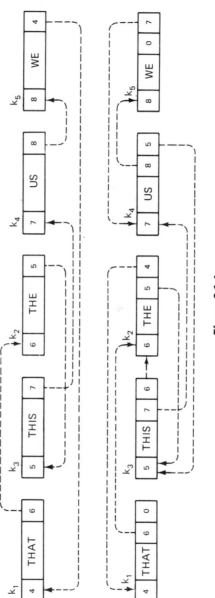

**Figure 2.1.4**

tions of a structure so that since $0 < b_i < 100000$, all additional numbers $b_i$ can be stored in memory locations that lie between z and z' in the structure.

The appropriate declaration is

**DCL** D(M) **FIXED BIN** (31), R(M) **FIXED BIN**;

where M is the number of memory locations.

```
LINK: PROC OPTIONS (MAIN); DCL (NEW, POS, IN) FIXED BIN;
   D(1), R(2) = 0; D(2) = 100000; R(1) = 2;
   /* THIS ESTABLISHES BEGINNING AND END OF A LIST */
   NEW = 3; /* THE VALUE OF NEW WILL BE THE ADDRESS OF
                   FIRST FREE MEMORY LOCATION THROUGHOUT */
   GET LIST (IN);
   DO WHILE (IN ¬ = 0);
      D(NEW) = IN;
      /* THUS THE NEXT NUMBER HAS BEEN STORED IN THE NEXT
         FREE MEMORY LOCATION; IT HAS TO BE INSERTED NOW
         INTO THE LIST AT THE APPROPRIATE PLACE */
      POS = 1; DO WHILE (IN > D(R(POS))); POS = R(POS); END;
      /* AT THIS STAGE IT IS KNOWN THAT THE CURRENT
         NUMBER HAS TO BE INSERTED IN THE LIST AFTER THE
         ELEMENT WITH ADDRESS POS */
      R(NEW) = R(POS); R(POS) = NEW; NEW = NEW + 1;
      IF NEW > M THEN CALL ERROR (1); /* IN THIS CASE NO
                   FREE STORAGE IS AVAILABLE */
      GET LIST (IN);
   END;
END;
```

The program segment above handles the sequence of numbers 11, 3, 19, 8, 0 as shown in Fig. 2.1.5.

## Exercises

**2.1.1** A sequence of positive whole numbers is given as input. Write a program that first stores the sequence as a linked structure A and then prints the entire structure in ascending order by determining the smallest number in A repeatedly, printing it, and removing it from A, until the structure A is empty.

**2.1.2** Are the results of the program segments in Examples 2.1.2(a) and 2.1.3(a) the same for all values of I?

**2.1.3** What happens if $I = 0$ in Example 2.1.2(c)?

**2.1.4** Improve the program segment in Example 2.1.2(e) so that only L steps are necessary. *Hint:* Go through the sequence $k_2, \ldots, k_n$ simultaneously from left to right and from right to left and make the appropriate changes.

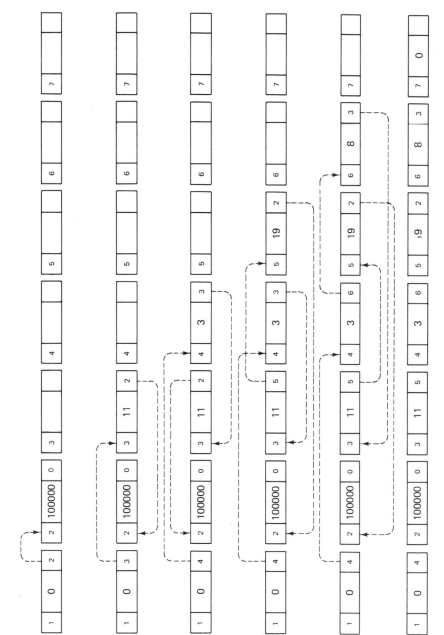

**Figure 2.1.5**

**2.1.5** Two sequences A and B of whole numbers are given as input. Write a program that determines whether B is a subsequence of A.

**2.1.6** Two positive whole numbers n and k are given as input. Suppose the numbers 1, 2, 3, . . . ,n are arranged circularly as in Fig. 2.1.6. Design a program that, beginning

**Figure 2.1.6**

with 1 and continuing clockwise, prints the current number, removes it from the circle, and then considers the kth next number in the list until the circle is empty. For example, for the values $n = 10$, $k = 3$, we would obtain the output 1, 4, 7, 10, 5, 9, 6, 3, 8, 2.

**2.1.7** A sequence $a_1, a_2, . . . , a_n$ of integer values is given as a linked structure. Design a program segment that prints the numbers of the sequence in the order $a_n$, $a_{n-1}, . . . , a_2, a_1$, without declaring an additional array. The given sequence is stored in memory locations that are declared by **DCL** (D(N), R(N), A) **FIXED BIN**;, where the variable A gives the first address of the sequence. *Hint:* Reverse the linking.

**2.1.8** Formulate a definition for the concept of a linear list without numbering the nodes as in Def. 2.1.1.

## Section 2.2 Stacks and Queues

The considerations mentioned in Sec. 2.1 indicate that the manipulation of nodes in the interior of a linear list can require considerable effort, whether sequential or linked allocation is used. For example, in sequential allocation, removing an interior node is very involved; in linked allocation, it is a problem to locate the ith node. Thus when linear lists are used, it makes sense to try to work only on the nodes at the beginning and end of the list.

**Definition 2.2.1** (Stacks, Queues, Deques) A *stack* is a linear list in which the manipulation of nodes takes place only at the beginning of the list.[1] A *queue* is a linear list in which nodes can be removed only at the beginning and nodes can be inserted only at the end of the list. A *deque*[2] is a linear list in which manipulation of nodes occurs only at the beginning or end of the list.

---

[1]Somewhat less precisely, we may also refer to a structure as a stack if nodes may be added or removed only at the beginning of a list but if the values of other nodes in the interior of the list may be used or altered. Such a structure is called a *peepable* stack.

[2]"Double-ended queue."

A stack can be illustrated by a stack of books lying on the floor. Only the top of the stack is immediately accessible, new books can be placed only on the top, and only the topmost book can be removed easily.

A stack can also be illustrated by B in the railway switching network in Fig. 2.2.1

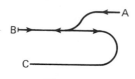

**Figure 2.2.1**

with arrivals on A and departures on C. (The direction of the traffic on rails A and C is in one direction as indicated.) The last car moved onto track B is the only one which is immediately accessible and which can be directly removed.

A queue is best illustrated by the example of a waiting line.

A deque can be visualized as a row of books on a bookshelf. Books can only be removed or added on the ends without leaving "gaps." The railway track B shown in Fig. 2.2.2 with arrivals on A and departures on C likewise illustrates a deque.

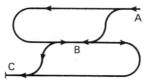

**Figure 2.2.2**

Stacks, queues, and deques can be stored sequentially or linked and treated as special cases of linear lists.

In our discussion of sequential allocation, suppose we have available in memory the storage domain M with m memory locations.

For the sequential allocation of a single stack S, the end node of S is often stored at the right end of M and an additional start pointer a is used. In this way, for example, we can remove a node by increasing $\rho a$ by 1.

For the simultaneous sequential allocation of two stacks S and T, it might seem reasonable to divide the storage domain M into two domains $M_1$ and $M_2$ with $m_1$ and $m_2$ memory locations ($m = m_1 + m_2$) and to use $M_1$ exclusively for stack S and $M_2$ exclusively for stack T but this is impractical. Such an arrangement could result in a memory overflow, even though additional memory space is available. Instead, stack S is stored sequentially (using step size 1) with the last node at the right end of M and stack T is stored sequentially (using step size $-1$) with the last node at the left end of M; we use two start pointers a and b for S and T, respectively. If this arrangement is used, then an overflow occurs only if S and T together actually require more than m memory locations; such a condition is indicated when $\rho b \geqslant \rho a$.

Figure 2.2.3(a) and (b) show the sequential allocation of two stacks S and T with

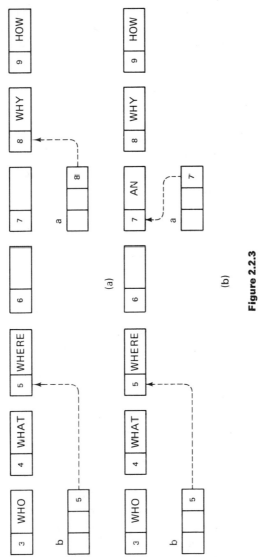

**Figure 2.2.3**

29

start pointers a and b and describe the allocation before and after the addition of a node to stack S.

For the sequential allocation of three or more stacks in m available memory locations, a similar arrangement is not possible. No matter how the stacks are stored sequentially to begin with, an overflow can arise later, even though additional memory space is available. In the case of an overflow either the program must terminate or the stack must be relocated by shifting the structure to the right or left. Since the ends of the stacks no longer correspond permanently to any particular memory locations, end pointers are used to identify the ends of the stacks.

The shifting of stacks requires a considerable amount of time. In order to avoid this loss of time, if a reallocation is necessary, additional memory space may be placed at the disposal of the stack. For example, we can just rearrange all stacks by allotting to all stacks proportionally $x\%$ of the memory space still available and assigning to every stack an additional share of the remaining $y\%$ that is proportional to the increase in size of the stack since the last reallocation. The values $x = 10$ and $y = 90$ are often suggested in the literature.

In the sequential allocation of a queue S, the first node is preferably stored at the left end of the available storage domain M and a start pointer a and an end pointer e are used. The removal of a node causes an increase of 1 in $\rho a$, the addition of a node causes an increase of 1 in $\rho e$, and the queue is empty whenever $\rho a > \rho e$.

In the method of storage just suggested, the queue is eventually shifted to the right because of repeated additions and deletions of nodes. Thus an overflow can arise even though additional memory space is available. To decrease the number of overflows, the usual procedure is to set the start pointer back to the left end of the storage domain, $\rho a = \min \{\alpha z \mid z \in M\}$, every time $\rho a > \rho e$ (i.e., every time the queue is empty). Whenever an overflow does occur, the entire queue can always be shifted far enough to the left so that the first node lies on the left end of the storage domain.

It is worthy of mention that we can get by without the shifting mentioned above if we think of the storage domain M as being circularly arranged and then use the first memory location of M immediately after the last memory location is filled. By applying this method it can be easily determined if (1) the queue is empty or (2) the storage domain is full, just by testing the start and end pointers. Unless care is taken, it is possible that $\rho a = \rho e + 1$ can occur as soon as either (1) the last node of the queue is removed or (2) the last vacant memory location of the storage domain is used.

In the sequential allocation of two or more queues in the same storage domain, shifting, as already mentioned for three or more stacks, is unavoidable. The sequential allocation of a deque is analogous to that for a queue. Here also shifting can be avoided by interpreting the storage domain as being "circular."

The problems of shifting that arise in the sequential allocation of more than two stacks, more than one queue, or more than one deque vanish when linked allocation is used.

The linked allocation of n stacks $S_1, S_2, \ldots, S_n$ using a set M of m memory locations can be accomplished as follows: Every stack $S_i$ is stored as a linked structure with start pointer $a_i$. All unused memory locations of M are stored in what is called a *free storage stack* V with start pointer b. Then $\rho a_i = 0$ or $\rho b = 0$ if the corresponding stack is empty.

If a node k is removed from stack $S_i$, the corresponding memory location is removed from stack $S_i$ and added to the free storage stack V. To add a node k to stack $S_i$ where k is to be stored in the first memory location of the free storage stack V, this node is removed from V and added to $S_i$. Example 2.2.1 illustrates the procedure in detail.

**Example 2.2.1** Suppose there are m memory locations available for use and each memory location consists of a whole-number data field and a pointer field with exactly one number. Five stacks $S_1, S_2, \ldots, S_5$ with start pointers $a_1, a_2, \ldots, a_5$ and a free storage stack V with start pointer b are stored as linked structures.

Appropriate declarations for a program segment are

**DCL** (D(M), R(M), A(5), B, T) **FIXED BIN**;

where D(J), R(J) represent a memory location and A(I) and B are used for start pointers; T is an auxiliary variable to be used later.

(a)   If the stacks $S_1, S_2, \ldots, S_5$ are empty, then

$A(I) = 0$      for $1 \leqslant I \leqslant 5$, $B = 1$;

$R(I) = I + 1$    for $1 \leqslant I \leqslant M - 1$;

and

$R(M) = 0$.

All memory locations therefore are allocated to the free storage stack.

(b)   The following program segment removes a node from a stack $S_i$.

```
BEGIN;
    IF A(I) = 0 THEN ERROR (1); /* STACK IS EMPTY AND NO
                        ELEMENT CAN BE REMOVED */
    T = R(A(I)); R(A(I)) = B; B = A(I); A(I) = T;
    /* THE CYCLIC EXCHANGE OF THE VALUES R(A(I)), B,
       AND A(I) PERFORMED ABOVE IS CHARACTERISTIC FOR
       THE REMOVAL OF A NODE FROM A STACK AND ADDING IT
       TO ANOTHER. FIGURE 2.2.4 ILLUSTRATES THE PROCEDURE
       BY REPRESENTING THE VALUES IN MEMORY, BEFORE AND
       AFTER THE PROCESS. THE PROGRAM ALSO WORKS IF
       THE STACK IS EMPTY. THEN A(I) = 0 */
END;
```

(c)   The following program segment adds a node whose value is given by the variable T to the stack $S_i$.

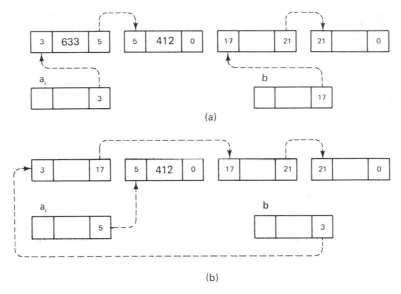

**Figure 2.2.4**

```
BEGIN;
    IF B = 0 THEN ERROR (1); /* NO SPACE AVAILABLE */
    D(B) = T; T = R(B); R(B) = A(I); A(I) = B; B = T;
    /* THIS PROGRAM SEGMENT ALSO WORKS IF THE STACK IS
       INITIALLY EMPTY. FIGURE 2.2.4 ILLUSTRATES THE
       PROCEDURE BY REPRESENTING THE VALUES IN MEMORY,
       BEFORE AND AFTER THE PROCESS */
END;
```

The linked allocation of a queue is accomplished as for a stack but a start pointer a and an end pointer e are used.

When adding a node to an empty list and when removing the last remaining node from a list, exceptional cases may arise that must be dealt with. For example, when adding to a nonempty queue only the end pointer needs to be adjusted; when adding to an empty queue start and end pointers must be adjusted. It would seem that the two cases must be handled separately in the program. Actually this and several other problem situations can be avoided if no separate declarations for the pointers are made but rather the pointers are interpreted as nodes of the list with unused data fields. This is a very practical programming consideration but the use of the technique tends to diminish the readability of the program; therefore, in program examples given here, start and end pointers usually are declared separately from the other nodes.

**Example 2.2.2** A queue S, consisting of whole number nodes, is stored as a linked structure with start pointer a and end pointer e. A free storage stack V is a linked structure with start pointer b. A node with value 1977 is to be added to the queue.

(a)  In the following program segment the declaration

**DCL (D(M), R(M), A, E, B) FIXED BIN;**

is assumed. D(I) and R(I) represent a memory location and A, E, and B serve as pointers. The empty queue is indicated by A $= 0$; i.e., $pa = 0$.

**BEGIN;**
   **IF B $= 0$ THEN ERROR (1);**
   **IF A $= 0$ THEN A $=$ B ELSE R(E) $=$ B;**
   **E $=$ B; D(B) $= 1977$; B $=$ R(B); R(E) $= 0$:**
**END;**

(b)  In the following program segment the declaration

**DCL (D(M), R(M)) FIXED BIN;**

is assumed. Here D(1), R(1) represent the start pointer a; D(2), R(2) represent the end pointer e; and D(3), R(3) represent the start pointer b. An empty queue is indicated by R(1) $= 0$ (i.e., $pa = 0$) and R(2) $= 1$ (i.e., $pe = \alpha a$). Thus the queue consists initially only of the start pointers [see Fig. 2.2.5(a)]. Notice that in the program segment no distinction between

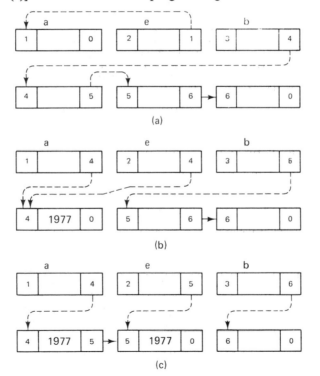

(a)

(b)

(c)

**Figure 2.2.5**

empty or nonempty queues is necessary. Figure 2.2.5 shows the repeated addition of a node to an initially empty queue: (a) before the addition of a node, (b) after addition of a node, and (c) after addition of two nodes.

```
BEGIN;
    IF R(3) = 0 THEN ERROR (1); /* THEN THE FREE STORAGE
                                      STACK IS EMPTY */
    R(R(2)) = R(3);
    /* NOTE THAT THE EFFECT OF THIS STATEMENT R(R(2)) = R(3)
       IS EQUIVALENT TO IF A = 0 THEN A = B ELSE R(E) = B
       IN PROGRAM A) */
    R(2) = R(3); D(R(3)) = 1977; R(3) = R(R(3)); R(R(2)) = 0;
END;
```

Besides the linked allocation just discussed, circularly linked allocation is often used for queues. In such a data structure, only the end pointer e (and not the start pointer a) is used since the address of the first node k can be determined from e by using $\alpha k = \rho\sigma\rho e$.

In the linked allocation of a deque using start and end pointers, an interesting problem arises: It is simple to add a node at the beginning or end of a deque but removing a node at the end is much more involved. The end pointer points first to the last node k but after k is removed, it should point to the predecessor k' of k. Because of the linking, k' of course points to k but not vice versa. In order to adjust the end pointer so that it points to k', the entire linked structure must be searched from beginning node on! As an alternative, two-way linking can be used.

In the remaining part of this section, several extensive and interesting applications of stacks will be discussed.

In many programming languages *arithmetic expressions* are permitted that are constructed from constants, variables, operation symbols, and parentheses. The evaluation of such an expression cannot proceed strictly from left to right because certain operations may have a higher *priority* than others (for example, $\times$ has a higher priority than $+$ so in the evaluation of $3 + 4 \times 5$ the $4 \times 5$ must be evaluated first). The parenthetical structure (if any) must also be considered. It is possible to determine, for every arithmetic expression, a *parenthesis-free expression* which can be evaluated strictly from left to right and which corresponds in value to the given arithmetic expression. Stacks have proved to be useful not only in the conversion of an arithmetic expression into a parenthesis-free one but also in the evaluation of parenthesis-free expressions. To facilitate defining the concept of *arithmetic* and *parenthesis-free expressions*, Backus systems are introduced.

**Definition 2.2.2** (Backus System) Let $\Sigma$ be a set of terminal symbols, not containing the symbols $::=$, $\langle$, $\rangle$, and $|$. By combining terminal symbols and enclosing them with $\langle$ and $\rangle$, we obtain a *variable*; by combining terminal symbols and variables, we obtain a *word*.

A *production* is of the form $v ::= w_1 | w_2 | \cdots | w_n$, where v is a variable and the $w_i$ (for $1 \leqslant i \leqslant n$) are words that are called the *alternatives of the variable v*. A *Backus system* B consists of a finite number of productions. If a Backus system B and a variable X are given, then X defines the set B(X) of all those words obtainable from X by replacing the first variable by one of its alternatives until there are no more variables.

In the rest of this section we shall use for the terminal symbol set $\Sigma$ the set $\{0, 1, 2, 3, 4, 5, 6, 7, 8, 9, +, -, \times, \div, (, ), .\}$ together with all the uppercase and lowercase letters of the alphabet.

**Definition 2.2.3** (Simple Arithmetic Expression) The variable $\langle$SAE$\rangle$ in the Backus system below defines the set of *simple arithmetic expressions*.

$\langle$SAE$\rangle ::= \langle$number$\rangle | \langle$SAE$\rangle\langle$op$\rangle\langle$SAE$\rangle | (\langle$SAE$\rangle)$
$\langle$number$\rangle ::= \langle$digit$\rangle. | \langle$digit$\rangle\langle$number$\rangle$
$\langle$digit$\rangle ..- 0 | 1 | 2 | 3 | 4 | 5 | 6 | 7 | 8 | 9$
$\langle$op$\rangle ::= + | - | \times | \div$

**Example 2.2.3** Some examples of simple arithmetic expressions are (a) 7., (b) 372., (c) (2. + 14.), (d) 3. $\times$ (5. - 2.) + 7.. The substitution process for d beginning with $\langle$SAE$\rangle$ is shown in Fig. 2.2.6. A single substitution (i.e., a single application of a production) is indicated by an arrow $\longrightarrow$; one or more substitution steps are indicated by $\overset{*}{\longrightarrow}$.

$\langle$SAE$\rangle \rightarrow \langle$SAE$\rangle \langle$op$\rangle \langle$SAE$\rangle \rightarrow \langle$SAE$\rangle \langle$op$\rangle \langle$SAE $\rangle \langle$op$\rangle \langle$SAE$\rangle$

$\overset{*}{\rightarrow} 3. \times \langle$SAE$\rangle \langle$op$\rangle \langle$SAE$\rangle \rightarrow 3. \times (\langle$SAE$\rangle) \langle$op$\rangle \langle$SAE$\rangle$

$\rightarrow 3. \times (\langle$SAE$\rangle \langle$op$\rangle \langle$SAE$\rangle) \langle$op$\rangle \langle$SAE$\rangle \overset{*}{\rightarrow} 3. \times (5. - 2.) + 7.$

**Figure 2.2.6**

The operators $+, -, \times, \div$ mean the usual addition, subtraction, multiplication, and (integer) division, respectively. Thus the value of 3. $\times$ (5. - 2.) + 7. is 16..

**Definition 2.2.4** (Parenthesis-Free Expression) The variable $\langle$PFE$\rangle$ in the following Backus system defines the set of *parenthesis-free expressions*.

$\langle$PFE$\rangle ::= \langle$number$\rangle | \langle$PFE$\rangle\langle$PFE$\rangle\langle$op$\rangle$
$\langle$number$\rangle ::= \langle$digit$\rangle. | \langle$digit$\rangle\langle$number$\rangle$
$\langle$digit$\rangle ::= 0 | 1 | 2 | 3 | 4 | 5 | 6 | 7 | 8 | 9$
$\langle$op$\rangle ::= + | - | \times | \div$

In parenthesis-free expressions, the operators are written after the operands rather than between them. Such an expression is said to be written using *postfix notation*.

Examples of parenthesis-free expressions are (a) 7., (b) 372., (c) 2. 14. +, (d) 3. 5. 2. — × 7. +, which correspond to the simple arithmetic expressions given in Example 2.2.3.

In the two following examples it will be shown how to determine the value of a parenthesis-free expression and, if given a simple arithmetic expression, how to construct the equivalent parenthesis-free expression. In each example it will be assumed that an expression separated into *elements* is given as input, where an element is either a number or one of the symbols +, —, ×, ÷, (, ), *, and * indicates the end of the expression.

**Example 2.2.4** (Evaluation of a Parenthesis-Free Expression) A parenthesis-free expression is given as input. The following program shows a simple technique for determining the value of the parenthesis-free expression using a sequentially stored stack with step size —1 and start pointer a. The declaration for the stack is **DCL** **D**(100) **FIXED BIN** (31);. The program does not check the given expression for validity.

```
EVALUATION: PROC OPTIONS (MAIN);
    DCL D(100) FIXED BIN (31), A FIXED BIN, Z CHAR (10)
                    VARYING;
    A = 0; /* A POINTS TO BEGINNING OF STACK */
    GET LIST (Z);
    DO WHILE (Z ¬= '#');
        IF NUMBER (Z) THEN DO;
            IF A >= 100 THEN CALL ERROR (1);
                    /* STACK OVERFLOW */
            A = A + 1;
            D(A) = CONV (Z);
            END;
        ELSE DO;
        IF Z = '+' THEN D(A − 1) = D(A − 1) + D(A); ELSE
        IF Z = '−' THEN D(A − 1) = D(A − 1) − D(A); ELSE
        IF Z = '*' THEN D(A − 1) = D(A − 1) * D(A); ELSE
        IF Z = '/' THEN D(A − 1) = D(A − 1)/D(A);
            A = A − 1;
            END;
        GET LIST (Z);
    END;
    PUT LIST (D(A));
END;
```

**Example 2.2.5** (Transformation of a Simple Arithmetic Expression into a Parenthesis-Free Expression) A simple arithmetic expression is given as input. The following program demonstrates a simple technique for determining the corresponding parenthesis-free expression, using a sequentially stored stack with step size —1 and start pointer a. The program does not check the given expression for validity.

```
TRANSFORMATION: PROC OPTIONS (MAIN);
    DCL (D(100), Z) CHAR (10) VARYING, A FIXED BIN;
    D(1) = '(';
    A = 1;
    GET LIST (Z);
    DO WHILE (Z ¬= '#');
        IF NUMBER (Z) THEN PUT LIST (Z);
        ELSE IF Z = '(' THEN DO;
                            A = A + 1;
                            D(A) = '(';
                        END;
        ELSE IF Z = ')' THEN DO;
                            DO WHILE (D(A) ¬= '(');
                                PUT LIST (D(A));
                                A = A - 1;
                            END;
                            A = A - 1;
                        END,
        ELSE IF (Z = '+') | (Z = '−') THEN DO;
                            DO WHILE (D(A) ¬= '(');
                                PUT LIST (D(A));
                                A = A - 1;
                            END;
                            A = A + 1; D(A) = Z;
                        END;
        ELSE IF (Z = '*') | (Z = '/') THEN DO;
                            DO WHILE ((D(A) = '*') | (D(A) = '/'));
                                PUT LIST (D(A));
                                A = A - 1;
                            END;
                            A = A + 1; D(A) = Z;
                        END;
        GET LIST (Z);
    END;
    DO WHILE (D(A) ¬= '(');
        PUT LIST (D(A));
        A = A - 1;
    END;
END;
```

Work through the program in Example 2.2.5 using the simple arithmetic expression 3. × (5. − 2.) + 7., i.e., with the input '3', '×', '(', '5', '−', '2', ')', '+', '7', '*'. The changes in the stack and the corresponding output produced are shown in Fig. 2.2.7.

Now if we work through the program of Example 2.2.4 in detail using the parenthesis-free expression 3. 5. 2. − × 7. +, we see that the output produced is the value 16; the changes in the stack are shown in Fig. 2.2.8.

Further attention will be given to the manipulation of expressions and the use of Backus systems in Chapter 3.

The problem of arranging the elements of a given set M in a partial ordering P,

| Stack | Output |
|---|---|
| ( | |
| ( | 3. |
| ( × | 3. |
| ( × ( | 3. |
| ( × ( | 3. 5. |
| ( × ( − | 3. 5. |
| ( × ( − | 3. 5. 2. |
| ( × | 3. 5. 2. − |
| ( | 3. 5. 2. − × |
| ( + | 3. 5. 2. − × |
| ( + | 3. 5. 2. − × 7. |
| ( | 3. 5. 2. − × 7. + |

**Figure 2.2.7**

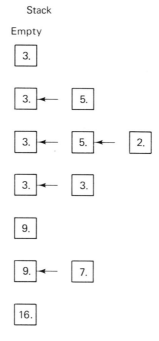

**Figure 2.2.8**

i.e., sorting the set M topologically (see Def. 1.1.6), arises in many various applications.

The set M might consist of numbers that are to be arranged in a sequence F in such a way that a comes before a′ in F if a divides a′ without a remainder. The set M may consist of problems that are to be ordered in a sequence F such that a comes before a' in F if problem a must be solved before problem a'. Or M could be a set of definitions that are to be ordered in a sequence F such that a comes before a' in F if the definition of a' requires the use of the definition of a, and so on. Essentially, a set M with partial ordering P can be topologically sorted by repeatedly determining an element $x \in M$ having no predecessor (relative to P) and removing it from the set. It is now necessary to define an efficient technique for determining an element with no predecessor. A recommended technique is presented using a concrete example.

**Example 2.2.6** (Topological Sort) Suppose we have as input a pair (n, m) followed by m pairs $(i_1, j_1), (i_2, j_2), \ldots, (i_m, j_m)$, which define a partial ordering on the n numbers $1, 2, \ldots, n$ in that each pair $(i_t, j_t)$ defines $i_t$ to be the predecessor of $j_t$, for $1 \leq t \leq m$, and $r = \{(i_1, j_1), (i_2, j_2), \ldots, (i_m, j_m)\}$ is a basis of P. It is assumed that r actually defines a partial ordering. The numbers 1 through n are to be printed in topologically sorted order.

The following program first reads the pairs $(i_t, j_t)$ for $1 \leq t \leq m$ successively and simultaneously builds a linear list F with n nodes $f_1, f_2, \ldots, f_n$ and n additional linear lists $G_1, G_2, \ldots, G_n$ and finally a stack S so that when the input process terminates, the following are true:

(a)   $f_i$ gives the number of predecessors of the number i (relative to r).
(b)   The list $G_i$ contains the successors of the number i (relative to r).
(c)   The stack S contains all numbers that have no predecessor.

Now the arrays F and S are systematically changed. The first node of S has as its value the number i with no predecessor. This is printed. Now for every j that is a successor of i (relative to r) (and this can be determined without a searching process by using the array $G_i$), the value of the node $f_j$ is decreased by 1 since the predecessor i of j no longer need be considered. If in doing this $of_j$ becomes equal to 0, then j is added to the stack S. Then again the first node of S is considered. The procedure terminates as soon as S is empty.

The list F is stored sequentially. The arrays $G_1, \ldots, G_n$ and the stack S are linked in memory with start pointers $ag_1, \ldots, ag_n$ and as, respectively. The corresponding declaration is **DCL (F(N), D(N + M), R(N + M), AG(N), AS) FIXED BIN;**.

```
TOPO: PROC OPTIONS (MAIN);
    DCL (N, M) FIXED BIN;
    GET LIST (N, M);
    BEGIN;
        DCL (F(N), AG(N), D(N + M), R(N + M), AS, T, FREE, I, J,
            AUX) FIXED BIN;
        FREE = 1; F, AG = 0; AS = 0;
        /*  FREE INDICATES FIRST FREE MEMORY LOCATION; ALL
            ELEMENTS OF F AND THE POINTER FIELDS OF THE START
            POINTERS ARE INITIALLY 0 */
```

```
DO T = 1 TO M;
    GET LIST (I, J);
    F(J) = F(J) + 1;
    /* THE PAIR (I, J) INDICATES THAT J IS SUCCESSOR
        OF I */
    R(FREE) = AG(I); D(FREE) = J; AG (I) = FREE; FREE = FREE + 1;
    /* THUS J IS TAKEN INTO THE LIST DETERMINED BY AG(I) */
END;
/*  THE INPUT HAS BEEN STORED NOW; IT REMAINS TO SET
    UP THE STACK S AS DESCRIBED IN C) ABOVE */
DO T = 1 TO N;
    IF F(T) = 0 THEN DO:
                        R(FREE) = AS;
                        D(FREE) = T;
                        AS = FREE;
                        FREE = FREE + 1;
                    END;
END;
/* NOW THE OUTPUT CAN BE OBTAINED STEP BY STEP */
DO WHILE (AS ¬= 0);
    I = D(AS); AS = R(AS); PUT LIST (I);
    /* SINCE I IS IN S IT HAS NO PREDECESSOR */
    AUX = AG(I);
    DO WHILE (AUX ¬= 0); /* IF AUX = 0 THEN I HAS
                            NO FURTHER SUCCESSORS */
        J = D(AUX);
        F(J) = F(J) − 1;
        IF F(J) = 0 THEN DO; /* J HAS TO BE ADDED TO STACK
                        S OF NUMBERS WITHOUT PREDECESSORS */
                        R(FREE) = AS;
                        D(FREE) = J;
                        AS = FREE;
                        FREE = FREE + 1;
                    END;
        AUX = R(AUX);
    END;
    END;
    END;
END;
```

For a better understanding of the program above, work through it using an example. Assume there is the input $(7, 9)$ and $r = \{(1, 2), (1, 3), (2, 4), (2, 5), (2, 6), (3, 5), (3, 7), (5, 7), (6, 7)\}$ that describes the partial ordering of seven numbers 1, 2, ..., 7 as shown in Fig. 2.2.9. An arrow goes from i to j if i is a predecessor of j (relative to r), i.e., if the pair (i, j) appears in the input. The arrangement of the data in memory at the end of the input process is described in Fig. 2.2.10.

Here, for example, $\delta f_5 = 2$ indicates that 5 has two predecessors relative to r; $\rho ag_4 = 0$ indicates that 4 has no successors. On the other hand, 1 has exactly two successors, namely 3 and 2, since $\delta \sigma \rho ag_1 = 3$ and $\delta \sigma \rho \sigma \rho ag_1 = 2$ and $\rho \sigma \rho \sigma \rho ag_1 = 0$. Since $\rho as = 10$ and $\delta \sigma 10 = 1$, $\rho \sigma 10 = 0$, the number 1 is initially the only one without a predecessor.

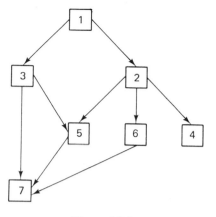

**Figure 2.2.9**

The program produces the topological sorting 1, 2, 4, 6, 3, 5, 7 that represents one of the possible topological sortings. The given program is quite efficient: Only $n + m$ steps are required. Sequential allocation is probably the most appropriate choice for the storage of the lists $F, G_1, G_2, \ldots, G_n$ and S since ready access to the ith node of F is needed and since no nodes are to be added or deleted. The arrays $G_1, \ldots, G_n$ require m memory locations altogether but the distribution of these memory locations among the arrays is not known at the beginning of the program; therefore *one* storage domain with a total of m memory locations should be used. If it is not to be assumed that the pairs $(i_t, j_t)$ are given in a particular order, sequential allocation is more difficult to program so linked allocation is chosen. The manipulation of S as a stack with linked allocation is optional because a queue S with sequential allocation, for example, could be chosen just as well.

As a transition into the next section, the Ackermann function will be introduced to show how stacks can be used in the calculation of recursive functions.

The *Ackermann function* $A(n, x, y)$ is defined for nonnegative whole numbers n, x, and y as follows:

$$A(n, x, y) = \begin{cases} x + 1, & \text{if } n = 0 \\ x, & \text{if } n = 1 \text{ and } y = 0 \\ 0, & \text{if } n = 2 \text{ and } y = 0 \\ 1, & \text{if } n = 3 \text{ and } y = 0 \\ 2, & \text{if } n \geqslant 4 \text{ and } y = 0 \\ A(n - 1, A(n, x, y - 1), x), & \text{if } n \neq 0 \text{ and } y \neq 0. \end{cases}$$

For example, the value of $A(2, 3, 1)$ is computed as follows:

$$A(2, 3, 1) = A(1, A(2, 3, 0), 3) = A(1, 0, 3) = A(0, A(1, 0, 2), 0)$$
$$= A(0, A(0, A(1, 0, 1), 0), 0) = A(0, A(0, A(0, A(1, 0, 0), 0), 0), 0)$$
$$= A(0, A(0, A(0, 0, 0), 0), 0) = A(0, A(0, 1, 0), 0) = A(0, 2, 0) = 3.$$

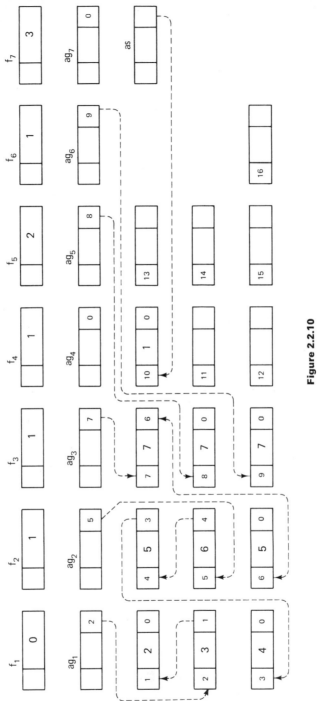

**Figure 2.2.10**

42

The Ackermann function has the remarkable property that

$$A (0, x, y) = x + 1$$
$$A (1, x, y) = x + y$$
$$A (2, x, y) = x \times y$$
$$A (3, x, y) = x^y$$

Thus it increases rapidly as n increases. Its practical value is slight; however, it is used in the theory of recursive functions as an example of a recursive function that is not simply recursive. Note that $A (n, x, y)$ either can be computed directly or can be replaced by $A (n - 1, t, x)$ as long as $t = A (n, x, y - 1)$ is known. It is natural to use a stack S in which the value of each node is a triple $(i, j, k)$ of numbers and for the computation of $A (n, x, y)$ to follow the procedure outlined here.

Initially the stack S consists of exactly one node with the value $(n, x, y)$. Now we repeatedly consider the node currently at the top of the stack, where two cases must be distinguished:

*Case 1:* [For the value $(n ,x, y)$ of the first node, where $n = 0$ or $y = 0$] Lct t be the value of $A (n, x, y)$ that can be computed directly; the first node is removed from S; if S is now empty, then t represents the value originally desired and the process terminates. Otherwise the value $(n', x', y')$ of the present first node is replaced by $(n' - 1, t, x')$ and the process continues.

*Case 2:* [For the value $(n, x, y)$ of the first node, where $n \neq 0$ and $y \neq 0$] A new node with a value of $(n, x, y - 1)$ is added to S and the process continues.

Figure 2.2.11 shows how the value of $A (2, 3, 1)$ is determined using the stack S. It is seen from the illustration that $A (2, 3, 1) = A (1, 0, 3) = A (0, 2, 0) = 3$.

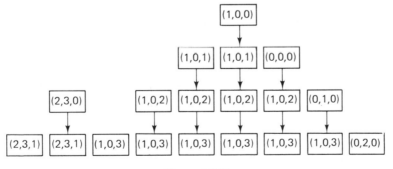

**Figure 2.2.11**

*Remarks and References*

The concept described in this book as a Backus system was introduced in Backus [1]. It also appears in the literature under the names *Backus normal form, Backus–Naur form, BNF, context-free grammar,* among others; see, for example, Ginsburg [1], Maurer [1]. The suggested solution for a topological sort arises from Knuth [1], whose book can generally be regarded as a standard reference on the subject of data structures. For the theoretical significance of the Ackermann function, see Hermes [1].

## Exercises

**2.2.1**   An initially empty storage domain consisting of 100 memory locations is given and is to be used in the sequential storage of a queue. A sequence of whole numbers is given as input. A number $n > 0$ indicates that n is to be added to the queue; $n = -1$ indicates that an element is to be removed from the queue, and $n = 0$ signals the end of the input. Design a program segment that manipulates the queue as a circular structure and prints error messages as soon as unusual conditions are detected.

**2.2.2**   For two arbitrary stacks X and Y an operation $X \longrightarrow Y$ is defined that removes an element from X and adds it to Y. Three stacks A, B, and C are given as input. Stack A originally contains the n elements $1, 2, 3, \ldots, n$ in this order with 1 at the top of the stack. Stacks B and C are initially empty. By repeated application of the operations $A \longrightarrow B$ and $B \longrightarrow C$, the elements $1, 2, 3, \ldots, n$ are brought into the stack C, whereby a certain ordering (*permutation*) $i_1, i_2, \ldots, i_n$ is produced. (The procedure described may be visualized using Fig. 2.2.1 if the numbers $1, 2, \ldots, n$ are interpreted as freight cars on track A that can be switched to track C only by moving in the direction indicated by the arrows.)
(a)   For $n = 4$, determine all possible permutations $i_1, i_2, i_3, i_4$ that can be obtained.
(b)   Let g(n) denote the number of different permutations $i_1, i_2, \ldots, i_n$ that can be obtained. Determine a recursion formula for g(n) and use it to compute g(5) and g(6). Also compute $\lim_{n \to \infty} [g(n)/n!]$ using the inequality $n! > n^n e^{-n}$ (for $n \geqslant 3$).

**2.2.3**   A sequence $F = a_1, a_2, \ldots, a_k$ of whole numbers $a_1 \leqslant a_2 \leqslant \cdots \leqslant a_k$ and a free storage stack V are stored as simple linked structures with start pointers af and av. Design a program segment that, for every i, where $1 \leqslant i \leqslant k - 1$, where $a_i = a_{i+1}$, removes the number $a_{i+1}$ from the chain and adds the vacated memory location to the free storage stack V. The declaration **DCL** (D(N), R(N), AF, AV) **FIXED BIN**; should be used for the data field and pointer field of the memory locations and the start pointers.

**2.2.4**   Design a program for the simultaneous sequential storage of five stacks using m memory locations. If a reallocation by shifting becomes necessary, all stacks should be rearranged so that unoccupied memory locations are equally distributed among the stacks. Initially all five stacks are empty. Input consists of pairs (i, j) of whole numbers where $1 \leqslant \text{abs} (i) \leqslant 5$. The pair (i, j) with $i > 0$ indicates that a node with value j is to be added to the ith stack; the pair (i, j) with $i < 0$ indicates that a node is to be removed from the ith stack. The program should print the arrangement of the five stacks before and after every reallocation.

**2.2.5**  Improve the program in Example 2.2.4 so that it will check whether the given expression really is a valid parenthesis-free expression.

**2.2.6**  Let $r = \{(i, j) \mid \mod (i, j) = 0, j < i \leqslant 100\}$ be a relation on $M = \{2, \ldots, 100\}$.
(a)  Prove that r is a partial ordering.
(b)  Design a program to print the elements of M topologically sorted.

**2.2.7**  Write a program that computes the value $A(n, x, y)$ of the Ackermann function for an arbitrary triple $(n, x, y)$, using a stack as explained in the text. The program should terminate if the numbers, the required number of memory locations, or the necessary number of recursion steps exceed the three given values a, b, and c, respectively.

**2.2.8**  Write a program that uses a stack to compute the value $f(m, n)$ for any pair of whole numbers $m, n \geqslant 0$ using

$$f(m, n) = \begin{cases} m + n + 1 & \text{if } m \times n = 0 \\ f[m - 1, f(m, n - 1)] & \text{if } m \times n \neq 0. \end{cases}$$

### Section 2.3   Stacks and Procedures

In Sec. 2.2 a stack was used in the computation of a recursive function. This was an application of a general principle: In the process of replacing program segments with procedure calls by equivalent program segments without procedure calls, stacks are found to be convenient working tools. Such substitutions must be performed, for example, by a compiler if a program in a procedure-oriented programming language is to be translated into a programming language that is not procedure-oriented.

In this section it will be shown how in PL/I programs certain procedures (which may call on themselves) can be replaced by equivalent PL/I program segments without procedures, by using stacks for the storage of "return labels" and auxiliary variables. The technique can be used, for example, to convert PL/I programs with recursively used procedures into equivalent programs in a programming language, such as Fortran, for instance, which does not permit the recursive use of procedures. The technique further shows the versatility of stacks and also permits an insight to the nature of recursivity in programming languages.

For the explanations given in this section, let a *block* be a construction of the form **BEGIN ... END** or **PROCEDURE ... END** or **DO ... END** and call everything inside such a block A, but not inside any block contained in $\Lambda$, the *scope of block $\Lambda$*.

Now consider a PL/I program which consists of a block A and which contains, in the scope of a block B inside A, the declaration of a procedure f, the definition of which is block C. The declaration of procedure f and its calls are to be replaced by equivalent program segments in which no procedure calls are used. For simplicity the following conditions 1 through 3 should be satisfied:

(1)   All arguments are passed by value; i.e., each argument must be an expression different from a single variable name. The type of f (if f is a function procedure) and the type of each parameter and each local variable of f is **FIXED BIN**. Arrays appear neither as arguments nor as local values in the procedure body C. There are no transfer instructions leading out of the procedure body. All labels used locally in procedure body C must be different from those that are valid in B.[3]

(2)   If f is a function procedure, then every call on f must have the form $v = f(a_1, a_2, \ldots, a_s)$, where $a_1, a_2, \ldots, a_s$ are the arguments and v is a variable.

(3)   No procedure call, be it of the form **CALL** $f(a_1, a_2, \ldots, a_s)$ or $v = f(a_1, a_2, \ldots, a_s)$, may appear directly after **THEN** or **ELSE**.[4] Calls on f may appear only in the scope of B or C (the latter permits recursive calls).[5] A **RETURN** statement must be of the form either **RETURN** or **RETURN** (t), where the expression t does not contain the name of a programmer-defined function.

To begin with, let f be a procedure that does not return a value with parameters $f_1, f_2, \ldots, f_s$ and local variables $f_{s+1}, f_{s+2}, \ldots, f_t$. If in the given program there are k calls on f, then RETF(1), RETF(2), $\ldots$, RETF(k) are k new labels (of a label array with name RETF), SF is an additional name (for a stack that gives the current values of the parameters, the local variables, and the return labels using the $t + 1$ components of the topmost node), ZF is an additional name (which corresponds to a start pointer for the sequentially stored stack SF), and JUMPF is an additional label (which is used to jump over the modified procedure body if it is not to be executed).

An equivalent program without procedure f can be obtained by following suggestions 1 through 6:

(1)   Add to the declarations for block B

**DCL** (SF(T + 1, 100), ZF) **FIXED BIN**;

The elements SF(1, I), SF(2, I), $\ldots$, SF(T + 1, I) represent the $t + 1$ components of the ith node of the stack SF. The elements SF(1, I), $\ldots$, SF(S, I) serve as parameters; SF(S + 1, I), $\ldots$, SF(T, I) are local variables; and SF(T + 1, I) is for the return.

---

[3]This is necessary in order to avoid conflict between labels that could arise in the processing of C. Systematic naming of all labels is a simple solution to this potential problem.

[4]Certain cases, such as **IF** $x > 0$ **THEN** f(a, b);, must be avoided since a call f(a, b) is replaced by more than one instruction. Such situations can always be avoided through suitable modifications in the program; in the example above, use **IF** $x \leqslant 0$ **THEN GOTO** H; f(a, b); H:;.

[5]The procedure call must be replaced by a transfer to a modified procedure body, the statements defining the procedure, and a return to the point after the call. For further observations, see Example 3.1.5.

(2)     Add to the declarations for block B:

   **DCL RETF(K) LABEL**;

(3)     $ZF = 0$; is inserted as the first statement after the declarations in block B.
        The value $ZF = 0$ indicates that the stack SF is initially empty.

(4)     If **CALL** $f(a_1, a_2, \ldots, a_s)$ is the ith textual occurrence of a call of the
        procedure f, then that call is replaced by the program segment

   **IF** $ZF \geqslant 100$ **THEN CALL ERROR** (1);
   $SF(1, ZF + 1) = a_1$; $SF(2, ZF + 1) = a_2$; $\cdots$; $SF(S, ZF + 1) = a_s$;
   $SF(T + 1, ZF + 1) = I$; $ZF = ZF + 1$; **GOTO** F;
   RETF(I): $ZF = ZF - 1$;

   In the above, RETF(I) stands for RETF(1) if $I = 1$, for RETF(2) if $I = 2$,
   etc. If $ZF \geqslant 100$, then the stack SF (the choice of 100 for its size being
   quite arbitrary) is too small for the nesting of calls occurring. Note that
   the statement $SF(T + 1, ZF + 1) = I$; provides for a possible jump back
   to RETF(I) at a later time by means of **GOTO** RETF($SF(T + 1, ZF)$);.
   The label f in **GOTO** f; is used to jump to the beginning of the modified
   procedure body (see 5c below).

(5)     Let X be the procedure body of f modified according to 5a through 5d:
(5a)    The declarations of local variables are removed.
(5b)    Every parameter and every local variable $f_i$ is replaced by $SF(I, ZF)$.
(5c)    Add to the beginning of the procedure body C the statement **GOTO**
        JUMPF; F: and replace each **RETURN** statement by the statement **GOTO**
        RETF($SF(T + 1, ZF)$);.
(5d)    The **END** of the procedure body C is replaced by **GOTO** RETF($SF(T + 1,$
        $ZF)$); JUMPF:.
(6)     The entire procedure declaration of f is removed from B and the program
        segment X is inserted immediately after the declarations remaining in B.

**Example 2.3.1** (Removing a Recursive Procedure) Consider the program

```
WITH: PROC OPTIONS (MAIN);
   DCL (N, M) FIXED BIN;
   F: PROCEDURE (F1, F2) RECURSIVE;
      DCL (F1, F2, F3) FIXED BIN;
      IF F1 > F2 THEN GOTO FINISH;
      IF MOD (F2, F1) = 0 THEN F3 = F1 + 1;
                          ELSE F3 = F1 + 3;
      CALL F(+F3, F2 − 1);
      FINISH: PUT LIST (F1, F2);
   END F;
   GET LIST (N, M); CALL F(+N, +M);
END;
```

Convince yourself that this program with input n = 4, m = 16 prints the following sequence of pairs:

    13, 11;
    12, 12;
     9, 13;
     6, 14;
     5, 15;
     4, 16;

An equivalent program without procedures may be obtained using the technique described. Let k = 2 (two calls on f), let t = 3 (two parameters, one local variable), and let block A be the same as block B:

```
WITHOUT: PROC OPTIONS (MAIN);
    DCL (N, M) FIXED BIN, ERROR ENTRY (FIXED DEC);
    DCL (SF(4, 100), ZF) FIXED BIN; /* ACCORDING TO 1 ABOVE */
    DCL RETF(2) LABEL; /* ACCORDING TO 2 ABOVE */
    ZF = 0; /* ACCORDING TO 3 ABOVE */
    /* THE FOLLOWING IS OBTAINED ACCORDING TO 6) ABOVE */
    GOTO JUMPF; F: IF SF(1, ZF) > SF(2, ZF) THEN GOTO FINISH;
    IF MOD (SF(2, ZF), SF(1, ZF)) = 0 THEN
        SF(3, ZF) = SF(1, ZF) + 1; ELSE SF(3, ZF) = SF(1, ZF) + 3;
    IF ZF >= 100 THEN CALL ERROR (1);
    SF(1, ZF + 1) = SF(3, ZF); SF(2, ZF + 1) = SF(2, ZF) − 1;
    SF(4, ZF + 1) = 1; ZF = ZF + 1; GOTO F;
    RETF(1): ZF = ZF − 1;
    /* THE LAST FOUR LINES CORRESPOND TO CALL F(+F3, F2 − 1) */
    FINISH: PUT LIST (SF(1, ZF), SF(2, ZF));
    GOTO RETF(SF(4, ZF)); JUMPF:;
    /* ACCORDING TO 6) THE PART GOTO JUMPF; ... JUMPF:;
        REPLACES THE PROCEDURE DECLARATION */
    GET LIST (N, M);
    IF ZF >= 100 THEN CALL ERROR (1);
    SF(1, ZF + 1) = N; SF(2, ZF + 1) = M;
    SF(4, ZF + 1) = 2; ZF = ZF + 1;
    GOTO F; RETF(2): ZF = ZF − 1;
    /* THE LAST THREE LINES CORRESPOND TO CALL F(+N, +M) */
END;
```

Figure 2.3.1 shows the stack SF and the printed output obtained during the execution of the program, using the input n = 4, m = 16, specifically the output produced before the execution of each GOTO F;.

Work through the program for n = 4, m = 16 using Fig. 2.3.1 and notice in particular that there are five transfers to the label RETF(1).

For function procedures, we proceed just as we did to eliminate subroutine procedures from PL/I programs. Let f be a function procedure with parameters $f_1, f_2, \ldots, f_s$ and local variables $f_{s+1}, \ldots, f_t$. Let RETF(1), ..., RETF(K), JUMPF, ZF, and SF be defined as for subroutine procedures, except that the nodes of stack SF have an additional component available that is used to store the function value.

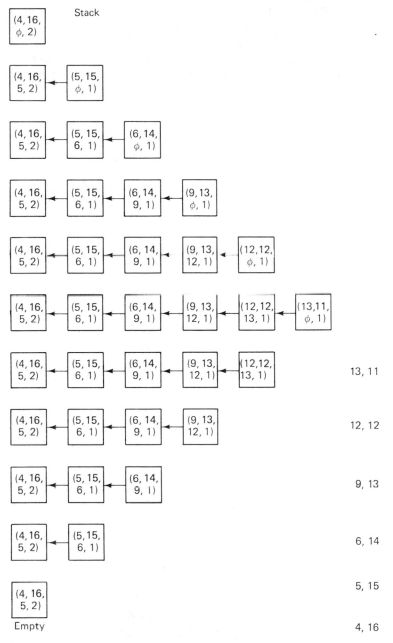

**Figure 2.3.1**

We shall use points 1 through 5 with several slight modifications. In 1, we use
**DCL** SF(T + 2, 100) **FIXED BIN**; instead of **DCL** SF(T + 1, 100) **FIXED BIN**;.
The element SF(T + 2, I) is used for the storage of the function value. In 4, we are
concerned with the replacement of the assignment statement $v = f(a_1, a_2, \ldots, a_n)$.
We replace it as in 4, but after RETF(I): ZF = ZF − 1;, the additional assignment
statement $v = $ SF(T + 2, ZF + 1); is inserted, which accomplishes the assignment
of the computed function value.

In 5c each statement **RETURN**(y); is replaced by **DO**; SF(T + 2, ZF) = y;
**GOTO** RETF(SF(T + 1, ZF)); **END**;, where y is an arbitrary expression.

**Example 2.3.2** (Removing a Recursive Function Procedure) The following program accepts the input n, x, y and computes and prints the value of the Ackermann
function A (n, x, y) using the recursively defined function procedure A.

```
ACK: PROC OPTIONS (MAIN);
     DCL (T, N, X, Y) FIXED BIN;
     A: PROCEDURE (N, X, Y) RECURSIVE RETURNS (FIXED BIN);
        DCL (N, X, Y, Z) FIXED BIN;
        IF N = 0 THEN RETURN (X + 1);
        IF Y = 0 THEN DO;
                        IF N = 1 THEN Z = X;
                        ELSE IF N = 2 THEN Z = 0;
                        ELSE IF N = 3 THEN Z = 1;
                        ELSE Z = 2; RETURN (Z);
                  END;
        Z = A(+N, +X, Y − 1);
        Z = A(N − 1, +Z, +X); RETURN (Z);
     END A;
     GET LIST (N, X, Y);
     T = A(+N, +X, +Y);
     PUT LIST (T);
END;
```

By removing procedure A we obtain

```
ACK2: PROC OPTIONS (MAIN);
      DCL (T, N, X, Y, SA(6, 100), ZA) FIXED BIN,
          ERROR ENTRY (FIXED DEC (1));
      DCL (RETA(3), A) LABEL; ZA = 0; /* NOW COMES THE
                              MODIFIED PROCEDURE BODY */
      GOTO JUMPA;
      A: IF SA(1, ZA) = 0 THEN DO; SA(6, ZA) = SA(2, ZA) + 1;
         GOTO RETA(SA(5, ZA)); END; IF SA(3, ZA) = 0 THEN DO;
             IF SA(1, ZA) = 1 THEN SA(4, ZA) = SA(2, ZA);
             ELSE IF SA(1, ZA) = 2 THEN SA(4, ZA) = 0;
             ELSE IF SA(1, ZA) = 3 THEN SA(4, ZA) = 1;
             ELSE SA(4, ZA) = 2;
             DO; SA(6, ZA) = SA(4, ZA); GOTO RETA(SA(5, ZA));
               END; END;
```

IF ZA > = 100 **THEN CALL** ERROR (1);
SA(1, ZA + 1) = SA(1, ZA); SA(2, ZA + 1) = SA(2, ZA);
SA(3, ZA + 1) = SA(3, ZA) − 1; SA(5, ZA + 1) = 1;
ZA = ZA + 1; **GOTO** A; RETA(1): ZA = ZA − 1;
SA(4, ZA) = SA(6, ZA + 1); /* CORRESPONDS TO
                    Z = A(+N, +X, Y − 1) */
IF ZA > = 100 **THEN CALL** ERROR (1);
SA(1, ZA + 1) = SA(1, ZA) − 1; SA(2, ZA + 1) =
SA(4, ZA); SA(3, ZA + 1) = SA(2, ZA); SA(5, ZA + 1)
= 2; ZA = ZA + 1; **GOTO** A; RETA(2): ZA = ZA − 1;
SA(4, ZA) = SA(6, ZA + 1); /* CORRESPONDS TO
                    Z = A(N − 1, +Z, +X) */
**DO**; SA(6, ZA) = SA(4, ZA); **GOTO** RETA(SA(5, ZA));
**END**; /* CORRESPONDS TO **RETURN** (Z) */
**GOTO** RETA(SA(5, ZA)); JUMPA: ;
**GET LIST** (N, X, Y); **IF** ZA > = 100 **THEN CALL** ERROR (1);
SA(1, ZA + 1) − N; SA(2, ZA + 1) − X; SA(3, ZA + 1)
= Y; SA(5, ZA + 1) = 3; ZA = ZA + 1; **GOTO** A;
RETA(3): ZA = ZA − 1; T = SA(6, ZA + 1);
/* CORRESPONDS TO T = A(+N, +X, +Y) */
**PUT LIST** (T);
     **END**;

The technique described for the replacement of procedures can be improved in several respects. Conditions 1 through 3 can be relaxed. Also, instead of a separate stack for each procedure we could introduce one stack for all the procedures. Using this technique we would have to pay particular attention to variables that are local to a procedure P but global to another procedure Q, a situation that is illustrated in Fig. 2.3.2 for the variable A.

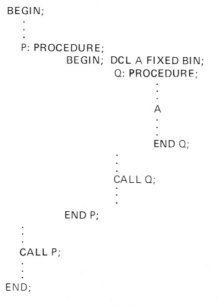

```
            BEGIN;
              .
              .
              .
            P: PROCEDURE;
                  BEGIN; DCL A FIXED BIN;
                        Q: PROCEDURE;
                              .
                              .
                              .
                            A
                              .
                              .
                              .
                            END Q;
                              .
                              .
                              .
                        CALL Q;
                              .
                              .
                              .
                      END P;
              .
              .
            CALL P;
              .
              .
            END;
```

**Figure 2.3.2**

## Exercises

**2.3.1** Determine the output of the program in Example 2.3.1 for
(a) $n = 2$, $m = 20$, (b) $n = 3$, $m = 20$.

**2.3.2** What happens in the program of Example 2.3.1 if we substitute **PUT LIST** (F1, F3); for **PUT LIST** (F1, F2);?

**2.3.3** The greatest common divisor $g(m, n)$ of two whole numbers m and n can be determined using the recursion formula

$$g(m, n) = \begin{cases} m, & \text{if } n = 0 \\ g(n, \text{mod } (m, n)), & \text{if } n \neq 0. \end{cases}$$

Write a program that uses a recursively defined procedure $g(m, n)$ to determine the greatest common divisor of several pairs of numbers. Then substitute for that procedure a nonrecursive one, using exactly the technique described in the text.

**2.3.4** For three whole numbers a, b, c > 0, the remainder (a, b, c) is defined recursively by

$$\text{remainder } (a, b, c) = \begin{cases} \text{remainder}\left(a^2, \dfrac{b}{2}, c\right), & \text{for } a < c \text{ and } b \geqslant 2, \text{ b even} \\ \text{mod}\left[a \times \text{remainder}\left(a^2, \dfrac{b-1}{2}, c\right)\right], & \text{for } a < c \text{ and } b \geqslant 3, \text{ b odd} \\ a, & \text{for } a < c \text{ and } b = 1 \\ \text{remainder } [\text{mod } (a, c), b, c], & \text{for } a \geqslant c. \end{cases}$$

[Notice that remainder (a, b, c) determines the value of mod $(a^b, c)$.] Write a recursive program to compute remainder (a, b, c) for several triples of numbers. Then convert this recursive program into a nonrecursive one using the technique described in the text.

## Section 2.4 Compressed, Indexed, and Scatter Storage

When working with linear lists in which several nodes have the same value V, we may sometimes simply not store these nodes and conclude that where a node does not appear in the structure it has the value V. This is the basic concept of *compressed storage*.

**Definition 2.4.1** (Compressed Storage) Let $F = k_1, k_2, \ldots, k_n$ be a sequence of nodes in which several nodes have the same value V. Let $F' = k'_1, k'_2, \ldots, k'_n$ be a sequence obtained from F by replacing each node $k_i$ by the node $k'_i$, where $\omega k'_i = (i, \omega k_i)$. Thus every node $k'_i$ carries along as a value the *original position* of $k_i$ in F.

Now let $F'' = k''_1, k''_2, \ldots, k''_m$ be a subsequence of $F'$, obtained by deleting all nodes k', for which $\omega k' = (i, V)$. Any method of storing F'' is called a *compressed storage* of F, in which nodes having value V are *suppressed*.

Compressed storage is always used along with another type of storage. We use the term *sequential compressed* if compressed and sequential storage are used and the term *linked compressed* if compressed and linked storage are used.

**Example 2.4.1** Figure 2.4.2(a) shows a sequential compressed storage and Fig. 2.4.2(b) shows a linked compressed storage of the linear list represented graphically in Fig. 2.4.1. Nodes having the value * are suppressed. Thus, for example, SHE $= \omega_2 k_3'' = \omega k_{\omega_1 k''_3} = \omega k_6$ and, in general, $\omega_2 k_i'' = \omega k_{\omega_1 k''_i}$; that is, the value $\omega_2 k_i''$ of the second component of $k_i''$ is the value of that node $k_p$ whose position in F is given by the first component of $k_i''$, $p = \omega_1 k_i''$.

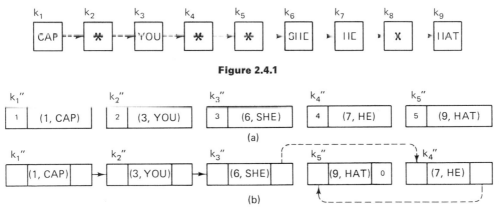

Figure 2.4.1

(a)

(b)

Figure 2.4.2

The obvious advantage of compressed storage lies in the possible reduction of storage space requirements.

If a linear list is stored in compressed form, then the value of the ith node is not so easily determined as when sequential storage is used. When using linked compressed storage it is necessary to search all used memory locations; while in the case of sequential compressed storage an efficient binary search (see Sec. 2.7) is possible. The advantages and disadvantages of linked compressed storage as compared to sequential compressed storage are similar to the advantages and disadvantages of linked storage as compared to sequential storage.

The next example illustrates an interesting application of compressed storage.

**Example 2.4.2** Given as input there is a sequence $m = m_1, m_2, \ldots, m_{10000}$ followed by a sequence $n = n_1, n_2, \ldots, n_{10000}$ of whole numbers, where less than 8% of the values in m are different from zero. We wish to design a program to compute

$$\text{SUM} = \sum_{i=1}^{10000} m_i n_i.^6$$

---

[6] That is, the *inner product* of the vectors m and n is to be computed.

In the following program, first the sequence m is sequentially compressed in memory (zeros are suppressed) and then the elements of n are read and the desired SUM is determined.

```
COM: PROC OPTIONS (MAIN);
    DCL (D1(800), D2(800)) FIXED BIN;
    /* FOR THE COMPRESSED STORAGE OF M */
    DCL (I, P, INP, SUM) FIXED BIN;
    P = 1;
    DO I = 1 TO 10000;
        GET LIST (INP);
        IF INP ¬= 0 THEN DO;
                        D1(P) = I;
                        D2(P) = INP;
                        P = P + 1;
                    END;
    END; /* NOW M IS STORED IN COMPRESSED FORM */
    D1(P) = 99999;
    SUM = 0;
    P = 1;
    DO I = 1 TO 10000;
        GET LIST (INP);
        DO WHILE (I > D1(P));
            P = P + 1;
        END;
        IF (I = D1(P)) & (INP ¬= 0) THEN DO;
                        SUM = SUM + D2(P) * INP;
                        P = P + 1;
                    END;
    END;
    PUT LIST (SUM);
END;
```

Another possibility in the storage of linear lists is offered by *indexed storage*. The fundamental concept consists of replacing the list B by several lists $B_1, B_2, \ldots, B_m$ (which altogether exactly comprise the nodes of B) and then using an additional *index list* whose m nodes give the beginning nodes of the m lists $B_1, B_2, \ldots, B_m$ for the purpose of finding the nodes.

**Definition 2.4.2** (Indexed Storage) Let $B = (K, R)$ be a linear list with the sequence of nodes $F = k_1, k_2, \ldots, k_n$ and let $K_1, K_2, \ldots, K_m$ be a partitioning of K. Arrange the nodes of the sets $K_1, K_2, \ldots, K_m$ in sequences $F_1, F_2, \ldots, F_m$ in any way as long as $F_1, F_2, \ldots, F_m$ are subsequences of F, and denote the beginning nodes of these sequences with $g_1, g_2, \ldots, g_m$. If the sequences $F_1, F_2, \ldots, F_m$ are stored with an additional *index sequence* or *index list* having nodes $X = x_1, x_2, \ldots, x_m$ with $\omega_1 x_i = \alpha g_i$ for $1 \leqslant i \leqslant m$, then F is said to be stored using *indexed storage*.

If a node k belongs to the ith subsequence $F_i$, then k is said to have *index* i.

It is sometimes appropriate to modify the indexed allocation just described by carrying along with the nodes of the subsequences $F_1, F_2, \ldots, F_m$ the initial position of the nodes in F, as is done with compressed storage. Also, if desired, the ith node

$x_i$ of the index list may contain additional information besides the address of the beginning node of $F_i$. The partitioning of K into a sequence of subsets $K_1, K_2, \ldots, K_m$ results from combining all nodes having a certain property P in one set or sequence.

The actual advantage of indexed allocation is that, to locate a node k with property P, it is not necessary to search through all the nodes of K. Since in the partitioning of K all nodes with property P are assigned to a sequence T, only the nodes of T need be searched, and the address of the beginning node of T can be found in the index list.

In partitioning K we often use what is called an *index function* g that yields, for each node k, the index i of k; i.e., $g(k) = i$. In general, the index function depends on only $\pi_F k$ (the position of k in F) or on the value $\omega_j k$ of the jth component of a node k; this component is then called the *key*.

**Example 2.4.3** Let $F = k_1, k_2, \ldots, k_9$ be a sequence of nodes with

$$\omega k_1, \omega k_2, \ldots, \omega k_9 = (17, YOU), (23, HE), (60, IT), (90, SHE), (166, THEY),$$
$$(177, THEM), (250, US), (288, WE), (300, SO).$$

(a)   The index function

$g_a(k) = 1 + (\pi k - 1) \div 3$

produces the subsequences of F:

$F_1 = (17, YOU), (23, HE), (60, IT)$

$F_2 = (90, SHE), (166, THEY), (177, THEM)$

$F_3 = (250, US), (288, WE), (300, SO)$

or, if the initial positions are carried along,

$F_1 = (1, 17, YOU), (2, 23, HE), (3, 60, IT)$

$F_2 = (4, 90, SHE), (5, 166, THEY), (6, 177, THEM)$

$F_3 = (7, 250, US), (8, 288, WE), (9, 300, SO)$.

Since $g_a$ depends only on the position $\pi k$ of the node k, to find $k_6$, for example, it is necessary to search only the subsequence $F_{g_a(6)} = F_2$ and not the entire sequence F.

(b)   The index function

$g_b(k) = 1 + \mod (\pi k - 1, 3)$

yields (carrying along the initial positions)

$F_1 = (1, 17, YOU), (4, 90, SHE), (7, 250, US)$

$F_2 = (2, 23, HE), (5, 166, THEY), (8, 288, WE)$

$F_3 = (3, 60, IT), (6, 177, THEM), (9, 300, SO)$.

Since $g_b$ depends only on the position $\pi k$ of the node k, it is necessary to search only the subsequence $F_{g_b(6)} = F_3$ and not the entire sequence F to locate $k_6$.

(c)    The index function

$$g_c(k) = 1 + \omega_1 k \div 100$$

yields the subsequences

$F_1 = (17, \text{YOU}), (23, \text{HE}), (60, \text{IT}), (90, \text{SHE})$

$F_2 = (166, \text{THEY}), (177, \text{THEM})$

$F_3 = (250, \text{US}), (288, \text{WE})$

$F_4 = (300, \text{SO}).$

Since $g_c$ depends only on the value $\omega_1 k$ of the first component of k, to find a node k with key 177 (i.e., with $\omega_1 k = 177$), only the subsequence $F_{g_c(177)} = F_2$ must be searched.

With indexed storage an arbitrary storage technique A can be used for the index list X and an arbitrary storage technique B can be used for the sequences $F_1, F_2, \ldots,$ $F_n$. To indicate specifically which techniques are used, we speak of an *A-indexed-B* storage technique.

In actual practice, the use of a sequential-indexed-linked technique is favored because it represents a certain compromise between sequential and linked storage. First, as with linked allocation, it is not necessary to undertake extensive reallocation during the addition and deletion of nodes. On the other hand, to locate a node, it is not necessary to search the entire sequence as would be the case with linked allocation, but rather it is sufficient to search a subsequence.

**Example 2.4.4** Figure 2.4.3 shows a sequential-indexed-linked allocation with index sequence $X = x_1, x_2, x_3, x_4$ corresponding to Example 2.4.3(c) with index function

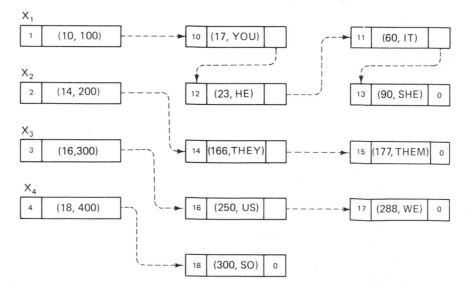

**Figure 2.4.3**

$g_c$. Notice that $\omega_1 x_i$ gives the address of the beginning node of the subsequence $F_i$ and $\omega_2 x_i$ contains additional information that facilitates the computation of $g_c(t)$ for a given key t, using the formula $g_c(t) = \min \{i \,|\, t < \omega_2 x_i\}$. The index of a node with key t can therefore be determined by searching the index sequence until a node $x \in X$ is found for which the key t is smaller then $\omega_2 x$.

The index list used with indexed storage can itself be stored as an indexed structure. Arbitrary nesting of indexed allocations is therefore possible.

**Example 2.4.5** Figure 2.4.4 shows the linked-indexed-linked-indexed-linked storage of a list $B = (K, R)$ with the sequence of nodes $F = k_1, k_2, \ldots, k_{10}$ for which

$$\omega k_1, \omega k_2, \ldots, \omega k_{10} = (338, Z), (145, A), (136, H), (214, I), (146, C), (334, Y),$$
$$(333, P), (127, G), (310, O), (322, X).$$

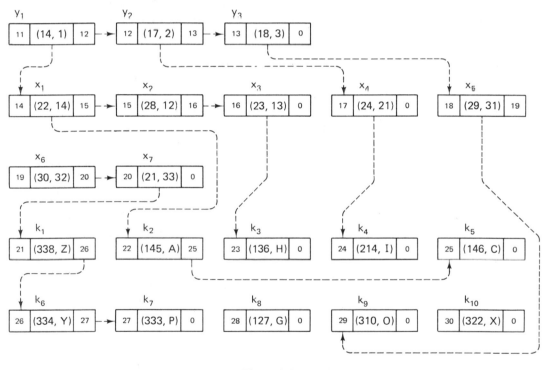

**Figure 2.4.4**

First, all nodes whose first components agree in the first two digits are put into a sequence. The nodes belonging to the index sequence $X = x_1, x_2, \ldots, x_7$ contain these two digits as additional information. The index sequence X is itself indexed with index sequence $Y = y_1, y_2, y_3$ by collecting nodes together that agree in the first digit of the additional information. The nodes of Y contain this digit as additional information. To locate a node with key t, whose first digit is $t_1$ and whose first two digits are $t_{1,2}$, we first search Y until we find a node y for which $\omega_2 x = t_1$. Next we search the linked nodes of X, beginning with address $\omega_1 y$, until a node x is found for which $\omega_2 x = t_{1,2}$. The linked nodes beginning at address $\omega_1 x$ are then searched until finally the node k is found with key t, i.e., with $\omega_1 k = t$.

As an example, suppose we wish to locate the node with key $t = 127$. We find that $\omega_2 y_1 = \delta_2 \sigma 11 = 1$ so we search beginning with $\omega_1 y_1 = 14$. Now $\delta_2 \sigma 14 \neq 12$ but $\rho \sigma 14 = 15$ and $\delta_2 \sigma 15 = 12$. Therefore we continue the search with $\delta_1 \sigma 15 = 28$ and find $\delta_1 \sigma 28 = 127$, the desired node.

By using an appropriate nesting of indexed storage, the node sequences $F = k_1, k_2, \ldots, k_n$ can be stored so that a node k with a given key or with a given position in F can be found in very few steps of searching. This method can be described conveniently using trees. (See Chapter 3 and, in particular, Sec. 3.3 on balanced trees.)

If a set of nodes is to be searched frequently for a node for which the value of a certain component (the *key*) is given, then *scatter storage* is a useful technique. For our discussion of scatter storage it can be assumed without loss of generality that the keys are positive whole numbers and are always the first components of the nodes.

**Definition 2.4.3** (Scatter Storage) Let $B = (K, R)$ be a linear list with nodes $k_1, k_2, \ldots, k_n$ and let M be a storage area consisting of m memory locations whose first memory location has address e. Let $s : K \longrightarrow \{0, 1, 2, \ldots, m - 1\}$ be a one-to-one function. If, for every $k \in K$, $\alpha k = e + s(\omega_1 k)$, then we say the list B is stored using *scatter storage* and the function s is called a *scatter function* or a *hash function*. The advantage of scatter storage is the obvious ease with which a node k having a given key $\omega_1 k$ can be located.

**Example 2.4.6** Let $B = (K, R)$ be a linear list with 15 nodes $k_1, \ldots, k_{15}$ where

$$\omega k_1 = (12, E), \quad \omega k_2 = (33, B), \quad \omega k_3 = (65, X), \quad \omega k_4 = (9, Z),$$
$$\omega k_5 = (38, A), \quad \omega k_6 = (71, Y), \quad \omega k_7 = (82, M), \quad \omega k_8 = (63, B),$$
$$\omega k_9 = (75, Z), \quad \omega k_{10} = (15, V), \quad \omega k_{11} = (24, V), \quad \omega k_{12} = (57, R),$$
$$\omega k_{13} = (54, E), \quad \omega k_{14} = (88, R), \quad \omega k_{15} = (98, S).$$

If we use the scatter function $s(n) = n \div 5$ and a storage area with 20 memory locations, the first having address $e = 1$, then Fig. 2.4.5 shows the scatter storage of B.

If, for example, we wish to locate the node k with key $n = 71$, we can find it directly using $\alpha k = 1 + s(71) = 15$.

Let $k_1, k_2, \ldots, k_n$ again be a sequence of n nodes, let M be a storage area of size m, and let s be a function

$$s : \{k_1, k_2, \ldots, k_n\} \longrightarrow \{0, 1, \ldots, m - 1\}.$$

Even for a large choice of m it is usually difficult to find a sufficiently simple one-to-one function s.[7] For this reason, scatter storage is often used even if s is not a one-

---

[7] For example, if we choose 25 pseudo-random numbers between 1 and 400, then the chances are about 50% that two of the numbers are the same!

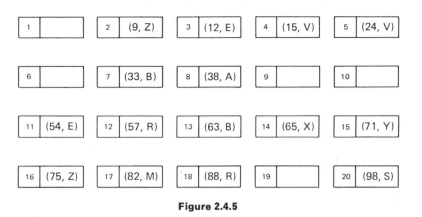

**Figure 2.4.5**

to-one function. If the scatter function s associates a memory location z with t nodes (where t > 1), then a *collision* or *hash clash* has occurred and we have an *overflow* of t — 1 nodes; this overflow must be dealt with in some way. Several possibilities suggest themselves:

(a) All overflows are stored as a single linear list separate from M.
(b) The overflows of each memory location are stored as a linear "overflow list" outside M.
(c) Overflow items are stored in memory locations of M that are not yet used.

Alternative a is particularly easy to program but only practical if there are only a few overflow items. In alternative b every memory location of M requires a pointer field to point to the beginning node of the corresponding overflow list; then additional memory space is required for the overflow list itself. In contrast, no storage space except that used for M is required in alternative c. In the literature two variations of c, c1 and c2, are proposed. In variation c1 the nodes $k_1, k_2, \ldots, k_n$ are stored consecutively. If in the process a node k is associated with the address of a memory location z that is already in use, then k is stored in that neighboring free memory location z' for which abs ($\alpha z - \alpha z'$) is as small as possible. In variation c2 no overflows are stored in the "first pass," but rather in the "second pass" overflows are stored in those memory locations of M that were not associated with any node in the first pass. Thus by using c2 an undesirable situation associated with variation c1 can be avoided, that of a memory location z being already taken by an overflow before the address of z is generated the first time by the scatter function.

The method of handling overflows, the choice of the scatter function s, and the *load factor* n/m are all important in determining the frequency with which collisions occur in scatter storage. Actual practice has shown that a load factor between 0.5 and 0.9 is satisfactory, as long as s yields a "sufficiently" uniform distribution of memory location addresses.

We shall now determine the average number of probes required to locate a node k with a given key $\omega_1 k$; method b is used for handling overflows and linked storage is used for the overflow lists. An "ideal" scatter function s is assumed, where a node has probability $p = 1/m$ of being associated with any given memory location.

The probability that a memory location z will be associated with exactly r nodes (where $0 \leqslant r \leqslant n$) is given by the binomial distribution

$$P_r = \left(\frac{n}{r}\right)\left(\frac{1}{m}\right)^r\left(1 - \frac{1}{m}\right)^{n-r}$$

For large m, this binomial distribution becomes the Poisson distribution

$$p_r = \frac{(n/m)^r}{r!}e^{-n/m} = \frac{\beta^r}{r!}e^{-\beta},$$

where $\beta = n/m$ is the load factor.

If a memory location z is associated with exactly r nodes that are linked in memory, then one probe is required to find the first node, two probes are required for the second node, etc., making a total of

$$v = 1 + 2 + \cdots + r = \frac{r(r+1)}{2} \text{ probes.}$$

The random variable v is Poisson distributed and has an expected value

$$E(v) = \sum_{r=0}^{\infty} \frac{1}{2}r(r+1)p_r = \frac{1}{2}e^{-\beta}\sum_{r=0}^{\infty} r(r+1)\frac{\beta^r}{r!}$$

and from this[8] we obtain

$$E(v) = \frac{1}{2}\beta^2 + \beta.$$

Therefore in order to find all nodes associated with an arbitrary memory location, an average of $(\beta^2/2) + \beta$ probes are necessary.

In all we have m memory locations and n nodes; thus on the average

$$\frac{m}{n}\left(\frac{1}{2}\beta^2 + \beta\right) = 1 + \frac{\beta}{2}$$

probes are required per node.

---

[8]  $$\sum_{r=0}^{\infty} r(r+1)\frac{\beta^r}{r!} = \sum_{r=0}^{\infty} r^2\frac{\beta^r}{r!} + \sum_{r=0}^{\infty} r\frac{\beta^r}{r!}, \qquad \sum_{r=0}^{\infty} r\frac{\beta^r}{r!} = \beta e^\beta;$$

from

$$f(\beta) = e^\beta = \sum_{r=0}^{\infty} \frac{\beta^r}{r!}$$

we obtain, by two differentiations,

$$f''(\beta) = e^\beta = \frac{1}{\beta^2}\sum_{r=0}^{\infty} r^2\frac{\beta^r}{r!} - \frac{1}{\beta}e^\beta$$

and from this the value

$$\sum_{r=0}^{\infty} \frac{r^2\beta^r}{r!}.$$

The significance of this result is that the average number of probes necessary to find an arbitrary node depends not on the absolute sizes of n and m but rather on the load factor $\beta = n/m$.

The average number of probes needed to locate a node using scatter storage is

$$P_1(\beta) = 1 + \frac{\beta}{2}$$

if alternative b is used for handling the overflows. If alternative c1 is used, however, it can be shown that the average number of probes is

$$P_2(\beta) = \frac{1}{2}\left(1 + \frac{1}{1-\beta}\right)$$

where

$$\lim_{\beta \to 1} \text{abs}\,[P_2(\beta)] = \infty.$$

For smaller values of $\beta$ both techniques are quite useful; for example, $P_1(0.5) = 1.25$ and $P_2(0.5) = 1.5$.

Of the many techniques for choosing a scatter function presented in the literature, we mention here two that are commonly used. The number m gives the size of the storage area that is available.

**Definition 2.4.4** (Division–Remainder Technique) Choose $p = \max\{i\,|\,i \leqslant m,$ i a prime number$\}$ and let the scatter function be $s(n) = \text{mod}\,(n, p)$. If there are, for example, n = 12 keys, F = 34, 112, 502, 86, 93, 66, 708, 801, 913, 500, 600, 88, and if we desire a load factor $\beta = n/m = 0.6$, then we would use m = 20 and p = max $\{i\,|\,i \leqslant 20,$ i a prime number$\} = 19$. For the given keys, the function $s(n) = \text{mod}\,(n, 19)$ yields the values 15, 17, 8, 10, 17, 9, 5, 3, 1, 6, 11, 12, which includes only one overflow.

**Definition 2.4.5** (Selection Technique) Let $d(j, n)$ denote the jth digit (from the right) of the decimal number n, as defined in the PL/I segment

```
D: PROCEDURE (J, N);
   RETURN (MOD (N/(10 ** (J − 1)), 10)); END;
```

Let r be an arbitrary number less than the number of digits in the key. Let $j_1 > j_2 > \cdots > j_r$ be r different numbers and let $g(n) = d(j_1, n) \times 10^{r-1} + d(j_2, n) \times 10^{r-2} + \cdots + d(j_r, n)$; i.e., $g(n)$ is that number obtained from n by selecting the digits numbered $j_1, j_2, \ldots, j_r$ (from the right).

As a scatter function s we choose $s(n) = [g(n) \times m] \div 10^r$. If, as in the example above, we have the n = 12 keys F and $\beta = 0.6$, then

$$r = \min\{i\,|\,10^i \geqslant 20\} = 2.$$

If we choose $j_1 = 2, j_2 = 1$, then we have

$$g(n) = d(2, n) \times 10 + d(1, n) \quad \text{and} \quad s(n) = g(n) \div 5;$$

therefore

$$s(34) = 6, \quad s(112) = 2, \quad s(502) = 0, \quad s(86) = 17,$$
$$s(93) = 18, \quad s(66) = 13, \quad s(708) = 1, \quad s(801) = 0,$$
$$s(913) = 2, \quad s(500) = 0, \quad s(600) = 0, \quad s(88) = 17,$$

which includes five overflows.

The positions $j_1, j_2, \ldots, j_r$ necessary in the selection technique are to be chosen, as much as possible, so that $d(j_i, n)$ produces each of the digits $0, \ldots, 9$ equally often for each i for the key under consideration.

Using scatter storage it is not possible to determine the original ith node of the stored linear list. In compressed or indexed storage, however, the original position is carried along.

Our discussion of scatter storage has been based on the principle that the address produced by the scatter function is interpreted as the address of a single memory location. In the literature, however, this address is often understood to be the beginning address of a block of memory locations, where a collision does not occur until all memory locations of the block are in use.

A broader application of scatter storage is given in Sec. 2.6.

*Remarks and References*

A detailed treatment of scatter storage techniques may be found in Knuth [2]. Other useful references are Berztiss [1], Harrison [1], and Stone [1]. The computation of collision probability was carried out with reference to Heising [1]. Experimental results for several variations of scatter storage may be found in Lum [1].

## Exercises

**2.4.1**  Between two cities A and B there is a railroad shuttle service. The trains leave A and B at whole-minute intervals, and the duration of the trip is different (depending on the number of stops) but never longer than 56 minutes. The train traffic leaving A and B, respectively, is given by the two sequences $a_1, a_2, \ldots$ and $b_1, b_2, \ldots$. Here $a_i = 0$ if at the ith minute no train leaves A; $a_i > 0$ if at the ith minute a train does leave A and arrives in B after $a_i$ minutes. The meaning of the values $b_i$ is analogous. Design a program that stores the sequences $a_1, a_2, \ldots$ and $b_1, b_2, \ldots$ using compressed storage and computes the total number of trains required for the shuttle service. Assume that a train arriving in A (or B) can depart again after no less than 5 minutes. For simplicity, it can be assumed that no trains leave A and B between 2: 00 and 3: 00 inclusive.

**2.4.2**  A sequence of positive whole numbers, whose end is indicated by a 0, is given as input. Write a program segment that reads in the numbers, one after the other, and stores them sequentially-indexed-linked, where numbers that agree in the 1's and 10's digits, respectively, are placed in a subset. The index list therefore consists of 100 nodes.

**2.4.3**   Given as input is a set $n_1, n_2, \ldots, n_t$ of whole-number keys. Develop a simple formula to determine the places $j_1, j_2, \ldots, j_r$ of the key that produce a uniform distribution for the scatter function in the selection technique for scatter storage.

**2.4.4**   Let $m = 2^{31}$, $y_0 = 568731$, $y_i = \mod (15625 \times y_{i-1} + 22221, m)$, and $x_i = $ floor $(1000 \times y_i/m)$ for $1 \leqslant i \leqslant 800$. The numbers $x_1, \ldots, x_{800}$ represent 800 pseudo-random numbers between 0 and 999. Write a program for scatter storing the $x_i$ using the scatter function $s(n) = n$, where

(a)   All overflows are stored as a single additional sequence.

(b)   Each overflow is stored in a memory location that is not yet used.

The program should determine and print the number of collisions in the two cases a and b.

**2.4.5**   As input there is a sequence of triples $(x_i, y_i, p_i)$. Each triple represents a German word $x_i$, the English equivalent $y_i$, and the frequency of usage (expressed as a percentage) of the word $x_i$ in a "typical German text." The sequence of pairs $(x_i, y_i)$ is to be treated as a linear list with nodes $k_i$ and is to be stored sequentially-indexed-linked so that nodes agreeing in the first two letters of the first component (the German word) are placed in a linked structure. The nodes in this linked structure are to be arranged by decreasing frequency of usage so that frequently used words can be quickly found. Use this data structure in a program to perform a word-by-word translation of simple German sentences. If no translation is given for a particular German word, simply leave it untranslated.

## Section 2.5   Multidimensional Arrays

**Definition 2.5.1** (Rectangular Array) A *rectangular array* of order $(m, n)$ is a data structure $B = (K, R)$ where K consists of $m \times n$ nodes

$$K = \{k_{i,j} \mid 1 \leqslant i \leqslant m, 1 \leqslant j \leqslant n\}^9$$

and R consists of the two relations

$$ROW = \{(k_{i,j}, k_{i,j+1}) \mid 1 \leqslant i \leqslant m, 1 \leqslant j \leqslant n - 1\}$$

and

$$COL = \{(k_{i,j}, k_{i+1,j}) \mid 1 \leqslant i \leqslant m - 1, 1 \leqslant j \leqslant n\}.$$

A rectangular array is also called a *two-dimensional array* or a *matrix*. A node $k'$ is said to be a *row successor* of k if $(k, k') \in ROW$ and $k'$ is a *column successor* of k if $(k, k') \in COL$.

Rectangular arrays can be represented graphically by using a rectangular scheme as shown in Fig. 2.5.1.

Rectangular arrays are found in the most diverse contexts. For example, the coefficients of a system of linear equations, the distribution of houses in a neighborhood having a rectangular network of streets, the population density of a territory

---

[9] We sometimes write $k_{ij}$ instead of $k_{i,j}$ if no misunderstanding is possible.

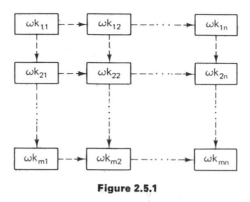

**Figure 2.5.1**

determined by longitude and latitude degrees, the current arrangement of chessmen on the squares of a chessboard, and the direct rail connections between cities all can be represented in a natural way using rectangular arrays.

**Definition 2.5.2** (Row Order and Column Order) Let $B = (K, R)$ be a rectangular array of order $(m, n)$ with

$$R = \{ROW, COL\},$$
$$ROW = \{(k_{i,j}, k_{i,j+1}) \mid 1 \leqslant i \leqslant m, 1 \leqslant j \leqslant n - 1\}$$

and

$$COL = \{(k_{i,j}, k_{i+1,j}) \mid 1 \leqslant i \leqslant m - 1, 1 \leqslant j \leqslant n\}.$$

The *row order* arrangement of nodes of $B$ is the sequence of nodes $k_{11}, k_{12}, \ldots,$ $k_{1n}, k_{21}, k_{22}, \ldots, k_{2n}, \ldots, k_{m1}, k_{m2}, \ldots, k_{mn}$. Any method of storing the row-order arrangement of $B$ is called a *row-order allocation* of $B$. Any method of storing a similarly defined *column-order* arrangement is called a *column-order allocation* of $B$.

For the commonly used sequential row-order storage (with step size $s$) of a rectangular array $B$ as given above, we find $\alpha k_{ij} = \alpha k_{11} + s[n(i - 1) + (j - 1)]$. Thus the address of the node $k_{ij}$, that is, the node in the *ith row* and the *jth column*, can be computed directly from the address of the node in the first row and first column and the numbers $i$ and $j$.

If many of the nodes in a rectangular array have the same value, then it is reasonable to suppress the storage of these nodes and use a compressed row-order storage method or some variation thereof.

**Definition 2.5.3** (Triangular Matrix and Band Matrix) Let $F = k_{11}, k_{12}, \ldots,$ $k_{nn}$ be the row-order arrangement of the nodes of a rectangular array $B = (K, R)$ of order $(n, n)$.[10] The structure $B$ is called a *triangular matrix* if all nodes $k_{ij}$ with $j > i$ have the same value or if all nodes "above the main diagonal" can be ignored for some other reason. The structure $B$ is called a *band matrix* with *band width* $b$, if all nodes with abs $(i - j) > b$ have the same value or if all nodes "more than b places

---

[10]$B$ is therefore square.

away from the main diagonal" can be ignored for some other reason. A triangular matrix therefore is often stored by removing, from the sequence F, nodes $k_{ij}$ for which $j > i$ and storing the remaining subsequence sequentially (with step size s). This method of storage requires only $n(n + 1)/2$ memory locations instead of $n^2$, and the address of the node in the ith row and jth column can be determined using

$$\alpha k_{ij} = \alpha k_{11} + s\left[\frac{i(i - 1)}{2} + (j - 1)\right].$$

Likewise in a band matrix we remove from the sequence F the unused nodes $k_{ij}$ for which $abs\,(i - j) > b$ and store the remaining subsequence of $(2b + 1)n - b(b + 1)$ nodes. These nodes are, however, not stored sequentially (with step size s) in $(2b + 1)n - b(b + 1)$ memory locations, but rather in $(2b + 1)n - 2b$ memory locations in such a way that

$$\alpha k_{i+1, i+1} = \alpha k_{i,i} + s(2b + 1)$$

holds for $1 \leqslant i \leqslant n - 1$. The address of the node in the ith row and jth column can be determined using the formula

$$\alpha k_{ij} = \alpha k_{11} + s[(i - 1)(2b + 1) + (j - i)].$$

**Example 2.5.1** Figure 2.5.2(a) shows a triangular matrix and a method of storing it, using $s = 1$, is seen in Fig. 2.5.2(b). Figure 2.5.3(a) shows a band matrix with band

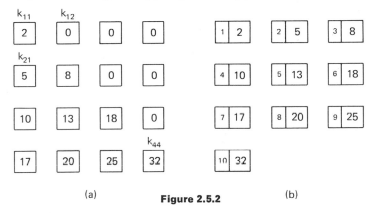

(a)            **Figure 2.5.2**            (b)

width $b = 2$ (in which the "band" is indicated with two additional straight lines) and a method of storing it, using $s = 1$, is seen in Fig. 2.5.3(b). In the triangular matrix, for example, $\alpha k_{32} = \alpha k_{11} + 4 = 5$, while in the band matrix $\alpha k_{32} = \alpha k_{11} + 9 = 10$. Notice that in the storage of the band matrix $\sigma 4$ and $\sigma 23$ are not used.

**Definition 2.5.4** (Compressed Storage) Let $F = k_{11}, k_{12}, \ldots, k_{mn}$ be the row-order arrangement of nodes in a rectangular array $B = (K, R)$ of order $(m, n)$, where several nodes in F have the same value V. Let $F' = k'_{11}, k'_{12}, \ldots, k'_{mn}$ be a sequence of nodes, obtained from F, in which each node $k_{ij}$ is replaced by $k'_{ij}$ and $\omega k'_{ij} = (i, j, \omega k_{ij})$; thus $k'_{ij}$ indicates in which row and column $k_{ij}$ occurred in the original array B. Let $F''$ be that subsequence of $F'$ obtained by deleting all nodes $k'$ where

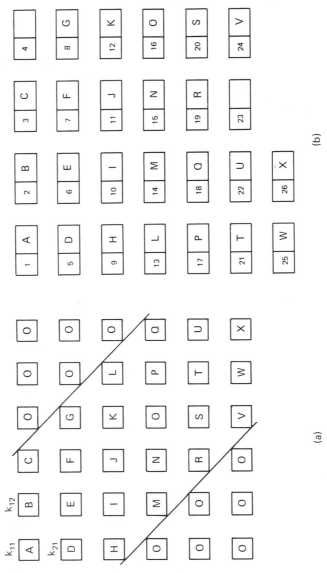

**Figure 2.5.3**

$\omega k' = (i, j, V)$. Any method of storing $F''$ in which the storage of nodes with value V is suppressed is called a *compressed* storage of B.

There are also some practical variations of compressed storage. For example, in the transition from F to $F'$, each node $k_{ij}$ can be replaced by $k'_{ij}$, where $\omega k'_{ij} = (p, \omega k_{ij})$ and $p = \pi_F k_{ij}$. The corresponding row i and the column j can be calculated from p by using $i = 1 + (p - 1) \div n$ and $j = 1 + \mod (p - 1, n)$.

A sequential compressed storage of the rectangular array of Fig. 2.5.4(a) is given in Fig. 2.5.4(b), where the storage of nodes with value * is suppressed. Since $\delta\sigma 4 = (3, 4, \text{YES})$, then, for example, $\omega k_{34} = \text{YES}$.

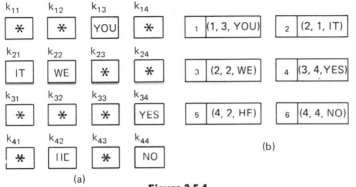

(a)

(b)

**Figure 2.5.4**

When using sequential compressed storage for a rectangular array, the process of locating a node $k_{ij}$ can be greatly accelerated by applying a binary search (see Sec. 2.7).

It is often convenient to use a combination of indexed and compressed storage for an array $B = (K, R)$ of order $(m, n)$. For example, we may divide K into m classes in such a way that for any i $(1 \leqslant i \leqslant m)$ the nodes in row i are put into a linear array $B_i$ of length n with relation ROW (the row successor relation). Thus, for example, sequential-indexed-compressed linked storage with index array X can be used, in which the ith node $x_i$ of X gives the address of the beginning node of the compressed linked array $B_i$.

Although when using this type of storage the column successor of a given node k cannot be found directly, this storage technique does prove itself useful in many cases, as demonstrated in the next example.[11]

**Example 2.5.2** (Shortest Distance) A pair of numbers (n, m), where $1 \leqslant n \leqslant 1000$, $1 \leqslant m \leqslant 2000$, followed by m triples $(i_1, j_1, f_1), \ldots, (i_m, j_m, f_m)$ and a whole number g are given as input. Each triple $(i_t, j_t, f_t)$, where $1 \leqslant i_t, j_t \leqslant n$ for $1 \leqslant t \leqslant m$, indicates that there exists a direct train connection (i.e., with no other cities in between) between

---

[11]A variation of the sequential-indexed-compressed linked storage has actually already been used in Example 2.2.6 (topological sort) if we interpret the sequence of start pointers $ag_1$, $ag_2$, $\ldots$, $ag_n$ as an index list.

the two cities $i_t$ and $j_t$, in both directions, of length $f_t$ miles. It can be assumed that $i_t < j_t$ for $1 \leqslant t \leqslant m$. We wish to develop a program that determines for the city $g\, (1 \leqslant g \leqslant n)$, and every city j that can be reached from g, the length of the shortest connection from g to j.

For this program we have the train connections, as described above, appropriately stored: a linear array E of length n with nodes $e_1, e_2, \ldots, e_n$, a queue S, and a number u much larger than any possible distance occurring in the problem. This is the procedure to be followed:

(a) The value $\omega e_i$ assigns at each point in time the shortest train connection from g to i yet found. Thus $\omega e_i = u$ means that so far no connection from g to i has been found and $\omega e_i = 0$ indicates that i is the given city, i.e., that $i = g$. So at the beginning $\omega e_i = u$ for $i \neq g$ and $\omega e_g = 0$.

(b) If a value i occurs in the queue S, then i can be reached from g by way of a connection of length $\omega e_i$; it is then to be determined whether there are possibly shorter connections than any yet found, from g via city i to other cities j. The queue S initially consists of exactly one node with value g.

(c) If a connection of length h, where $0 < h < \omega e_j$, from g to j is found, then $\omega e_j$ is replaced by this value h and j is added to the queue S, as long as j does not already appear in S.

(d) For finding new or shorter connections to cities from g, the value i of the first node of the queue S is always used: since i appears in S, there is a connection from g to i; each j that can be reached directly from i is considered. We let h $= \omega e_i +$ direct distance from i to j; if $h < \omega e_j$, then we proceed according to step c. After considering all direct connections from i, i is removed from S.

(e) The process terminates as soon as the queue S is empty. Each $e_i$ with $0 < \omega e_i < u$ means that at this point in time the shortest distance from g to i is $\omega e_i$ miles.

Work through the given procedure using the input $(7, 10)$, $(1, 2, 13)$, $(1, 3, 8)$, $(1, 5, 30)$, $(1, 7, 32)$, $(2, 6, 9)$, $(2, 7, 7)$, $(3, 4, 5)$, $(4, 5, 6)$, $(5, 6, 2)$, $(6, 7, 17)$, 6. This input describes the railway network for seven cities 1, 2, $\ldots$, 7 as illustrated in Fig. 2.5.5. The problem is to determine the shortest connections from city 6.

Starting with the array E (using $u = 99999$)

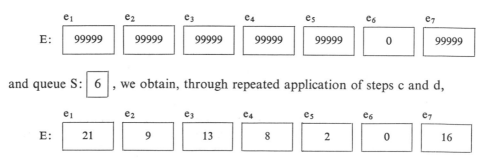

|  | $e_1$ | $e_2$ | $e_3$ | $e_4$ | $e_5$ | $e_6$ | $e_7$ |
|---|---|---|---|---|---|---|---|
| E: | 99999 | 99999 | 99999 | 99999 | 99999 | 0 | 99999 |

and queue S: 6 , we obtain, through repeated application of steps c and d,

|  | $e_1$ | $e_2$ | $e_3$ | $e_4$ | $e_5$ | $e_6$ | $e_7$ |
|---|---|---|---|---|---|---|---|
| E: | 21 | 9 | 13 | 8 | 2 | 0 | 16 |

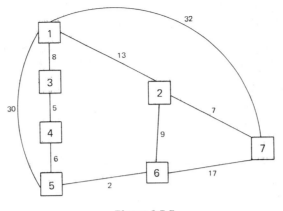

**Figure 2.5.5**

so that, for example, since $\omega e_1 = 21$, the shortest connection from 6 to 1 is 21 miles long.

To obtain an efficient program, the given direct connections must be appropriately stored. In consideration of this the following two important points should be noted:

(a)   For each city i, we must be able to determine in a small number of steps all cities j that have a direct connection with city i.

(b)   The total storage area required must not be "unreasonably" large.

Because of point a it would be unsuitable to store the triples $(i_1, j_1, f_1), \ldots, (i_m, j_m, f_m)$ as they appear in input, as a linear array of length m. Because of point b on the other hand, it would not be feasible to store the input as a rectangular array B of order (n, n) with nodes $k_{ij}$ uncompressed so that $\omega k_{ij} = f$, where cities i and j have a direct connection of length f.

A sequential-indexed-compressed linked storage of the rectangular array B with an index array X of length n, however, satisfies both demands a and b. The value of the ith node $x_i \in X$ is the address of the beginning node of an array $B_i$, where the value of each node of $B_i$ is a pair (j, f) indicating that a direct connection of length f exists between city i and city j.

The list X is stored sequentially. For this there is the declaration **DCL** X(N) **FIXED BIN**;. The arrays $B_1, B_2, \ldots, B_n$ are stored linked and are declared using **DCL** (D1(2 * M), D2(2 * M), R1(2 * M)) **FIXED BIN**;. (There are 2m memory locations used because each input triple produces two entries in $B_i$ and $B_j$.) The array E is sequentially stored and the declaration **DCL** E(N) **FIXED BIN**; is used. The queue S with end pointer es and length os is stored circularly linked so that it can be determined in one comparison whether i presently belongs to S or not: this is provided for using the declaration **DCL** (S(N), RS(N), ES, OS) **FIXED BIN**;, which is to be interpreted as follows: S(I) = I or S(I) = −I depending on whether i belongs to S or not. The array RS always points to the next node of the queue S.

```
DIST: PROC OPTIONS (MAIN);
    DCL (N, M) FIXED BIN; GET LIST (N, M);
    BEGIN;
        DCL (D1(2 * M), D2(2 * M), R1(2 * M), X(N), S(N), RS(N),
            E(N), ES, OS, G, H, I, J, K, F, P, Q) FIXED BIN;
        X = 0; P = 1;
        DO K = 1 TO M;
            GET LIST (I, J, F);
            D1(P) = J; D2(P) = F; R1(P) = X(I); X(I) = P; P = P + 1;
            D1(P) = I; D2(P) = F; R1(P) = X(J); X(J) = P; P = P + 1;
        END; /* THE DIRECT CONNECTIONS ARE STORED */
        GET LIST (G);
        DO K = 1 TO N;
            E(K) = 99999;
            S(K) = −K;
        END;
        E(G) = 0; ES, S(G), RS(G) = G; OS = 1;
        /* NOW E AND S ARE PREPARED ACCORDING TO A. AND B. */
        DO WHILE (OS ¬= 0);
            P = RS(ES); I = S(P); S(P) = −P; RS(ES) = RS(P);
            /* CITY I IS NOW CONSIDERED ACCORDING TO D. */
            OS = OS − 1; Q = X(I);
            DO WHILE (Q ¬= 0);
                J = D1(Q); F = D2(Q); Q = R1(Q); H = E(I) + F;
                IF H < E(J) THEN DO;
                                    E(J) = H;
                                    IF S(J) = −J THEN DO;
                                    IF OS = 0 THEN RS(J) = J;
                                        ELSE DO;
                                                RS(J) = RS(ES);
                                                RS(ES) = J;
                                            END;
                                        S(J), ES = J; OS = OS + 1;
                                    END;
                                END;
            END;
        END;
        DO K = 1 TO N;
            IF (E(K) > 0) & (E(K) < 99999) THEN PUT LIST
                            (G, K, E(K));
        END;
    END;
END;
```

For the direct connections shown in Fig. 2.5.5, the arrays $B_1, \ldots, B_7$ with index array X are stored as shown in Fig. 2.5.6. Thus, for example, $\omega x_5 = 17$ and $\delta\sigma 17 = (6, 2)$ indicate that there is a direct connection of length 2 miles from city 5 to city 6.

Working through the examples of Fig. 2.5.5 and 2.5.6 by hand using $g = 6$ is somewhat tedious. The output finally obtained would be (6, 1, 21), (6, 2, 9), (6, 3, 13), (6, 4, 8), (6, 5, 2), (6, 7, 16); i.e., the shortest connection from city 6 to city 1, for example, is 21 miles long.

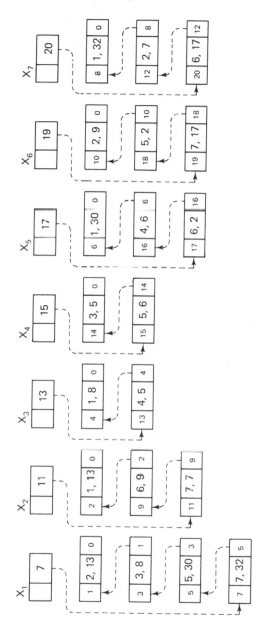

**Figure 2.5.6**

If in the compressed storage of a rectangular array it is necessary to be able to determine directly for any arbitrary node not only the row successor but also the column successor, then we use *compressed rectangular linked* storage.

**Definition 2.5.5** (Compressed Rectangular Linked Storage) Let $F = k_{11}, k_{12}, \ldots, k_{mn}$ be the row-order arrangement of nodes of a rectangular array $B = (K, R)$ of order $(m, n)$, where several nodes in $F$ have the same value $V$. By replacing each node $k_{ij}$ by a node $k'_{ij}$, where $\omega k'_{ij} = (i, j, k_{ij})$, we obtain a sequence $F' = k'_{11}, k'_{12}, \ldots, k'_{mn}$. Then by deleting all nodes $k'$ with $\omega k' = (i, j, V)$ we obtain from this a sequence $F'' = k''_1, k''_2, \ldots, k''_t$.

Any method of storing $F''$ in memory locations with two pointer fields is called a *compressed rectangular linked* storage of $B$ if for every node $k \in F''$ the following hold:

(a) If $k'$ is the first node after $k$ in $F''$ with $\omega_1 k = \omega_1 k'$, then $\rho_1 k = \alpha k'$; if there is no such node, then $\rho_1 k = 0$.

(b) If $k''$ is the first node after $k$ in $F''$ with $\omega_2 k = \omega_2 k'$, then $\rho_2 k = \alpha k''$; if there is no such node, then $\rho_2 k = 0$.

Therefore, in compressed rectangular linked storage, the first pointer field points to the next node in the same row with a value not equal to $V$ (if one exists) and the second pointer field indicates the next node in the same column with a value other than $V$ (if one exists). In this storage technique, two additional linear arrays are used, the *row beginning* and *column beginning*, whose ith node indicates the address of the first node with value not equal to $V$ in the ith row or column, respectively.

**Example 2.5.3** The rectangular array shown in Fig. 2.5.4(a) is pictured in Fig. 2.5.7 as a compressed rectangular linked structure. Here $R = r_1, r_2, r_3, r_4$ and $C = c_1, c_2, c_3, c_4$ represent the sequentially stored linear arrays *row beginning* and *column beginning*.

**Definition 2.5.6** (m-Dimensional Arrays and Standard Storage Form) A data structure $B = (K, R)$ is said to be an *m-dimensional array* of order $(n_1, n_2, \ldots, n_m)$, where $K$ consists of $n_1 \times n_2 \times \cdots \times n_m$ nodes

$$K = \{k_{i_1, i_2, \ldots, i_m} \mid 1 \leqslant i_t \leqslant n_t \text{ for } 1 \leqslant t \leqslant m\},^{12}$$

and $R$ consists of the relations $N_1, N_2, \ldots, N_m$, where

$$(k_{i_1, i_2, \ldots, i_m}, k_{j_1, j_2, \ldots, j_m}) \in N_r$$

if and only if $i_t = j_t$ for all $t \neq r$ and $i_r = j_r - 1$. Let $m + 1$ numbers $p_0, p_1, \ldots, p_m$ be defined by

$$p_t = \begin{cases} n_{t+1} \times n_{t+2} \times \cdots \times n_m & \text{for } 0 \leqslant t \leqslant m - 1 \\ 1 & \text{for } t = m. \end{cases}$$

---

[12] Or simply $k_{i_1 i_2 \ldots i_m}$ instead of $k_{i_1, i_2, \ldots, i_m}$ if no misunderstanding is possible.

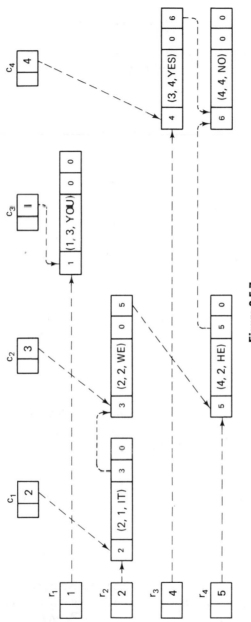

**Figure 2.5.7**

Then the sequence $p_1, \ldots, p_m$ is called the *dope vector* of B. If $F' = k'_1, k'_2, \ldots, k'_{p_0}$ is the sequence of nodes K such that

$$k_{i_1 i_2 \ldots i_m} = k'_{b+1} \quad \text{where } b = \sum_{t=1}^{m} (i_t - 1)p_t,$$

then $F'$ is called the *row ordering* of the nodes of B and any method of storing $F'$ sequentially (with step size s) is a *standard form* of B.

Linear (or rectangular) arrays are obviously m-dimensional arrays for $m = 1$ (or $m = 2$), respectively. The standard form of a rectangular array B is simply the sequential row-order storage of B.

For the standard storage form of an m-dimensional array B (with step size s) we have

$$\alpha k_{i_1 i_2 \ldots i_m} = \alpha k_{1, 1, \ldots, 1} + s \times b, \qquad b = \sum_{t=1}^{m} (i_t - 1)p_t,$$

$p_t$ as above. To avoid calculating the quantities $p_t$ repeatedly, the values in the dope vector may be calculated once and then stored as an auxiliary array. Even taking this precaution, locating a node $k_{i_1 i_2 \ldots i_m}$ is costly; in particular, in the formula above, $m - 1$ multiplications are required. These multiplications can be avoided using *Iliffe's method*.

**Definition 2.5.7** (Iliffe's Method) Let $F_m = k_{1,1,\ldots,1}, k_{1,1,\ldots,2}, \ldots, k_{n1,n2,\ldots,nm}$ be the row-order arrangement of nodes of an m-dimensional array of order $(n_1, n_2, \ldots, n_m)$. For each t $(1 \leqslant t \leqslant m - 1)$, let $F_t$ be that subsequence of F that consists of only those nodes $k_{i_1 i_2 \ldots i_m}$ for which $i_{t+1} = i_{t+2} = \cdots = i_m = 1$. Clearly $F_t$ is a subsequence of $F_{t+1}$ $(1 \leqslant t \leqslant m - 1)$. If we store all arrays $F_1, F_2, \ldots, F_m$ sequentially and replace the value of each node $k_{i_1 i_2 \ldots i_m}$ in $F_t$ by the address of the same node in $F_{t+1}$ (for $t = 1, 2, \ldots, m - 1$), we then have *Iliffe's method* of storage. If a is the address of the first node of $F_1$, then the address aux of the node $k_{i_1 i_2 \ldots i_m}$ in $F_m$ can be determined by starting with $\text{aux} = a$ and computing $\text{aux} = \delta\sigma(\text{aux} + i_t - 1)$ for $t = 1, 2, \ldots, m - 1$ and then taking $\text{aux} = \text{aux} + i_m - 1$.

**Example 2.5.4** Let $F_3 = k_{111}, k_{112}, \ldots, k_{223}$ be the row-order arrangement of nodes of a three-dimensional array $B = (K, R)$. The sequences $F_2$ and $F_1$ are, in accordance with Def. 2.5.7,

$F_2: k_{111}, k_{121}, k_{211}, k_{221}$

$F_1: k_{111}, k_{211}.$

Figure 2.5.8(a) shows a sequential storage of the arrays $F_1, F_2, F_3$; while Fig. 2.5.8(b) shows Iliffe's method of storing B, obtained from Fig. 2.5.8(a) by replacing the nodes in $F_1$ and $F_2$ by the addresses of the same nodes in $F_2$ and $F_3$.

The node $k_{213}$ is found as follows: first $\text{aux} = 1$; then $\text{aux} = \delta\sigma(\text{aux} + i_1 - 1)$, so $\text{aux} = 5$; now $\text{aux} = \delta\sigma(\text{aux} + i_2 - 1)$, i.e., $\text{aux} = 13$; finally $\text{aux} = \text{aux} + i_3 - 1$, so $\text{aux} = 15$; and 15 is the desired address of $k_{213}$.

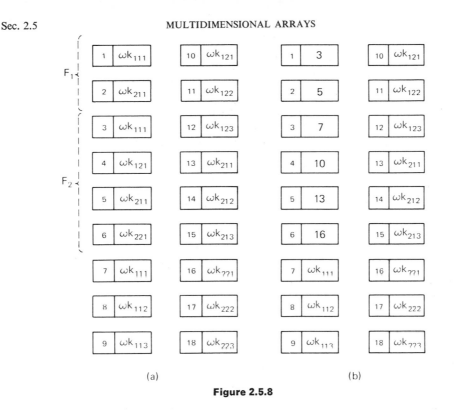

(a)                                         (b)

**Figure 2.5.8**

The storage area required for Iliffe's method is significantly greater than that for standard form; however, it is always less than twice as great. Iliffe's method may be thought of as nested indexed storage. It is an obvious and natural utilization of the fact that arrays can be interpreted as trees [see Sec. 3.1, for example, Fig. 3.1.5(c)].

*Remarks and References*

The technique used in Example 2.5.2 is actually the algorithm given by Ford [1].

## Exercises

**2.5.1**  Given as input there is a sequence of 100 numbers that represent the row-order arrangement $a_{1,1}, a_{1,2}, \ldots, a_{10,10}$ of the values of nodes in a matrix A of order (10, 10). Let B be a matrix of order (10, 10) whose nodes, in row order, have the values $b_{1,1}, b_{1,2}, \ldots, b_{10,10}$, where

$$b_{ij} = \sum_{k=1}^{10} a_{ik} \times a_{kj} \quad \text{for } 1 \leqslant i, j \leqslant 10$$

(B is therefore the *square* of A). Write a program that, starting with the described input, stores A using compressed rectangular linked allocation (in which nodes with value 0 are suppressed) and then computes the values of the nodes of B, prints them, and also stores B as a compressed rectangular linked structure.

**2.5.2**   Given as input there is a sequence of 600 numbers $a_{1,1,1}, a_{1,1,2}, \ldots, a_{10,6,10}$ that represents the row-order arrangement of values of the nodes in an array A of order (10, 6, 10). Write a program that stores A using Iliffe's method. Then the program should read in 50 triples (i, j, k) and print the corresponding values $a_{i,j,k}$.

**2.5.3**   Determine the dope vector for an array of order    (a) (2, 3, 4, 5). (b)   (5, 4, 3, 2).   (c)   (2, 2, 2, 10).   (d)   (9, 7, 7, 3, 2).

**2.5.4**   How many memory locations are required using Iliffe's method of storing an array of order   (a)   (2, 3, 4, 5)?   (b)   (5, 4, 3, 2)?   (c)   (2, 2, 2, 2, 2, 2)?

**2.5.5**   Improve the program discussed in Example 2.5.2 so that the program determines not only the length of the shortest connection but also the corresponding route. For example, in the network shown in Fig. 2.5.5, not only should (6, 1, 21) be produced but 6, 5, 4, 3, 1 should be printed too since the shortest connection from 6 to 1 with length 21 goes through 5, 4, and 3.

## Section 2.6   Merging and Sorting

In a data structure B = (K, R), frequently a certain component $\omega_i k$ of the node k $\in$ K is distinguished in that it has a value that uniquely identifies the node. Such a component of a node k is called a *key component* and its value is the *key* of k.

**Definition 2.6.1** (Sorted List) If B is a list with nodes $k_1, k_2, \ldots, k_n$ and if a (total) ordering r is defined on the keys $\{\omega_i k_1, \omega_i k_2, \ldots, \omega_i k_n\}$, then B is said to be *sorted* if the sequence $\omega_i k_1, \omega_i k_2, \ldots, \omega_i k_n$ of keys is sorted (relative to r).

*Agreement:*   Unless specifically stated otherwise, it will be assumed in the remainder of this book that conditions 1 through 3 are satisfied by the nodes under consideration.

(1)   The key component of a node is the first component.
(2)   The key is a whole number.
(3)   As an order relation r for the key, we shall use the usual $\leqslant$ relation.

Therefore, if the sequence $F = k_1, k_2, \ldots, k_n$ is a sorted sequence of nodes, then $\omega_i k_i \leqslant \omega_i k_j$ for $1 \leqslant i < j \leqslant n$ and we say that node $k_i$ is *less than* node $k_j$ and node $k_j$ is *greater than* $k_i$.

**Definition 2.6.2** (Merging Lists) Two sorted lists A and B of length (order) m and n, respectively, are *merged* into a sorted list C of length m + n if each node of A and each node of B is contained as a node in list C exactly once.

**Example 2.6.1** If A consists of five nodes with keys 6, 17, 23, 39, 47 and B consists of four nodes with keys 19, 25, 38, 60, then by merging lists A and B we obtain list C having nine nodes with keys 6, 17, 19, 23, 25, 38, 39, 47, 60. It is possible to merge more than two lists simultaneously into one sorted list.

Merging processes are necessary or desirable in many applications. The insertion of a series of new customers into an existing customer file is a typical merging process; merging proves to be useful in the preparation of tables (see Example 2.6.3), and a sorted list can be obtained from an unsorted list through a series of merging operations (see Example 2.6.5), etc.

In merging sorted lists A and B into a sorted list C, we usually begin with an initially empty list C and at each step add to C the first node $a_i$ of A or $b_j$ of B, whichever has the smaller key, that does not already appear in C.

**Example 2.6.2** (Merging Two Lists) As input we have two numbers m and n followed by $m + n$ positive whole numbers $a_1 \leqslant a_2 \leqslant \cdots \leqslant a_m$ and $b_1 \leqslant b_2 \leqslant \cdots \leqslant b_n$.

The $a_i$ and $b_i$ represent the keys of the sorted lists A and B. The keys of the list formed by merging A and B are to be produced by a program.

In the following program, the $m + n$ numbers are initially stored in a list W. The actual merging process is performed by calling the procedure "Merge (W, 1, $m + n$, m)."

A call on the procedure "Merge (W, low, up, L)" merges the sorted arrays W(low), W(low + 1), . . . , W(low + L − 1), and W(low + L), W(low + L + 1), . . . , W(up) into a single sorted sequence W(low), W(low + 1), . . . , W(up). For this, W(low), . . . , W(low + L − 1) are initially stored in an auxiliary array A and W(low + L), . . . , W(up) in an auxiliary array B. Also, the last nodes of A and B are defined as STOPPERS so that the process can be terminated as soon as either array has been completely scanned.[13]

In the case being considered here, the call "Merge (W, 1, $m + n$, m)" merges W(1), W(2), . . . , W(m) and W(m + 1), . . . , W(m + n) into a single sequence W(1), W(2), . . . , W(m + n).

```
M: PROC OPTIONS (MAIN);
    MERGE: PROCEDURE (W, LOW, UP, L);
        DCL (W(*), LOW, UP, L, A(L + 1), B(UP − LOW − L + 2), T,
            I, J, K, V) FIXED BIN;
        IF L ¬= 0 THEN DO;
            DO T = LOW TO LOW + L − 1:
                A(T − LOW + 1) = W(T);
            END;
            DO T = LOW + L TO UP;
                B(T − LOW − L + 1) = W(T);
            END;
```

---

[13]The procedure "Merge" is used in this general form later in Example 2.6.5.

```
            V, A(L + 1), B(UP − LOW − L + 2) = W(LOW + L − 1) +
                                                        W(UP) + 1;
        I = 1; J = 1; K = LOW;
        DO WHILE (A(I) ¬= V | B(J) ¬= V);
            DO WHILE (A(I) < B(J));
                W(K) = A(I);
                I = I + 1;
                K = K + 1;
            END;
            DO WHILE (A(I) > B(J));
                W(K) = B(J);
                J = J + 1;
                K = K + 1;
            END;
        END;
        END;
    END MERGE;
    GET LIST (M, N);
    BEGIN;
        DCL W(M + N) FIXED BIN;
        GET LIST (W);
        CALL MERGE (W, 1, M + N, +M);
        PUT LIST (W) SKIP;
    END;
  END M;
```

The work done by the program and the procedure "Merge" can be followed by hand using the input 2, 3, 3, 9, 5, 7, 8. Upon completion of the input process, $W(1) = 3$, $W(2) = 9$, $W(3) = 5$, $W(4) = 7$, and $W(5) = 8$. The call "Merge (W, 1, 5, 2)" first produces $A(1) = 3$, $A(2) = 9$, $A(3) = 18$ (STOPPER), $B(1) = 5$, $B(2) = 7$, $B(3) = 8$, and $B(4) = 18$ (STOPPER). After the procedure "Merge" is completed, we have $W(1) = 3$, $W(2) = 5$, $W(3) = 7$, $W(4) = 8$, and $W(5) = 9$, and we obtain the output 3, 5, 7, 8, 9.

To merge arrays A and B of lengths m and n, respectively, using the technique above, $m + n$ comparisons are necessary. For special values of m and n, techniques are known that require fewer comparisons. For example, for $m = 1$, a technique can be given using the binary search (Sec. 2.7) that requires only $\log_2 n$ comparisons.

**Example 2.6.3** (Currency Table) Three numbers $k_2, k_3, k_4$ are given that specify the rates of exchange of four currencies $W_1, W_2, W_3, W_4$. A unit of currency $W_1$ corresponds to $k_i$ units of currency $W_i$, $i = 2, 3, 4$. We want a program that, for the

| $W_1$ | $W_2$ | $W_3$ | $W_4$ |
|-------|-------|-------|-------|
| 0.714 | 1.000 | 0.785 | 0.571 |
| 0.909 | 1.273 | 1.000 | 0.727 |
| 1.000 | 1.400 | 1.100 | 0.800 |
| 1.250 | 1.750 | 1.375 | 1.000 |
| 1.428 | 2.000 | 1.570 | 1.142 |

**Figure 2.6.1**

first 100 units of the four currencies, gives the values in all currencies. For $k_2 = 1.4$, $k_3 = 1.1$, $k_4 = 0.8$, the beginning of the desired table is shown in Fig. 2.6.1.

This exercise can be viewed as a merging problem. For each of the four currencies $W_i$, a sorted array $F_i$ is computed whose jth node gives the value of j units of currency $W_i$ in units of currency $W_1$. By merging the four arrays $F_1, F_2, F_3, F_4$, a list RES is obtained, from which the desired table is easily constructed.

```
CUR1: PROC OPTIONS (MAIN);
      DCL (F1(101), F2(101), F3(101), F4(101), RES(400),
          K2, K3, K4) DEC FLOAT; /* THE ARRAYS F1, F2, F3, F4
          HAVE 101 ELEMENTS SINCE THE LAST IS USED AS A STOPPER */
      DCL I FIXED BIN;
      GET LIST (K2, K3, K4);
      DO I = 1 TO 100;
          F1(I) = I; F2(I) = I/K2; F3(I) = I/K3;
          F4(I) = I/K4; END;
      F1(101), F2(101), F3(101), F4(101) = 999999; /* STOPPER */
      CALL MERGE (F1, F2, F3, F4, RES);
      /* THE PROCEDURE MERGE, NOT DEFINED HERE, MERGES THE
          ARRAYS F1, F2, F3, F4 INTO A SINGLE ARRAY RES */
      DO I = 1 TO 100;
          PUT LIST (RES(I), RES(I) * K2, RES(I) * K3, RES(I) * K4);
      END;
   END;
```

The storage requirements for the program above can be reduced considerably if the computation of the four arrays, the merging into one array, and the printing are performed to some extent in parallel.

In the following program, only four arrays K, H, E, A of length 4 are used. The ith node of K gives the value of one unit of currency $W_1$ in units of currency $W_i$. The array H contains the reciprocals of the values of K. Array E contains 100 times the values of H as stoppers. The values in array A change during the execution of the program. The ith node of A specifies, for $j = 1, 2, \ldots, 100$ successively, the value of j units of currency $W_i$ in units of currency $W_1$.

```
CUR2: PROC OPTIONS (MAIN);
      DCL (K(4), H(4), E(4), A(4), MIN) DEC FLOAT, (I, POS)
          FIXED BIN;
      MINIMUM: PROCEDURE (A, MIN, POS);
          DCL A(*), MIN) DEC FLOAT, POS FIXED BIN;
          /* MINIMUM (A, MIN, POS) YIELDS THE SMALLEST VALUE
              A(I) OF THE FOUR VALUES A(1), A(2), A(3), A(4)
              AND ITS POSITION I */
          MIN = A(1); POS = 1;
          DO I = 2 TO 4;
              IF A(I) < MIN THEN DO;
                                  MIN = A(I);
                                  POS = I;
                              END;
          END;
      END MINIMUM;
```

```
/* NOW THE EXCHANGE RATES ARE READ AND THE ARRAYS
    H, E, AND A PREPARED */
K(1) = 1;
GET LIST (K(2), K(3), K(4));
A, H = 1/K;
E = 100 * H; /* THE ACTUAL COMPUTATION OF THE TABLE CAN
                NOW BEGIN */
CALL MINIMUM (A, MIN, POS);
DO WHILE (MIN <= 999990); /* MIN < 999999 WOULD BE
    RISKY DUE TO ROUNDOFF SINCE MIN IS FLOATING POINT */
    PUT LIST (MIN, MIN * K(2), MIN * K(3), MIN * K(4));
    A(POS) = A(POS) + H(POS);
    IF A(POS) > E(POS) THEN A(POS) = 999999;
                              /* 999999 AS STOPPER */
    CALL MINIMUM (A, MIN, POS);
  END;
END;
```

In the discussion below, several techniques are analyzed that allow us to obtain a sorted array B' by rearranging an array B. The nodes of the original array B are denoted throughout by the sequence $F = k_1, k_2, \ldots, k_n$.

**Definition 2.6.3** (Sorting by Insertion) A sorted array B' is obtained from B by first taking $k_1$ as the only node in B' and performing an *insertion* for $i = 2, 3, \ldots, n$:

*Insertion:*   The node $k_i$ is inserted in B' so that B' is a sorted array of length i.

A program for this technique, using linked allocation for B', has already been presented in Example 2.1.4. As clearly seen, to sort an array B of length n with a program like the one in Example 2.1.4, at most $n^2/2$ comparisons are required and on the average $n^2/4$ comparisons.[14] Thus the use of this technique should be limited to arrays of very small length. The number of required comparisons can be sharply reduced through a binary search (Sec. 2.7); however, this advantage is offset by the necessary shifts when sequential storage is used. On the other hand, if the array B' is stored as a tree (see Chapter 3), there is an efficient sorting technique that is dicussed in Example 3.2.6 (sorting using binary trees).

**Definition 2.6.4** (Sorting by Selection) The second obvious method of obtaining a sorted array B' from a given array B consists of determining, n times, the smallest node in B, adding it to the end of the (initially empty) array B', and removing it from B.

**Example 2.6.4** As input there is a number n and a sequence of n whole numbers. In the following program, the sequence of numbers is stored sequentially as a linear list and then, using selection, the nodes are sorted by rearranging them and without using additional memory space.

---

[14]For the insertion of $k_i$ at most i and on the average i/2 comparisons are required in the ith step.

```
SEL: PROC OPTIONS (MAIN);
    DCL N FIXED BIN; GET LIST (N);
    BEGIN;
        DCL (D(N), I, J, AUX) FIXED BIN;
        GET LIST (D);
        DO I = 1 TO N − 1;
            DO J = I + 1 TO N;
                IF D(I) > D(J) THEN DO;
                                        AUX = D(I);
                                        D(I) = D(J);
                                        D(J) = AUX;
                                    END;
            END;
        END;
        PUT LIST (D);
    END;
END;
```

When sorting using selection, $n^2$ steps are required for sorting n nodes. An improvement is possible using $n\sqrt{n}$ steps if the set of nodes of B is divided into $m \approx \sqrt{n}$ sets, $K_1, K_2, \ldots, K_m$, and for each of the sets $K_i$ the smallest node $g_i$ is determined. To find the smallest node of all, we merely consider the nodes $g_1, g_2, \ldots, g_m$.

A consideration of *sorting by quadratic selection* is not of practical importance since there are several more efficient sorting techniques.

**Definition 2.6.5** (Sorting by Merging) A sorted list B′ can be obtained from B by first dividing the sequence of nodes $F = k_1, k_2, \ldots, k_n$ into n sequences $F_1 = k_1$, $F_2 = k_2, \ldots, F_n = k_n$ each of length 1. One *pass* (defined below) is then repeated until only one sequence of length n remains.

*Pass:* The $m \geqslant 2$ sorted sequences $F_1, F_2, \ldots, F_m$ being considered are replaced by those m/2 [or (m + 1)/2] sorted sequences that are obtained by merging the sequences $F_{2i-1}$ and $F_{2i}$, for $i = 1, 2, \ldots$, into one sequence and by adding the sequence $F_m$ if m is odd.

Figure 2.6.2 shows the sorting of a sequence of n = 14 numbers using merging. The numbers in each sequence are separated here (and in later similar illustrations) by commas; the sequences are separated from one another by semicolons.

For the execution of one pass, n steps are required for n nodes. Since $\log_2 n$ passes are necessary, then, to sort n nodes by merging, $n \log_2 n$ steps are needed. The technique is therefore very efficient and thus applicable for large values of n. It can be

```
9;   7;   18;   3;  52;   4;   6;   8;   5;  13;  42;  30;  35;  26;
7,   9;    3,  18;   4,  52;   6,   8;   5,  13;  30,  42;  26,  35;
3,   7;    9,  18;   4,   6,   8,  52;   5,  13,  30,  42;  26,  35;
3,   4,    6,   7;   8,   9,  18,  52;   5,  13,  26,  30,  35,  42;
3,   4,    5,   6,   7,   8,   9,  13,  18,  26,  30,  35,  42,  52;
```

**Figure 2.6.2**

used even if the set of nodes to be sorted is too large for primary storage and *secondary storage* (such as magnetic tape) must be brought into use.

**Example 2.6.5** (Sorting by Merging) Given as input is a number n followed by n whole numbers $g_1, g_2, \ldots, g_n$. A program is given that sorts the sequence $g_1, g_2, \ldots, g_n$ by merging and prints the resulting sequence.

```
DCL N FIXED BIN;
GET LIST (N);
BEGIN;
    DCL (G(N), L, LOW, UP) FIXED BIN;
    MIN: PROCEDURE (U, V);
        DCL (U, V) FIXED BIN;
        IF U < V THEN RETURN (U); ELSE RETURN (V);
    END MIN;
    GET LIST (G);
    L = 1; LOW = 1;
    /* IN THE FOLLOWING LOOP TWO LISTS ARE MERGED INTO ONE */
    DO WHILE (L < N);
        UP = MIN (LOW + 2 * L − 1, +N);
        CALL MERGE (G, LOW, UP, L) /* MERGE AS DEFINED IN
                            EXAMPLE 2.6.2 */
        IF UP + L < N THEN LOW = UP + 1;
            ELSE DO;
                    L = L * 2;
                    LOW = 1;
                END;
        /* UP + L >= N MEANS AT MOST L REMAIN AND THEREFORE
            NO FURTHER MERGING IS POSSIBLE */
    END;
    PUT LIST (G);
END;
```

For better understanding, work through the program using input 5, 17, 3, 8, 9, 6.

**Definition 2.6.6** (Pocket Sorting) Let $d(j, n)$ denote the jth digit from the right in the decimal number n, as in Def. 2.4.5, and let $B_0, B_1, \ldots, B_9$ be 10 auxiliary arrays to serve as "pockets." Let the keys of the given array B be t-digit decimal numbers. To sort by pocket sorting, we perform a process consisting of a *distribution phase* and a *collection phase* for $j = 1, 2, \ldots, t$.

*Distribution phase:* The arrays $B_0, B_1, \ldots, B_9$ are empty at the beginning of the distribution phase. For $i = 1, 2, \ldots, n$ the ith node $k_i$ of B is added as the last node to the array $B_k$ where $k = d(j, \omega_1 k_i)$.

*Collection phase:* The sequences of nodes corresponding to the arrays $B_0, B_1, \ldots, B_9$ are combined in this order to form one sequence of nodes of a new array B.

Figure 2.6.3 illustrates the described sorting technique for the 14 two-digit ($t = 2$) keys of Fig. 2.6.2.

Original list

    B: 09, 07, 18, 03, 52, 04, 06, 08, 05, 13, 42, 30, 35, 26

After distribution phase

    $B_0$ : 30
    $B_1$ : empty
    $B_2$ : 52, 42
    $B_3$ : 03, 13
    $B_4$ : 04
    $B_5$ : 05, 35
    $B_6$ : 06, 26
    $B_7$ : 07
    $B_8$ : 18, 08
    $B_9$ : 09

After collection phase

    B: 30, 52, 42, 03, 13, 04, 05, 35, 06, 26, 07, 18, 08, 09

After distribution phase

    $B_0$ : 03, 04, 05, 06, 07, 08, 09
    $B_1$ : 13, 18
    $B_2$ : 26
    $B_3$ : 30, 35
    $B_4$ : 42
    $B_5$ : 52
    $B_6$ : empty
    $B_7$ : empty
    $B_8$ : empty
    $B_9$ : empty

After collection phase

    B: 03, 04, 05, 06, 07, 08, 09, 13, 18, 26, 30, 35, 42, 52

**Figure 2.6.3**

The technique of pocket sorting works like the mechanical sorting machine commonly used commercially. With appropriate programming, no comparisons are required for this technique; thus the efficiency of a sorting technique cannot be measured solely by the number of comparisons required. For this reason we have used, and shall continue to use, the number of "steps," not the number of comparisons, as a measure of efficiency.

The number of steps required for sorting n nodes with a t-digit key is t × n. Since in practice t is often equal to $\log_2 n$, pocket sorting and sorting by merging may be considered to be nearly equally efficient, as far as the number of required steps is concerned.

A frequent (but avoidable) disadvantage of pocket sorting is the large storage area necessitated by the auxiliary lists $B_0$, $B_1$, . . . , $B_9$. Two obvious means of reducing the storage requirements suggest themselves.

**Definition 2.6.7** (Bit Pocket Sorting) The keys are interpreted as binary numbers rather than decimal numbers: d(j, n) yields the jth bit from the right in the binary representation of the number n.

Several advantages result from this: first, only two auxiliary lists $B_0$ and $B_1$ are needed; second, in many computers locating the jth bit is particularly simple using shift operations; and, third, this technique is also well-suited for sorting with peripheral storage facilities (such as magnetic tape units).

**Definition 2.6.8** (Linking Pockets) We use the technique of pocket sorting but store the given array B as a linked list. The auxiliary arrays $B_0, B_1, \ldots, B_9$ then require no additional memory space in general since they can be materialized through appropriately chosen pointer fields.

This technique has the advantages that the required storage space is small, few steps are necessary, and no nodes need to be relocated.

The following example gives a program for the technique described. It is a fine illustration of the use of linked allocation. The function procedure d(j, n) from Def. 2.4.5 is assumed.

**Example 2.6.6** Two whole numbers n and t and a sequence $G = g_1, g_2, \ldots, g_n$ of n positive t-digit decimal numbers are given as input. We shall design a program that sorts the sequence G using pocket sorting and prints the sequence G.

The memory locations required for the storage of G are declared by **DCL** (G(N), R(N)) **FIXED BIN**;. The start pointer of G and the start and end pointers of the auxiliary arrays $B_0, B_1, \ldots, B_9$ are declared by **DCL** (AG, AB(0: 9), EB(0: 9)) **FIXED BIN**;.

```
POCKET: PROC OPTIONS (MAIN);
    DCL (N, T) FIXED BIN;
    GET LIST (N, T);
    BEGIN;
        DCL (G(N), R(N), AB(0: 9), EB(0: 9), I, J, K, AG, V)
            FIXED BIN;
        GET LIST (G);
        DO I = 1 TO N − 1;
            R(I) = I + 1;
        END;
        R(N) = 0;
        AG = 1;
        /* NOW THE NUMBERS ARE STORED LINKED */
        DO J = 1 TO T;
            AB, EB = 0;
            DISTRIBUTE: DO WHILE (AG ¬= 0);
                K = D(J, G(AG));
                V = AG; AG = R(AG);
                IF AB(K) = 0 THEN AB(K) = V;
                        ELSE R(EB(K)) = V;
                EB(K) = V;
                R(V) = 0;
            END;
            COLLECT: I = 0;
            DO WHILE (AB(I) = 0);
                I = I + 1;
            END;
```

```
        AG = AB(I); K = I + 1;
        DO WHILE (K <= 9);
            IF AB(K) ¬= 0 THEN DO;
                                R(EB(I)) = AB(K);
                                I = K; K = K + 1;
                            END;
                      ELSE K = K + 1;
            END;
        END;
        DO WHILE (AG ¬= 0);
            PUT LIST (G(AG));
            AG = R(AG);
        END;
      END;
  END;
```

For better understanding, work through the program above by hand using the input 5, 2, 09, 07, 18, 17, 52.

The two sorting techniques just discussed (sorting by merging and pocket sorting) are indeed extremely efficient with regard to the number of steps necessary for the sorting; however, in addition to the memory space required for the array being sorted, both techniques use additional storage in an amount proportional to the length of the given array. The additional storage is in the form of auxiliary arrays (as in Example 2.6.5 for the procedure "Merge") or in the form of pointer fields (as in Example 2.6.6). In contrast to this the technique of sorting by selection requires no additional storage space (see Example 2.6.4) but does require an undesirably large number of steps.

There are several well-known techniques that represent a reasonable compromise in that, to sort n nodes, an average of only $n \log_2 n$ steps are necessary and the additional storage requirements are proportional to $\log_2 n$. Two such techniques are discussed here.

**Definition 2.6.9** (Quicksort) If, for the given sequence of nodes $F = k_1, k_2, \ldots,$ $k_n$, n is less than or equal to 2, then the sequence can be sorted by using at most one interchange and the sort operation is completed. Otherwise F is arranged in a sequence of nodes $F', k_1, F''$, where $F'$ consists of all nodes k of F that are less than or equal to $k_1$, i.e., $\omega_1 k \leqslant \omega_1 k_1$ for $k \in F'$, and where $F''$ consists of all nodes k of F that are greater than $k_1$, i.e., $\omega_1 k > \omega_1 k_1$ for $k \in F''$. Thus F is split into two sequences $F'$ and $F''$ by $k_1$. The sequences $F'$ and $F''$ are then sorted by using Quicksort.

Figure 2.6.4 illustrates the process of sorting the sequence of $n = 14$ numbers from Fig. 2.6.2 using Quicksort.

When using Quicksort, the number of comparisons necessary for the sorting is strongly dependent on the arrangement of the n keys. If the given sequence is already nearly sorted, then approximately $n^2/2$ comparisons are necessary; whereas using the most advantageous arrangement only about $n \log_2 n$ are necessary. For example, to sort the sequence of 15 numbers 1, 2, 3, 4, 5, 6, 7, 8, 9, 10, 11, 12, 13, 14, 15, around

```
9,  7,  18,  3,  52,  4,  6,    8,    5,  13,  42,  30,  35,  26
7,  3,   4,  6,   8,  5;  9;  18,  52,  13,  42,  30,  35,  26
3,  4,   6,  5;   7;  8;  9;  13;  18;  52,  42,  30,  35,  26
3;  4,   6,  5;   7;  8;  9;  13;  18;  42,  30,  35,  26;  52
3;  4;   6,  5;   7;  8;  9;  13;  18;  30.  35,  26;  42;  52
3;  4;   5;  6;   7;  8;  9;  13;  18;  26;  30;  35;  42;  52
```

**Figure 2.6.4**

110 comparisons are needed; but to sort the same 15 numbers given in the sequence 8, 12, 14, 15, 13, 10, 11, 9, 4, 6, 7, 5, 2, 3, 1, only about 50 comparisons are needed.

If we let C(n) be the total number of comparisons necessary to sort all possible n! different sequences formed from the n numbers 1, 2, . . . , n using Quicksort, then $C(n)/n!$ is the average number of comparisons necessary for sorting n numbers. It is therefore of interest to determine the value of $C(n)/n!$.

If the key $\omega_1 k_1$ used in splitting the node sequence F in the Quicksort technique is the kth largest $(1 \leqslant k \leqslant n)$ occurring key, then n comparisons are necessary to split F, a total of $n \times n!$ comparisons for the n! possible arrangements. From the splitting process, two sequences of lengths $(n - k)$ and $(k - 1)$ remain. To sort all possible arrangements of $(n - k)$ and $(k - 1)$ numbers, $C(n - k)$ and $C(k - 1)$ comparisons, respectively, are necessary and every possible arrangement occurs $\binom{n-1}{k-1}(k-1)!$ and $\binom{n-1}{n-k}(n-k)!$ times, respectively, i.e., $\dfrac{(n-1)!}{(n-k)!}$ and $\dfrac{(n-1)!}{(k-1)!}$ times respectively. Therefore we have

$$C(n) = nn! + \sum_{k=1}^{n}\left[C(n-k)\frac{(n-1)!}{(n-k)!} + C(k-1)\frac{(n-1)!}{(k-1)!}\right]$$

$$= nn! + (n-1)!\,2\sum_{k=0}^{n-1}\frac{C(k)}{k!}$$

and from that

$$\frac{C(n)}{(n-1)!} = n^2 + 2\sum_{k=0}^{n-1}\frac{C(k)}{k!}$$

from which it follows by induction[15] that

$$\frac{C(n)}{(n-1)!} = -n^2 + 2n(n+1)\sum_{i=1}^{n}\frac{1}{i+1}.$$

---

[15]
$$\frac{C(n+1)}{n!} = (n+1)^2 + 2\sum_{k=0}^{n}\frac{C(k)}{k!}$$

$$= (n+1)^2 + \left[n^2 + 2\sum_{k=0}^{n-1}\frac{C(k)}{k!}\right] - n^2 + \frac{2C(n)}{n!}$$

$$= 2n + 1 + \frac{n+2}{n}\left[-n^2 + 2n(n+1)\sum_{i=1}^{n}\frac{1}{i+1}\right]$$

$$= -(n+1)^2 + 2(n+1)(n+2)\sum_{i=1}^{n+1}\frac{1}{i+1}.$$

Since, as is known,

$$\sum_{i=1}^{n} \frac{1}{i} < \ln n + 0.6 + \frac{1}{2n},$$

it follows that

$$\frac{C(n)}{n!} < 2n \ln n; \qquad \text{therefore } \frac{C(n)}{n!} < 1.4n \log_2 n.$$

The average effort in terms of comparisons is thus $n \log_2 n$ for Quicksort, exactly as for sorting by merging.

The following procedure "Quick (A, low, hi)" illustrates further how a sequence of numbers A(low), A(low + 1), . . . , A(hi) can be sorted using Quicksort without auxiliary arrays and without pointer fields for linking.[16] A "left pointer" i and a "right pointer" j point first to A(low + 1) and A(hi), respectively. Then the process *partition*, which splits the numbers into those $\leqslant$ A(low) and those $>$ A(low), is performed until the left and right pointers point to the same element.

*Partition:* The left pointer shifts one step to the right if it points to a number $\leqslant$ A(low); otherwise the right pointer advances to the left until it points to a number $\leqslant$ A(low); now the numbers to which the two pointers point are interchanged and the partitioning continues.

```
QUICK: PROCEDURE (A, LOW, HI) RECURSIVE;
DCL (A(*), LOW, HI) FIXED BIN;
    EXCHANGE: PROCEDURE (M1, M2);
        DCL (M1, M2, M3) FIXED BIN;
        M3 = M1; M1 = M2; M2 = M3;
    END EXCHANGE;
    SHORT: PROCEDURE (A, I, J);
        DCL (A(*), I, J) FIXED BIN;
        IF J − I = 1 THEN IF A(I) > A(I + 1) THEN CALL
                        EXCHANGE (A(I), A(I + 1));
    END SHORT;
    DCL (CUTPOINT, I, J) FIXED BIN;
    I = LOW + 1; J = HI; CUTPOINT = A(LOW);
    IF J ¬= 1 THEN DO;
    DO WHILE (I ¬= J);
        IF A(I) > CUTPOINT THEN DO;
            IF A(J) > CUTPOINT THEN J = J − 1;
                        ELSE DO;
                        CALL EXCHANGE (A(I), A(J));
                        I = I + 1;
                        END;
                        END;
                    ELSE I = I + 1;
        END;
```

---

[16]The only additional storage area is necessitated because "Quick" is a recursive procedure. If a stack were used instead of recursive, then $\log_2 n$ memory locations would be adequate for the stack.

```
PARTITION: IF A(I) > CUTPOINT THEN I = I − 1;
CALL EXCHANGE (A(I), A(LOW));
IF I − LOW > 2 THEN CALL QUICK (A, +LOW, I − 1);
            ELSE CALL SHORT (A, LOW, I − 1);
   IF HI − I > 2 THEN CALL QUICK (A, I + 1, +HI);
            ELSE CALL SHORT (A, I + 1, +HI);
                  END;
END QUICK;
```

If we split a sequence of n nodes not using the key of the first node as with Quicksort but using the arithmetic mean of the smallest and largest keys, then we have the *binary sort* that is more desirable than Quicksort in that in no case are more than $t \times n$ comparisons required for the sort, where

$$t = \log_2 (\max \{\omega_1 k \mid k \in F\} - \min \{\omega_1 k \mid k \in F\}).$$

The additional memory space required is the same as for Quicksort; however, the programming is somewhat more involved.

**Definition 2.6.10** (Binary Sort) From among the keys of the nodes the smallest and the largest are determined, and the arithmetic mean $\mu$ is calculated. From the sequence $F = k_1, k_2, \ldots, k_n$ of nodes, a sequence $F', F''$ is produced, in which the sequence $F'$ contains all nodes with key less than or equal to $\mu$ ($\omega_1 k \leqslant \mu$ for $k \in F'$) and in which the sequence $F''$ contains all nodes with key greater than $\mu$ ($\omega_1 k > \mu$ for $k \in F''$). If $F''$ contains no elements, then $F'$ is sorted and the sorting process is complete. Otherwise both $F'$ and $F''$ are sorted using binary sorting.

Figure 2.6.5 shows the sorting process for the 14 two-digit keys of Fig. 2.6.2.

When sorting using pocket sorting and binary sorting, the number of steps for sorting a linear list of length n depends on n and the nature of the keys.

```
9,  7,  18,  3,  52,  4,  6,  8,  5,  13,  42,  30,  35,  26
9,  7,  18,  3,  4,  6,  8,  5,  13,  26;  52,  42,  30,  35
9,  7,  3,  4,  6,  8,  5,  13;  18,  26;  30,  35;  52,  42
7,  3,  4,  6,  5,  8;  9,  13;  18;  26;  30;  35;  42;  52
3,  4,  5,  7,  6,  8;  9;  13;  18;  26;  30;  35;  42;  52
3,  4;  5;  6,  7;  8;  9;  13;  18;  26;  30;  35;  42;  52
3;  4;  5;  6;  7;  8;  9;  13;  18;  26;  30;  35;  42;  52
```

**Figure 2.6.5**

If we consider sorting techniques in which no manipulation of keys (other than comparisons) is allowed, then we see that there is no technique that sorts an arbitrary list of length n in less than $n \log_2 n$ comparisons.

To show this, suppose we have given an algorithm for sorting a sequence of n nodes that works only by comparing keys. After each comparison performed in the algorithm, there are two paths in the algorithm corresponding to the two possible results of the comparison. Altogether there are n! possible arrangements of n nodes, therefore there must be at least n! different paths[17] in the algorithm. For n! different paths, at least t comparisons are necessary, where $2^t \geqslant n!$.[18] Therefore $t \geqslant \log_2 n!$ where $\log_2 n! \approx n \log_2 n$ as asserted.

*Sorting by hashing* shows, rather impressively, that this lower bound of $n \log_2 n$ comparisons or steps for sorting n nodes can be significantly improved by using operations other than comparisons of keys.

**Definition 2.6.11** (Sorting by Hashing) The nodes $k_1, k_2, \ldots, k_n$ of the given array are first stored using scatter storage with a *monotone* scatter function s; i.e., $s(\omega_1 k) \leqslant s(\omega_1 k')$ if $\omega_1 k \leqslant \omega_1 k'$. Then the memory space used for the scatter storage is searched from left to right. The stored nodes are gathered together and overflow items are sorted if necessary.

An example should clarify the technique.

**Example 2.6.7** Given as input we have a sequence of 17000 different whole numbers between 0 and 19999. The following program sorts the sequence of numbers using hashing.

For the scatter storage we use a storage area of 10000 memory locations having a data field and a pointer field, where the pointer field points to an overflow area. For the storage of overflow items we use a linear array F of length 8500, stored sequentially. As a scatter function we use $s(n) = n \div 2$ so that at most one overflow per memory location can occur.

```
HASH: PROC OPTIONS (MAIN);
    DCL (D(10000), R(10000), F(8500), I, FREE, POS, M)
        FIXED BIN;
    /* D IS THE STORAGE AREA FOR THE SCATTER STORAGE,
       F IS FOR OVERFLOW */
    FREE = 1; /* ALWAYS POINTS TO THE FIRST FREE NODE OF F */
    R = -1; /* AN EMPTY MEMORY LOCATION IS INDICATED BY -1
            IN THE POINTER FIELD */
    DO I = 1 TO 17000;
        GET LIST (M);
        POS = FLOOR (M/2 + 1)
        IF R(POS) = -1 THEN DO;
                        D(POS) = M;
                        R(POS) = 0;
                    END;
                ELSE DO;
                    IF D(POS) > M THEN DO;
                            F(FREE) = D(POS);
                            D(POS) = M;
                        END;
```

---

[17]That is, n! different sequences of steps in the algorithm.

[18]Notice that j comparisons yield at most $2^j$ different paths.

```
                              ELSE F(FREE) = M;
                            R(POS) = FREE;
                            FREE = FREE + 1;
                          END;
             END; /* THE HASHING IS COMPLETE, OUTPUT BEGINS */
             DO I = 1 TO 10000;
                 IF R(I) ¬= −1 THEN DO;
                     PUT LIST D(I));
                     IF R(I) ¬= 0 THEN PUT LIST F(R(I)));
                 END;
             END;
         END;
```

It is not difficult to see that in the execution of the program above fewer than $(n \log_2 n)/2$ steps ($n = 17000$) are performed, a notable improvement over the lower bound mentioned earlier.

In actual practice, problems sometimes arise in which sorting techniques lead to efficient algorithms for solution, even though at first it is not apparent that sorting techniques are at all relevant to the problem solution.

**Example 2.6.8** Let $g(x_1, x_2)$ and $h(x_1, x_2)$ be arbitrary functions with whole-number arguments. We wish to determine the minimum of the function $f(x_1, x_2, x_3, x_4) =$ abs $[g(x_1, x_2) - h(x_3, x_4)]$ for $1 \leqslant x_1, x_2, x_3, x_4 \leqslant n$.

Computing $f(x_1, x_2, x_3, x_4)$ for all possible values would require $n^4$ steps and therefore for large values of $n$ would not be a reasonable approach. On the other hand, we could calculate the $n^2$ possible values of $g(x_1, x_2)$ and the $n^2$ possible values of $h(x_3, x_4)$ and then sort them together. The minimal difference of a pair $(g, h)$ or $(h, g)$, respectively, occurring in the sorted result gives the desired minimum. Using an efficient sort technique (such as the technique of sorting by merging), the necessary number of steps is reduced from $n^4$ to $n^2 \log_2 n$. The situation is similar if, for example, we wish to determine the intersection of two sets $C_1, C_2$ having $c_1, c_2$ elements (for example, if we wish to determine all persons belonging to two clubs $C_1$ and $C_2$). Instead of searching through all of $C_2$ for each element of $C_1$ and thus performing $c_1 \times c_2$ steps, the elements of both sets can be sorted together in $(c_1 + c_2) \log_2 (c_1 + c_2)$ steps and then all those elements occurring twice in succession can be chosen.

*Remarks and References*

Martin [1] presents a survey of sorting techniques. A rigorous development of sorting techniques may be found in Knuth [2]. For optimal sorts, see Ford [1]. The technique Quicksort originated with Hoare [1] and has been improved several times {see Van Emden [1]}. Among the techniques not discussed in this book, the *heap sort* {Williams [1]} is particularly interesting since this technique requires no more storage than Quicksort and no more than $n \log_2 n$ steps are needed to sort $n$ numbers.

## Exercises

**2.6.1** Complete Example 2.6.3 by writing the procedure "Merge (F1, F2, F3, F4, RES)."

**2.6.2** Write a program, similar to Example 2.6.5, but in which the numbers to be sorted are stored using linked storage. The merging is done not by actual relocation but rather by changing the linking.

**2.6.3** Write a program for sorting n numbers using bit pocket sorting and using a single auxiliary array that is sequentially accessible from both ends.

**2.6.4** Write a program to sort n numbers using a binary sort.

**2.6.5** The unordered membership lists of four clubs $C_1, C_2, C_3, C_4$ are given as input. No club has more than 250 members. Write a program to determine all those persons who are members of at least three of the clubs. *Hint:* If necessary, for simplification, it may be assumed that members are listed not by their names but by a positive whole number.

## Section 2.7   Searching Linear Lists

This section is divided into two parts. In the first we shall investigate how nodes in a linear list with given keys can be found; in the second we shall learn how to locate the node having the ith largest key in a linear list.

**Definition 2.7.1** (Search Problem) Given a linear array $B = (K, R)$ and given a sequence V of keys, the problem often is to determine for each key v in V the set of all nodes of K having key v.

Without loss of generality, it is assumed as already mentioned in Sec. 2.6 that the key component is always the first component and that the keys are whole numbers. The sequence F of nodes corresponding to the given array B is denoted by $F = k_1, k_2, \ldots, k_n$.

For simplicity, we first consider the particular search problem in which V consists of a single key and exactly one node with this key exists in the array B. The efficiency of a technique A for solving this specific search problem is often measured by the two numbers.

     Max (A) = maximum number of comparisons to find the node with given
           key,

and

     Avg (A) = average number of comparisons to find the node with given key.

To determine Avg (A) it is assumed that a node k with probability p(k) is found

where

$$\sum_{i=1}^{n} p_i = 1$$

where we write simply $p_i$ instead of $p(k_i)$. The number $p_i$ is also called the *relative usage frequency* of the node $k_i$, and it indicates that in t searches of the array B the node $k_i$ is found approximately $t \times p_i$ times. If we denote by $s_i$ the number of comparisons necessary to locate the node $k_i$ using technique A, then we obtain

$$\text{Max (A)} = \max \{s_i \,|\, i = 1, 2, \ldots, n\}$$

and

$$\text{Avg (A)} = \sum_{i=1}^{n} p_i s_i.$$

We now consider several techniques for locating a node with a given key v in a linear array B.

**Definition 2.7.2** (Sequential Search) The keys of the nodes $k_1, k_2, \ldots, k_n$ are compared with v until a node $k_i$ is found in which $\omega_1 k_i = v$. A sequential search is suitable not only for arrays that are sequentially stored but also for arrays that are stored using linking. Clearly

$$\text{Max (sequential search)} = n$$

and

$$\text{Avg (sequential search)} = \sum_{i=1}^{n} i p_i.$$

In view of the last formula, it is advisable in a sequential search to arrange the nodes so that $p_i \geqslant p_{i+1}$ for $i = 1, 2, \ldots, n - 1$. It is often the case that $p_i = 1/n$ for all i (in which all nodes have the same relative usage frequency); then

$$\text{Avg (sequential search)} = \sum_{i=1}^{n} i \frac{1}{n} = \frac{1}{n} \frac{n(n + 1)}{2} \approx \frac{n}{2}. \text{[19]}$$

In the case of equal relative usage frequencies for a sequential search, on the average, half of all the nodes must be checked, which for large arrays is too costly. The situation can be improved for different distributions of relative usage frequencies. For example, if

$$p_i = \frac{1}{e^a} \frac{a^{i-1}}{(i - 1)!}, \text{[20]}$$

---

[19]More precisely,

$$\sum_{i=1}^{n-1} i \frac{1}{n} + (n - 1) \frac{1}{n}$$

since the nth node just like the $(n - 1)$st is found after $n - 1$ steps.

[20]Poisson distribution with parameter a,

$$\sum_{i=1}^{\infty} p_i = 1.$$

then we obtain

$$\text{Avg (sequential search)} = \sum_{i=1}^{\infty} i \frac{1}{e^a} \frac{a^{i-1}}{(i-1)!} = a + 1.\text{[21]}$$

In this case the average search time is therefore independent of the length of the array!

Often it is known that the relative usage frequencies differ greatly from one another but the actual values are not available. In such cases the use of a *self-organizing list* is suggested. Each time a node is found, it is moved closer to the beginning of the list. Thus, frequently used nodes will have the tendency to migrate toward the beginning of the list in accordance with their relative usage frequencies. Two extreme strategies have been proposed in the literature. One is to move a node when found to the very head of the list; the other is to move the node just a single position closer to the head of the list. Recent investigations in Rivest [1] seem to indicate that the second ("transposition technique") provides better results.

When searching for a node with a given key, if it is not certain whether such a node actually occurs in the array, then it is necessary to anticipate reaching the end of the array. Example 2.7.1 shows, however, that when using a stopper it is not necessary to check at each step whether the last node of the array has already been reached.

**Example 2.7.1** As input, 101 whole numbers $v, a_1, a_2, \ldots, a_{100}$ are given that represent a key $v$ and the values $a_1, a_2, \ldots, a_{100}$ of the 100 nodes of an array B. First B is to be stored; then using a sequential search we are to search for a node with key $v$, where it is not certain that B really contains such a node.

(a)　Without using a stopper:

```
SEQ1: PROC OPTIONS (MAIN);
      DCL (A(100), I, V) FIXED BIN;
      GET LIST (V, A);
      I = 1;
      LOOP: IF V = A(I) THEN DO;
                             PUT LIST (V, I);
                             GOTO FIN;
                           END;
                  I = I + 1; IF I < = 100 THEN GOTO LOOP;
      PUT LIST (V, 'DOES NOT OCCUR');
      FIN:
      END;
```

---

[21]Indeed if we set

$$f(x) = \sum_{i=0}^{\infty} \frac{x^{i+1}}{i!} = x \sum_{i=0}^{\infty} \frac{x^i}{i!} = xe^x,$$

then

$$f'(x) = \sum_{i=0}^{\infty} (i+1)\frac{x^i}{i!} = e^x(x+1),$$

from which for $x = a$ the proposed relation follows.

(b)  Using a stopper:

```
SEQ2: PROC OPTIONS (MAIN);
    DCL (A(101), I, V) FIXED BIN;
    GET LIST (V,(A(I) DO I = 1 TO 100));
    I = 1; A(101) = V; /* V SERVES AS STOPPER */
    LOOP: IF V = A(I) THEN GOTO FIN;
        I = I + 1; GOTO LOOP;
    FIN: IF I = 101 THEN PUT LIST (V, 'DOES NOT OCCUR');
            ELSE PUT LIST (V, I);
    END;
```

In program b, notice that in the loop the test $i \leqslant 100$ is not necessary.

Search techniques significantly more efficient than the sequential search are possible if the given array B is sorted.

**Definition 2.7.3** (Binary Search) A sorted array B with the sequence of nodes $F = k_1, k_2, \ldots, k_n$ is assumed. To determine a node with given key v we begin with $i = 1, j = n$ and perform the following *bisecting step* repeatedly. The auxiliary values i and j indicate that, at a given point in time, the search has already been confined to the subsequence $k_i, k_{i+1}, \ldots, k_j$.

*Bisecting step:* Let $m = (i + j) \div 2$ be the "middle" of the remaining sequence of nodes. If $v = \omega_1 k_m$, then the desired node $k_m$ has been found and we are finished. Otherwise the bisecting step is repeated, with a new value $j = m - 1$ if $v < \omega_1 k_m$ (for then the desired node lies in the sequence $k_i, k_{i+1}, \ldots, k_{m-1}$) and with a new value $i = m + 1$ if $v > \omega_1 k_m$ (for then the desired node lies in the sequence $k_{m+1}, k_{m+2}, \ldots, k_j$).

The binary search is then useful only if the mth node of B can easily be determined, that is, if B is stored sequentially.

**Example 2.7.2** (Binary Search) Figure 2.7.1(a) shows a linear array with 15 nodes. The binary search for the node with key $v = 27$ can be followed using the table in Fig. 2.7.1(b) that shows the changes of the values i, j, and m. The desired node $k_5$ is found after four bisecting steps as indicated in Fig. 2.7.1(c).

To simplify the calculation of Max (binary search) and Avg (binary search), we shall assume equal relative usage frequencies and we shall consider only the case $n = 2^t - 1$. We wish to determine how many times is it necessary to perform the bisecting step (which contains one comparison with three possible results).

If $t = 1$, then the bisecting step is performed exactly once. Otherwise we obtain $m = 2^{t-1}$ and either the process stops or another bisecting step must be carried out for the $2^{t-1} - 1$ nodes $k_1, k_2, \ldots, k_{m-1}$ or $k_{m+1}, k_{m+2}, \ldots, k_n$. Thus

$$\text{Max (binary search)} = t = \log_2 (n + 1) \approx \log_2 n.$$

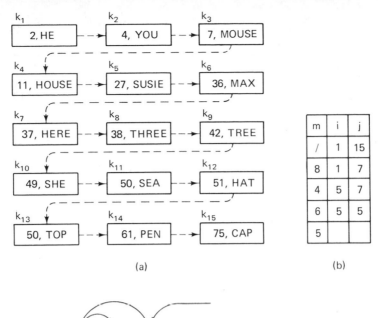

$$k_1, k_2, k_3, k_4, k_5, k_6, k_7, k_8, k_9, k_{10}, k_{11}, k_{12}, k_{13}, k_{14}, k_{15}$$

(c)

**Figure 2.7.1**

Since in the ith bisecting step $2^{i-1}$ nodes can be found,

$$\text{Avg (binary search)} = \frac{1}{n}(1 + 2 \times 2^1 + 3 \times 2^2 + \cdots + t \times 2^{t-1})$$

$$= \frac{1}{n}\sum_{i=1}^{t} i2^{i-1} \approx -1 + \log_2 n.\text{[22]}$$

The binary search is therefore much faster than the sequential search; however, it does demand that the given array be stored sequentially, which is a serious disadvantage when additions and deletions must be made to the list. A technique that is often preferred involves interpreting the given array as a *tree*; this topic will be covered in Sec. 3.3. Another convenient compromise, the *m-block search*, is particularly applicable to indexed storage.

---

[22]Using induction it is easy to prove

$$\sum_{i=1}^{t} i2^{i-1} = 2^t(t-1) + 1$$

and, therefore, with $t = \log_2 (n + 1)$, that

$$\frac{1}{n}\sum_{i=1}^{t} i2^{i-1} = \frac{1}{n}\{(n + 1) [\log_2 (n + 1) - 1] + 1\}$$

$$= \log_2 (n + 1) - 1 + \frac{\log (n + 1)}{n} \approx -1 + \log_2 n.$$

**Definition 2.7.4** (m-Block Search) Suppose we are given a sorted array B with nodes $F = k_1, k_2, \ldots, k_n$ and m numbers $n_1, n_2, \ldots, n_m$, where $n_1 + n_2 + \cdots + n_m = n$. We divide F into m subsequences (or blocks) $F_1, F_2, \ldots, F_m$ in which the first $n_1$ nodes of F are chosen as the sequence $F_1$, the next $n_2$ nodes as the sequence $F_2$, and so on. To find a node with key v, consider for $j = 1, 2, \ldots$ the last node of $F_j$ until, for the last node k of $F_j$, $v \leqslant \omega_1 k$ holds; i.e., the desired node occurs in the subsequence $F_j$. Then apply a sequential search to $F_j$.[23]

**Example 2.7.3** (m-Block Search) Let nine nodes $k_1, k_2, \ldots, k_9$ be given with keys 3, 7, 18, 21, 35, 36, 40, 47, 60. Let $m = n_1 = n_2 = n_3 = 3$. To find $v = 35$ we first construct the three blocks $F_1 = k_1, k_2, k_3$; $F_2 = k_4, k_5, k_6$; and $F_3 = k_7, k_8, k_9$. Of the last nodes $k_3, k_6, k_9$ of the blocks $F_1, F_2, F_3, k_6$ (the last node of $F_2$) is the first for which $v \leqslant \omega_1 k_6$. Thus the desired node lies in $F_2$ and the node $k_5$ with $v = \omega_1 k_5$ is found in $F_2$ by using a sequential search.

The m-block search is suitable for both sequential and linked storage. To evaluate Max (m-block search) and Avg (m-block search) we again assume equal relative usage frequencies.

Since to find a node in the ith block i comparisons are required to find the block and as many as $n_i$ more are needed to find the node within the block, we see that

$$\text{Max (m-block search)} = \max\{i + n_i \,|\, i = 1, 2, \ldots, m\}$$

and

$$\text{Avg (m-block search)} = \frac{1}{n} \sum_{i=1}^{m} \sum_{j=1}^{n_i} (i + j).$$

If we use only blocks of equal lengths $n_1 = n_2 = \cdots = n_m = f$ (and $f = n/m$), then we obtain

$$\text{Max (m-block search)} = m + f$$

and

$$\text{Avg (m-block search)} = \frac{m + f + 2}{2} \approx \frac{f + m}{2}.$$

Clearly $f + m$ becomes minimal for the given product $f \times m = n$ when $f = m$. Therefore when using blocks of equal length it is best to use $n_1 = n_2 = \cdots = n_m = m \approx \sqrt{n}$, and then we obtain

$$\text{Max (m-block search)} \approx 2\sqrt{n}$$

and

$$\text{Avg (m-block search)} \approx \sqrt{n}.$$

The values for Max (m-block search) and Avg (m-block search) can be further improved by using blocks of different lengths. The best choice for the length $n_{m-i}$ of the ith to the last block is $n_{m-i} \approx i + 1$. For example, for 36 nodes using the

---

[23]Since $F_j$ is searched sequentially, the given array F does not actually have to be sorted. It is sufficient that every node in $F_i$ be smaller than every node in $F_j$ if $i < j$.

choice $m = 8$, $n_1 = 8$, $n_2 = 7$, $n_3 = 6$, $n_4 = 5$, $n_5 = 4$, $n_6 = 3$, $n_7 = 2$, $n_8 = 1$, the Max (m-block search) is about 33% better and the Avg (m-block search) is about 7% better than if we had chosen $m = n_1 = n_2 = \cdots = n_6 = 6$.

In the particular search problems considered in the first part of this section, it was assumed that there is exactly one node in the given array having the given key. For the three given search techniques, however, it was necessary to bear in mind the possibility that none or several nodes could occur with the desired key; caution was required particularly in the programming of the binary search.

The situation is even more interesting if instead of a single key v a sorted sequence V of keys $V = v_1, v_2, \ldots, v_t$ is given and for each of these keys the corresponding node is to be found in the sorted array B. Particularly in the sequential search and the m-block search, it is then better not to re-initiate the search process for each key but rather to continue the search process from that point in array B that has already been searched. It is easy to see, for example, that Max (sequential search) drops from n to n/t.

Notice that the sequential search process just proposed for finding a sequence of keys V in an array B brings to mind the idea of merging V with B, performing only the comparisons (and not the relocations) of nodes. Conversely the merging of two arrays A and B of lengths m and n, respectively, can be achieved, for example, for $m = 1$ by determining the appropriate position in B with a binary search in only $\log_2 n$ steps (see Example 2.6.2) and inserting there the single node of array A.

To handle the problem of finding the ith largest node in a linear array B with nodes $F = k_1, k_2, \ldots, k_n$ it is first assumed for simplicity that all (whole-number) keys are different from one another. If F′ is the sequence obtained by sorting F, $F' = k'_1, k'_2, \ldots, k'_n$, then the ith largest node is the ith node from the right in F′, that is, node $k'_{n+1-i}$.

The ith largest node in an array B can then be determined by sorting B, but of course, according to Sec. 2.6, at least $n \log_2 n$ comparisons are necessary (if no other manipulation of the keys is to be made). In the following, it is shown that to locate the ith largest node sorting is unnecessary and only n steps are required.

Determining the largest node of an array B (i.e., the ith largest node where $i = 1$) is usually accomplished by considering n subsequences $F_i = k_1, k_2, \ldots, k_i$ (for $i = 1, 2, \ldots, n$) and computing the largest key $g(F_i)$ of $F_i$ using the formulas $g(F_1) = \omega_1 k_1$ and $g(F_i) = \max \{g(F_{i-1}), \omega_1 k_i\}$ for $i = 2, 3, \ldots, n$. Thus we go through the sequence $k_1, k_2, \ldots, k_n$ and carry along the "largest yet" key. For this technique $n - 1$ comparisons are necessary.

Clearly, at least n steps are necessary to determine the largest of n keys. Notice, however, that significantly fewer than n comparisons may suffice. Comparisons can be replaced to a certain extent by other operations so the number of necessary comparisons alone is not a reliable criterion for the efficiency of a technique. For example, the largest of $n = 2^t$ positive whole numbers $a_1, a_2, \ldots, a_n$ is determined using only $t = \log_2 n$ comparisons since at any given time in a single comparison half of the numbers can be ruled out as follows. If for $m = 2^t$ numbers $b_1, b_2, \ldots, b_m$ it is true that $b_1! + b_2! + \cdots + b_{m/2}! > b_{(m/2)+1}! + \cdots + b_m!$, then the largest of the numbers cannot occur among the m/2 numbers $b_{(m/2)+1}$, $b_{(m/2)+2}$, . . . , $b_m$; otherwise it cannot occur among the m/2 numbers $b_1$, $b_2$, . . . , $b_{m/2}$.

While the largest number in a sequence of numbers $a_1, a_2, . . . , a_n$ can be determined without difficulty in n steps, determining the ith largest number for arbitrary i in n steps is not so simple.

**Definition 2.7.5** (Finding the ith Largest Number by Elimination) Let $k \geqslant 5$ be an arbitrarily chosen odd number. The ith largest number in a sequence A of n different whole numbers is determined by *elimination* as follows:

*Step 1:* If n < 3k, then determine the ith largest number of A by sorting and the task is completed.

*Step 2:* Divide A into $f = n \div k$ subsequences $B_1, B_2, . . . , B_f$ of k numbers each, where b = mod (n, k) numbers are left over.

*Step 3:* Determine the middle number [i.e., the (k + 1)/2 largest number] of each of the f subsequences $B_1, B_2, . . . , B_f$ by sorting; from the sequence of numbers $b_1, b_2, . . . , b_f$ obtained, determine the middle number M [i.e., the f/2 largest or (f + 1)/2 largest] by elimination.

*Step 4:* Let j be the number of numbers in A that are $\geqslant$ M. If j = i, then M is the desired number and the task is completed. If j > i, then replace n by j − 1, remove all numbers $\leqslant$ M from A, and determine the ith largest of the remaining sequence of numbers in A by elimination. Finally if j < i, then replace n by n − j, remove all numbers $\geqslant$ M from A, and determine the (i − j)th largest of the remaining sequence of numbers by elimination.

**Example 2.7.4** For the n = 28 numbers 6, 3, 2, 7, 8; 17, 0, 9, 13, 10; 5, 11, 20, 21, 23; 1, 4, 25, 29, 12; 31, 14, 26, 15, 19; 30, 33, 24; we wish to determine the i = thirteenth largest number for k = 5 by elimination.

Step 2 yields the $t = n \div k = 28 \div 5 = 5$ subsequences

| $B_1$ | $B_2$ | $B_3$ | $B_4$ | $B_5$ | Remainder |
|-------|-------|-------|-------|-------|-----------|
| 6     | 17    | 5     | 1     | 31    | 30        |
| 3     | 0     | 11    | 4     | 14    | 33        |
| 2     | 9     | 20    | 25    | 26    | 24        |
| 7     | 13    | 21    | 29    | 15    |           |
| 8     | 10    | 23    | 12    | 19    |           |

Step 3 sorts the subsequences

| $B_1$ | $B_2$ | $B_3$ | $B_4$ | $B_5$ | Remainder |
|-------|-------|-------|-------|-------|-----------|
| 2     | 0     | 5     | 1     | 14    | 30        |
| 3     | 9     | 11    | 4     | 15    | 33        |
| 6     | 10    | 20    | 12    | 19    | 24        |
| 7     | 13    | 21    | 25    | 26    |           |
| 8     | 17    | 23    | 29    | 31    |           |

and determines the middle number $M = 12$ from the sequence of middle numbers 6, 10, 20, 12, 19. Notice that at least one-fourth of all the given numbers must be $\leqslant M$ and at least one-fourth of all the given numbers must be $\geqslant M$.

Step 4 yields $j = 16$. Since $j > i = 13$, n is replaced by $j - 1 = 15$ and now we need only determine the thirteenth largest number of the remaining sequence $A = 13, 17, 20, 21, 23; 25, 29, 14, 15, 19; 26, 31, 30, 33, 24$.

Step 2 yields the $t = n \div k = 15 \div 5 = 3$ subsequences

| $B_1$ | $B_2$ | $B_3$ |
|-------|-------|-------|
| 13 | 25 | 26 |
| 17 | 29 | 31 |
| 20 | 14 | 30 |
| 21 | 15 | 33 |
| 23 | 19 | 24 |

Step 3 yields, by sorting these subsequences, the three middle numbers 20, 19, 31, and thus $M = 20$.

Step 4 now yields $j = 10$. Since $j < i = 13$, n is replaced by $n - j - 4$, and i is replaced by $i - j = 2$, and we need only determine the second largest in the remaining sequence $A = 13, 14, 17, 15$.

Step 1 produces the desired number 15.

For an analysis of the elimination algorithm given in Def. 2.7.5, let $s(n)$ be the maximum number of comparisons needed to sort n elements using a particular sort technique. Then there is an upper bound $g(n)$ for the number of comparisons needed to locate the ith largest of n numbers by elimination, for which

(1)　$g(n) = s(n)$　　　for $n < 3k$

(2)　$g(n) \leqslant s(k)\dfrac{n}{k} + g\left(\dfrac{n}{k}\right) + n + g\left(\dfrac{3}{4}n\right) = n\left[1 + \dfrac{s(k)}{k}\right] + g\left(\dfrac{n}{k}\right) + g\left(\dfrac{3}{4}n\right).$

The individual terms in formula 2 are obtained as follows: $s(k)(n/k)$ to sort the $f \leqslant n/k$ subsequences $B_1, B_2, \ldots, B_f$ each having k elements and to determine $b_1, b_2, \ldots, b_f$; $g(n/k)$ to find the middle number of the numbers $b_1, b_2, \ldots, b_f$; n to divide the numbers into those $< M$ and those $> M$; $g(3n/4)$ since in step 4 the ith largest of at most $3n/4$ remaining numbers must be determined.

We now show that $g(n)$ is equal to n.

*Assertion:*　Let $k \geqslant 5$. If $\gamma$ is a number such that

$$\gamma \geqslant \frac{4[k + s(k)]}{k - 4} \quad \text{and} \quad s(t) \leqslant \gamma t \quad \text{for } t = 1, 2, \ldots, 3k - 1,$$

then $g(n) \leqslant \gamma n$ for all n.

*Proof:*　(By induction) For $n < 3k$, $g(n) = s(n) \leqslant \gamma n$ by hypothesis. Assume the assertion is true for all $m \leqslant n$. Then

$$g(n+1) \leqslant (n+1)\left[1 + \frac{s(k)}{k}\right] + g\left(\frac{n+1}{k}\right) + g\left[\frac{3(n+1)}{4}\right]$$

$$\leqslant (n+1)\gamma\left[\frac{k+s(k)}{\gamma k} + \frac{1}{k} + \frac{3}{4}\right] \leqslant (n+1)\gamma.$$

Notice that the proof is possible only for $(1/k) + \frac{3}{4} < 1$, i.e., only for $k \geqslant 5$. If we take $s(k) = k \log_2 k$ (as for sorting by merging), then, for example, for $k = 21$ we obtain $\gamma \geqslant 26$.

By improving the elimination technique, $\gamma$ can be decreased to less than 6; however, the elimination technique is primarily of theoretical interest. To determine the ith largest of n numbers by sorting, a technique can be given with approximately $5n \log_2 n$ steps; whereas using elimination at least $60n$ steps are necessary. This is less than the effort required for sorting only when n is very large (say $n \geqslant 5000$), which seldom occurs in actual practice.

**Example 2.7.5** The following program accepts as input three numbers n, i, k followed by n numbers $a_1, a_2, \ldots, a_n$. The ith largest of these n numbers is determined; k gives the size of the subsequences used. Two procedures "Sort" and "Search" are used in the program; these are given first.

```
SORT: PROCEDURE (A, G1, G2);
       DCL (A(*), G1, G2, I, J, AUX) FIXED BIN;
       DO I = G1 TO G2 − 1;
           DO J = I + 1 TO G2;
               IF A(I) > A(J) THEN DO;
                                    AUX = A(I);
                                    A(I) = A(J);
                                    A(J) = AUX;
                               END;
           END;
       END;
END SORT;
SEARCH: PROCEDURE (A, I, N, K) RETURNS (FIXED BIN) RECURSIVE;
       DCL (A(*), I, N, K, L) FIXED BIN, SORT ENTRY ((*)
           FIXED BIN, FIXED BIN, FIXED BIN);
       /* SEARCH (A, I, N, K) YIELDS THE ITH LARGEST OF THE
          NUMBERS A(1) THROUGH A(N) USING ELIMINATION; K
          INDICATES THE SIZE OF THE SUBSEQUENCES */
       IF N < 3 * K | K = 1 THEN DO;
                               CALL SORT (A, 1, N);
                               RETURN (A(N − I + 1));
                           END; /* STEP 1 IS FINISHED */
       BEGIN;
           DCL (B(FLOOR(N/K)), M, F, J, V, T) FIXED BIN;
           F = FLOOR (N/K);
           DO T = 1 TO F;
               CALL SORT (A, (T − 1) * K + 1, T * K);
               B(T) = A((T − 1) * K + FLOOR((K + 1)/2));
           END; /* B CONTAINS THE MIDDLE NUMBER OF THE
                                           SUBSEQUENCE */
```

```
T = FLOOR (F/2) + 1;
M = SEARCH (B, T, F, K); /* THE NUMBER M IS NOW
        DETERMINED IN ACCORDANCE WITH STEP 3 */
J = 0;
DO T = 1 TO N;
    IF A(T) > = M THEN J = J + 1;
END; /* THERE ARE J NUMBERS GREATER THAN OR EQUAL
                TO M */
IF J = I THEN RETURN (M);
IF J > I THEN DO;
                V = 1;
                DO T = 1 TO N;
                    IF A(T) > M THEN DO;
                            A(V) = A(T);
                            V = V + 1;
                            END;
                END;
                RETURN (SEARCH (A, I, J - 1, K)),
            END;
        V = 1;
        DO T = 1 TO N;
            IF A(T) < M THEN DO;
                            A(V) = A(T);
                            V = V + 1;
                        END;
        END;
        RETURN (SEARCH (A, I - J, N - J, K));
    END;
END SEARCH;
```

The main program consists of one call of "Search" and the necessary input/output instructions.

```
APPL: PROC OPTIONS (MAIN);
    DCL (N, I, K) FIXED BIN, SEARCH ENTRY ((*) FIXED BIN,
        FIXED BIN, FIXED BIN, FIXED BIN) RETURNS (FIXED BIN);
    GET LIST (N, I, K);
    BEGIN;
        DCL (A(N), M) FIXED BIN;
        GET LIST (A);
        M = SEARCH (A, I, N, K);
        PUT LIST (M);
    END;
END;
```

*Remarks and References*

A short survey of search techniques appears in Price [1]. The m-block search is analyzed rigorously in Six [1]. In particular, it is demonstrated that the use of blocks of different lengths yields the best results. The technique of determining the ith largest number by elimination originated with Blum [1].

## Exercises

**2.7.1**   Write a translating program as outlined in Exercise 2.4.5, but use sequential storage, no percent frequencies, and the binary search. It should be assumed that the input triples give the German words in alphabetical order.

**2.7.2**   Given as input is a sorted sequence of numbers $a_1, a_2, \ldots, a_n$ followed by a sequence of "questions" $b_1, b_2, \ldots, b_m$. Write a program that first stores the numbers $a_1, a_2, \ldots, a_n$ sequentially and then for each "question" $b_i$ determines all j for which $a_j = b_i$ with a binary search. The program should also work if there is no such j or if there are several such j's.

**2.7.3**   Modify the program in Exercise 2.7.2 so that, in the binary search, instead of the values i, j, m used in Def. 2.7.3, only two values are used: $d = j - i$ and m (that is, only the "length of the interval" and the "midpoint" rather than both end points and the midpoint).

**2.7.4**   Given as input is a sequence of number pairs $A = (a_1, b_1), (a_2, b_2), \ldots,$ $(a_n, b_n)$ and a sequence of numbers $C = c_1, c_2, \ldots, c_m$ with $m > 3n$, where each $c_i \in C$ appears among the $a_i$; the sequence C therefore contains repeats. Write a program that stores A linked and then for each $c_i \in C$ uses a sequential search to determine and print those $b_j$ for which $a_j = c_i$.
(a)   The program should treat A as self-organizing.
(b)   The program should store A so that a pair $(a_i, b_i)$ precedes a pair $(a_j, b_j)$ in the linking if $a_i$ occurs more often in C than $a_j$ (i.e., A is linked in order of decreasing relative usage frequency).
In both cases a and b the program should not only solve the search problem stated but also print the number of search steps used.

**2.7.5**   Compute Avg (sequential search) for a sorted array with n nodes, if (a) two arbitrary keys $v_1 < v_2$, (b) three arbitrary keys $v_1 < v_2 < v_3$ are considered simultaneously. *Hint:* Let $h(v_1, v_2)$ be the number of comparisons to locate two arbitrary keys $v_1 < v_2$.

$$\text{Avg (sequential search)} = \frac{2}{(n-1)n} \sum_{v_1 < v_2} h(v_1, v_2).$$

**2.7.6**   Generalize Exercise 2.7.5 to t keys $v_1 < v_2 < \cdots < v_t$.

$$\textit{Hint:} \quad \sum_{a=0}^{n} \binom{a}{b} = \binom{n+1}{b+1} \qquad \text{for a, b, n} \geqslant 0.$$

# 3 Trees

## Section 3.1 Trees and Methods of Storing Trees

A *tree* B consists of a node k, designated as the *root* of B, which has as *successors* $n \geqslant 0$ roots of n other trees $B_1, B_2, \ldots, B_n$ (the *subtrees* of B).

**Definition 3.1.1** (Tree) A data structure $B = (K, R)$ is called a *tree* if R consists of exactly one relation N that satisfies conditions a through c.

(a) There is exactly one node W, called the *root* of the tree, which has no predecessor.

(b) Each node except the root W has exactly one predecessor.

(c) For each node k different from W, there is a sequence of nodes $W = k_0$, $k_1, \ldots, k_n = k$ (for $n \geqslant 1$) in which $k_i$ is the successor of $k_{i-1}$ (for $1 \leqslant i \leqslant n$).

**Definition 3.1.2** (Notational Conventions) The end nodes of a tree (i.e., the nodes having no successors) are often called *terminal nodes* or *leaves*. The *degree of a node* k is the number of successors of k. The largest degree of any node occurring in a tree is called the *degree of the tree*.

A sequence $W = k_0, k_1, \ldots, k_n$ as described in condition c of Def. 3.1.1 is called a *branch of length n* to the node $k = k_n$. The length of a branch to a node k is denoted by $\lambda k$.

**Definition 3.1.3** (Ordered and Complete Trees) A tree $B = (K, R)$ of degree n is said to be *ordered* if for every successor $k'$ of k it is also specified whether $k'$ is the first, second, . . . , nth successor of k.[1]

---

[1] We can interpret the relation $N \in R$ as consisting of n pairwise disjoint relations $N_1, N_2, \ldots, N_n$, $N = N_1 \cup N_2 \cup \cdots \cup N_n$, where $(k, k') \in N_i$ implies that $k'$ is the ith successor of k.

A tree B = (K, R) of degree n is called *complete* if every node has either n successors or none at all.

In the graphical representation of a tree, a successor k′ of k is usually placed below the node k, so to connect the corresponding rectangles an undirected line segment is sufficient. For ordered trees the successors of a node k are arranged from left to right in the order "first successor," "second successor," . . . . If there is an ith successor k′ of k but no (i − 1)st, then the line going from k to k′ is marked by i. Figure 3.1.1(a) and (b) show different representations of the same (complete) tree of degree 2. Notice that the two trees represented are equivalent as trees but different as ordered trees.

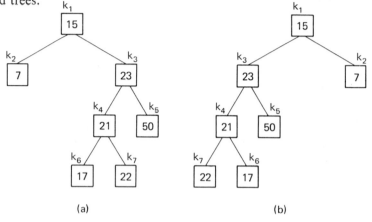

(a)                                                                         (b)

**Figure 3.1.1**

Figure 3.1.2 shows three different ordered trees. Each of the trees has $k_1$ as the root and $k_2, k_4, k_5, k_6$ as leaves. In Fig. 3.1.2(a), notice though that $k_1$ has no third successor, in (b) $k_1$ has no second successor, and in (c) $k_1$ has no first successor.

Tree structures are used in many kinds of applications, often to define a hierarchical relationship. For example, Fig. 3.1.3(a) shows the structure of a family (Max has two sons Edward and Otto, etc.). A tree could also be used to show the divisions in a firm, the arrangement of geographical areas into subdivisions, or the construction of a set out of disjoint subsets as in Fig. 3.1.3(b) (which we can interpret as a representation of the relation A = B ∪ C ∪ D, B = E ∪ H, E = R ∪ S, C = V ∪ W).

Ordered trees also indicate, in addition to a hierarchical connection, a certain ordering of the subtrees of a node, and this is useful in many cases.

Examples are the organization of a book into volumes, chapters, and sections as shown in Fig. 3.1.4(a) or the representation of the structure of a sentence as in Fig. 3.1.4(b) where we see not only that the sentence consists of a subject and predicate but also that the subject precedes the predicate.

Trees are generalizations of arrays. Notice, for example, the one-dimensional array A of order 3 in Fig. 3.1.5(a), the two-dimensional array B of order (2, 3) in Fig. 3.1.5(b), and the three-dimensional array C of order (2, 2, 2) in Fig. 3.1.5(c) are represented as ordered trees; whereas the ordered tree in Fig. 3.1.4(a) does not correspond to any array.

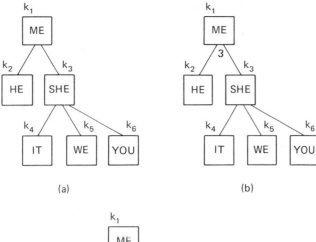

(a)                              (b)

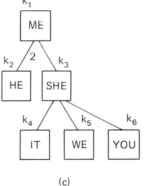

(c)

**Figure 3.1.2**

Arithmetic expressions can be represented in several ways by ordered trees. Some possible representations of the simple arithmetic expression $((3. \times (5. - 2.)) + 7.)$ are given in Fig. 3.1.6, where Fig. 3.1.6(c) corresponds to Def. 2.2.3 and the substitution process shown in Fig. 2.2.6. The tree shown in Fig. 3.1.6(c) is called the *derivation tree* of the expression $((3. \times (5. - 2.)) + 7.)$.

In working with tree structures it is often desirable to deal with the nodes and leaves of an ordered tree in a certain order, just as elements of an array are usually manipulated in a certain order.

**Definition 3.1.4** (Preorder, Postorder, Yield) Let $B = (K, R)$ be a tree of degree n. The nodes of B are traversed in *preorder* by first taking the root and then traversing the nodes of the subtrees in *preorder*. The nodes of B are traversed in *postorder* by first traversing the nodes of the subtrees in *postorder* and then taking the root. A *yield* of B is obtained as follows: if B consists of only one node, then take this node; otherwise, take the *yields* of the subtrees of B. For ordered trees, preorder, postorder, and yield are uniquely defined since the subtrees of a tree are always considered in the sequence "first subtree," "second subtree," ..., from left to right.

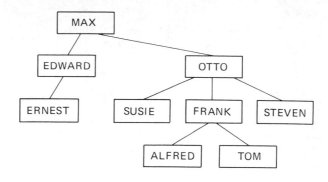

(a)

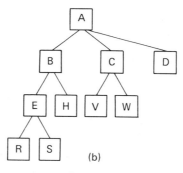

(b)

**Figure 3.1.3**

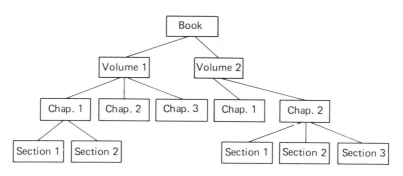

(a)

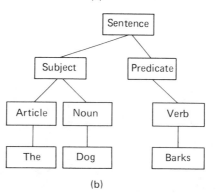

(b)

**Figure 3.1.4**

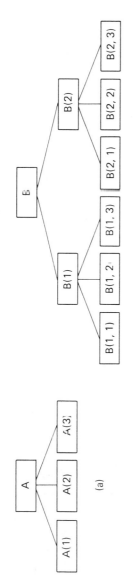

(a)

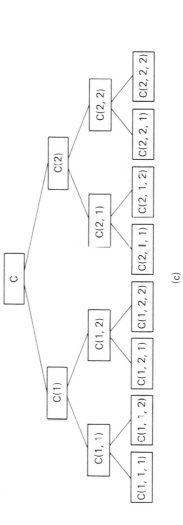

(b)

(c)

**Figure 3.1.5**

107

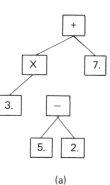

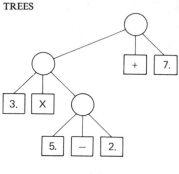

(a)　　　　　　　　　　　　(b)

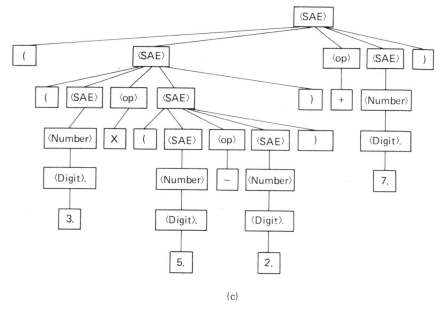

(c)

**Figure 3.1.6**

**Example 3.1.1** A preorder of the nodes in the tree of Fig. 3.1.1(a) is 15, 7, 23, 21, 17, 22, 50; another is 15, 23, 50, 21, 22, 17, 7. The (unique) postorder of nodes in the ordered tree of Fig. 3.1.1(a) is 7, 17, 22, 21, 50, 23, 15. The yield of the ordered tree in Fig. 3.1.2(b) is HE, IT, WE, YOU; the nodes of the tree in Fig. 3.1.6(a) taken in postorder are 3., 5., 2., $-$, $\times$ 7., $+$ ; and the yield is 3., 5., 2., 7.. For the tree in Fig. 3.1.6(c) the yield is ((3. $\times$ (5. $-$ 2.)) $+$ 7.).

For many applications it is necessary to be able to give a linear representation of a tree. For this purpose *level numbers* are introduced.

**Definition 3.1.5** (Level Numbers, Representation of a Tree Using Level Numbers) Let B $=$ (K, R) be a tree. If each node k is associated with a positive number $\nu k$, then these numbers are called *level numbers* (for the tree B), if conditions a and b are satisfied:

(a)   If k' is a successor of k, then $\nu k' > \nu k$.

(b)   If k' and k'' are successors of the same node k, then $\nu k' = \nu k''$.

A *level-number representation* of the tree B is obtained by writing all nodes of the tree along with their level numbers in a preorder.

**Example 3.1.2**  Two possible level-number representations of the tree in Fig. 3.1.1(a) are

$$1\,k_1,\, 2\,k_2,\, 2\,k_3,\, 3\,k_4,\, 4\,k_6,\, 4\,k_7,\, 3\,k_5$$

and

$$2\,k_1,\, 26\,k_2,\, 26\,k_3,\, 27\,k_4,\, 30\,k_6,\, 30\,k_7,\, 27\,k_5.$$

Since $k_6$ and $k_7$ are successors of the same node, $\nu k_6 = \nu k_7$; since $k_4$ is a successor of $k_3$, $\nu k_4 > \nu k_3$; and so on. Notice that the level-number representation of an unordered tree or a complete, ordered tree uniquely defines the tree. The level-number representation of an ordered (not complete) tree, however, does not always uniquely define the ordered tree. For example, $1\,k_1,\, 2\,k_2,\, 2\,k_3,\, 3\,k_4,\, 3\,k_5,\, 3\,k_6$ is a level-number representation of the three different ordered trees in Fig. 3.1.2(a) through (c).

In order to gain uniqueness of representation, we may construct a complete ordered tree by inserting additional "filler nodes." The tree shown in Fig. 3.1.7 is a complete, ordered tree formed from the ordered tree in Fig. 3.1.2(b) by adding a filler node $k_7$ with $\omega k_7 = $ **.

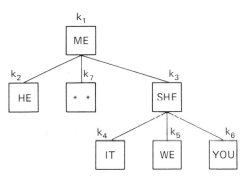

**Figure 3.1.7**

The level-number representation $1\,k_1,\, 2\,k_2,\, 2\,k_7,\, 2\,k_3,\, 3\,k_4,\, 3\,k_5,\, 3\,k_6$ defines in a unique way a complete, ordered tree of degree 3. Another linear representation of trees that is closely related to level-number representation is *parenthetical representation*.

**Definition 3.1.6**  (Parenthetical Representation) Let $B = (K, R)$ be a tree. A *parenthetical representation* of B is obtained by following the rules a and b:

(a)   If the tree B consists of only one node, then that node is the parenthetical representation.

(b)  If the tree B consists of a root W with subtrees $B_1, B_2, \ldots, B_n$, then the parenthetical representation of B is the root W, followed by a left bracket, followed by the parenthetical representations of $B_1, B_2, \ldots, B_n$, separated by commas, followed by a right bracket.

An ordered tree has a unique parenthetical representation, but only in the case of complete, ordered trees is there a one-to-one correspondence between trees and parenthetical representations.

**Example 3.1.3**  A parenthetical representation of the tree in Fig. 3.1.1(a) is $k_1$ $[k_2, k_3 [k_4, [k_6, k_7], k_5]]$. The parenthetical representation $k_1 [k_2, k_3 [k_4, k_5, k_6]]$ represents the three different ordered trees in Fig. 3.1.2(a) through (c); $k_1 [k_2, k_7, k_3 [k_4, k_5, k_6]]$ is the parenthetical representation of the complete ordered tree of Fig. 3.1.7. The parenthetical representation of the values of the nodes in the tree of Fig. 3.1.6(a) is $+ [\times [3., - [5., 2.]], 7.]$.

When working with tree structures, the following operations are frequently required:

(1)  Find a node with a given property.
(2)  Search through all the nodes of a tree in a certain order.
(3)  Determine the predecessor of a certain node.
(4)  Determine all successors of a certain node.
(5)  Remove a subtree.
(6)  Replace a given leaf by a tree.

When choosing a method of storing a tree, it is necessary to consider which of the operations 1 through 6 are to be performed and how frequently, how fast these operations can be carried out for the particular method of storage chosen, and how large the anticipated storage area is to be.

For simplicity in the following discussion, unless specified otherwise, we shall consider only ordered trees in which each node with m successors has exactly one first, second, $\ldots$, mth successor.

**Definition 3.1.7** (Standard Form, Inverse Form, Extended Standard Form)  Let $B = (K, R)$ be a tree of degree n with $R = \{N\}$. When B is stored in *standard form*, the relation N is realized as a linked structure; i.e., each node k points, using a certain pointer field (with n components), to its $m \leqslant n$ successors; thus in the case of ordered trees only the first m components of the pointer field are different from zero. A beginning node is often used (which points to the root of the tree) and for large values of n indirect allocation may be used for the pointer field (see Sec. 1.4). When B is stored in *inverse form*, the relation $N^{-1} = \{(k', k) \mid (k, k') \in N\}$ is realized using linked allocation; i.e., each node $k'$ points, using a certain pointer field, to its predecessor. *Extended standard form* is a combination of standard and inverse form; i.e., both relations N and $N^{-1}$ are realized using linked allocation. In all three of these methods of storing B, unused components of pointer fields are set equal to zero.

As might be guessed from the names of the methods, standard form and extended standard form are the preferred methods. The utility of inverse form is limited since when using this type of storage only operation 3, determining the predecessor, is easily performed.

**Example 3.1.4** (Storing a Tree with a Given Level-Number Representation) As input a number m followed by m pairs $(l_1, w_1), \ldots, (l_m, w_m)$ is given; these define a tree of degree 3 with m nodes $k_1, k_2, \ldots, k_m$ in level-number representation. The level number of the node $k_i$ is given by $l_i$, $\nu k_i = l_i$; the value of node $k_i$ is the character string $w_i$, $\omega k_i = w_i$. The following program stores the given tree in extended standard form. The input is not checked for validity. The arrays R11, R12, R13 specify the three successors of a node (that is, they serve as the three components of the pointer fields necessary for standard form); the array R2 indicates the predecessor of a node (that is, it is the pointer field necessary for the inverse form). The arrays D and LEV are used for the values and level numbers, respectively, of the nodes.

```
LEVEL: PROC OPTIONS (MAIN);
    DCL M FIXED BIN;
    GET LIST (M);
    BEGIN;
        DCL (R11(M), R12(M), R13(M), R2(M), LEV(M), I, J)
            FIXED BIN, D(M) CHAR (10) VARYING;
        R11, R12, R13, R2 = 0;
        GET LIST (LEV(1), D(1)); /* THE ROOT OF THE TREE */
        DO I = 2 TO M;
            GET LIST (LEV(I), D(I));
            J = I − 1;
            IF LEV(I) > LEV(J) THEN DO;
                            R2(I) = J;
                            R11(J) = I;
                    END;
                ELSE DO;
                        DO WHILE (LEV(I) < LEV(J));
                            J = R2(J);
                        END;
                        R2(I) = R2(J);
                        J = R2(J);
                        IF R12(J) = 0 THEN
                            R12(J) = I;
                        ELSE R13(J) = I;
                    END;
        END;
    END;
END;
```

Work through the program by hand using the input

9, 1 MAX, 2 EDWARD, 3 ERNEST, 2 OTTO, 3 SUSIE,
3 FRANK, 4 ALFRED, 4 TOM, 3 STEVEN

The result is shown in Fig. 3.1.8.

| I | LEV (I) | D(I) | R11(I) | R12(I) | R13(I) | R2(I) |
|---|---------|------|--------|--------|--------|-------|
| 1 | 1 | MAX | 2 | 4 | 0 | 0 |
| 2 | 2 | EDWARD | 3 | 0 | 0 | 1 |
| 3 | 3 | ERNEST | 0 | 0 | 0 | 2 |
| 4 | 2 | OTTO | 5 | 6 | 9 | 1 |
| 5 | 3 | SUSIE | 0 | 0 | 0 | 4 |
| 6 | 3 | FRANK | 7 | 8 | 0 | 4 |
| 7 | 4 | ALFRED | 0 | 0 | 0 | 6 |
| 8 | 4 | TOM | 0 | 0 | 0 | 6 |
| 9 | 3 | STEVEN | 0 | 0 | 0 | 4 |

**Figure 3.1.8**

**Example 3.1.5** (Preorder) A tree of degree 7, whose nodes have whole-number values, is given in extended standard form. The elements $D(P)$, $R1(1, P)$, $R1(2, P)$, ..., $R1(7, P)$, and $R2(P)$ represent the data field, the seven components of the first pointer field (for the successors of a node), and the second pointer field (for the predecessor of a node). The value of the variable W is the address of the root of the tree. The following program segments illustrate different techniques for expressing the values of the nodes of the tree in preorder.

In program segment A, we use the information about predecessors that is supplied by the inverse form.

```
A: BEGIN; DCL (P, I) FIXED BIN; P = W;
      DOWN: PUT LIST (D(P));
            NEW: DO I = 1 TO 7;
                  IF R1(I, P) > 0 THEN DO;
                              R1(I, P) = −R1(I, P);
                              P = −R1(I, P);
                              GOTO DOWN;
                        END;
                  END; /* TO KEEP FROM HANDLING SUBTREES MORE
                  THAN ONCE, POINTER FIELD COMPONENTS ALREADY
                  USED ARE MADE NEGATIVE. THE FOLLOWING PLACE
                  IN THE PROGRAM IS REACHED ONLY WHEN A NODE
                  COMES UP, ALL OF WHOSE SUBTREES HAVE ALREADY
                  BEEN HANDLED */
                  DO I = 1 TO 7;
                        R1(I, P) = −R1(I, P);
                  END; /* ALL POINTER FIELD COMPONENTS ARE AGAIN
                                                      POSITIVE */
                  IF R2(P) > 0 THEN DO;
                              P = R2(P);
                              GOTO NEW;
                        END;
      END;
```

In the two program segments B and C, the information about predecessors (furnished by the inverse form) is not used. Rather in program segment B a stack S is used, which contains the addresses of the roots of the subtrees not yet handled; while in program segment C a recursive procedure F is used.

```
B: BEGIN; DCL (S(M), P, I, Q) FIXED BIN; /* SUITABLE M */
       Q = 1; S(1) = W;
       DO WHILE (Q ¬ = 0);
           P = S(Q); PUT LIST (D(P)); Q = Q − 1;
           DO I = 7 TO 1 BY −1;
               IF R1(I, P) > 0 THEN DO;
                                    Q = Q + 1;
                                    S(Q) = R1(I, P);
                               END;
           END;
       END;
   END;


C: BEGIN;
   F: PROCEDURE (P) RECURSIVE;
       DCL (P, I) FIXED BIN;
       PUT LIST (D(P));
       DO I = 1 TO 7;
           IF R1(I, P) ¬ = 0 THEN CALL (F(+R1(I, P));
       END;
   END F;
   CALL F(+W);
   END;
```

Note that **CALL** F(+R1(I, P)) cannot be replaced directly according to Sec. 2.3 since it occurs immediately after a **THEN**. Surrounding the call by **BEGIN** and **END** does not help either since then the call is no longer in the scope of the block containing the declaration of F as required in Sec. 2.3. The following program segment D is clearly equivalent to C, however, and meets all requirements mentioned in Sec. 2.3.

```
D: BEGIN;
   F: PROCEDURE (P) RECURSIVE;
       DCL (P, I) FIXED BIN;
       PUT LIST (D(P));
       I = 1;
       S: IF R1(I, P) = 0 THEN GOTO H;
       CALL F(+R1(I, P));
       H: I = I + 1; IF I < = 7 THEN GOTO S;
   END F;
   CALL F(+W);
   END;
```

From program segment D we can obtain, in accordance with Sec. 2.3, an equivalent program segment E without a procedure call.

```
E: BEGIN;
   DCL (SF(3, 100), ZF) FIXED BIN;
   DCL RETF(2) LABEL; ZF = 0;
   GOTO JUMPF;
   F: PUT LIST (D(SF(1, ZF)));
   SF(2, ZF) = 1; S: IF R1(SF(2, ZF), SF(1, ZF)) = 0
                  THEN GOTO H;
   IF ZF > = 100 THEN CALL ERROR (1);
   SF(1, ZF + 1) = R1(SF(2, ZF), SF(1, ZF));
   SF(3, ZF + 1) = 1; ZF = ZF + 1; GOTO F; RETF(1): ZF = ZF − 1;
   /* ABOVE THREE LINES CORRESPOND TO CALL F(+R1(I, P)) */
   H: SF(2, ZF) = SF(2, ZF) + 1; IF SF(2, ZF) < = 7 THEN GOTO S;
   GOTO RETF(SF(3, ZF)); JUMPF:
   IF ZF > = 100 THEN CALL ERROR (1);
   SF(1, ZF + 1) = W; SF(3, ZF + 1) = 2; ZF = ZF + 1;
   GOTO F; RETF(2): ZF = ZF − 1;
   /* ABOVE THREE LINES CORRESPOND TO CALL F(+W) */
   END;
```

Work through the different programs letting $W = 1$, using the tree defined in Fig. 3.1.9 and represented graphically in Fig. 3.1.10; in particular, compare program segments D and E.

| P | D(P) | R1(1, P) | R1(2, P) | R1(3, P) | R1(4, P) | R1(5, P) | R1(6, P) | R1(7, P) | R2(P) |
|---|------|----------|----------|----------|----------|----------|----------|----------|-------|
| 1 | 15 | 2 | 12 | 10 | 13 | 8 | 7 | 0 | 0 |
| 2 | 14 | 0 | 0 | 0 | 0 | 0 | 0 | 0 | 1 |
| 3 | 13 | 0 | 0 | 0 | 0 | 0 | 0 | 0 | 13 |
| 4 | 12 | 0 | 0 | 0 | 0 | 0 | 0 | 0 | 13 |
| 5 | 11 | 0 | 0 | 0 | 0 | 0 | 0 | 0 | 13 |
| 6 | 10 | 0 | 0 | 0 | 0 | 0 | 0 | 0 | 13 |
| 7 | 9 | 0 | 0 | 0 | 0 | 0 | 0 | 0 | 1 |
| 8 | 8 | 0 | 0 | 0 | 0 | 0 | 0 | 0 | 1 |
| 9 | 7 | 0 | 0 | 0 | 0 | 0 | 0 | 0 | 13 |
| 10 | 6 | 0 | 0 | 0 | 0 | 0 | 0 | 0 | 1 |
| 11 | 5 | 0 | 0 | 0 | 0 | 0 | 0 | 0 | 13 |
| 12 | 4 | 14 | 0 | 0 | 0 | 0 | 0 | 0 | 1 |
| 13 | 3 | 15 | 11 | 4 | 3 | 5 | 9 | 6 | 1 |
| 14 | 2 | 0 | 0 | 0 | 0 | 0 | 0 | 0 | 12 |
| 15 | 1 | 0 | 0 | 0 | 0 | 0 | 0 | 0 | 13 |

**Figure 3.1.9**

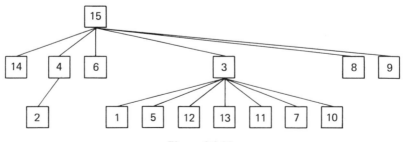

**Figure 3.1.10**

*Remarks and References*

A detailed discussion of trees is found in Knuth [2]. See also Berztiss [1] and Stone [1] for some interesting material on trees and other data structures.

## Exercises

**3.1.1**   The values of the nodes of a tree B in level-number representation are 1 X, 2 A, 2 B, 3 E, 3 Y, 4 Z, 5 R, 4 L, 3 W, 4 T, 2 U, 3 N, 3 F, 2 G.
(a)   Represent B graphically.
(b)   Write the values of the nodes of B in a postorder.
(c)   Determine the yield of B.
(d)   Give a parenthetical representation of B.
(e)   Graphically represent an extended standard form of B.

**3.1.2**   Write a program that accepts as input a tree B of degree 3, with integer nodes, given in parenthetical form, and stores it in standard form.

**3.1.3**   A tree B of degree 8 is given in standard form. The nodes have character strings as values and the pointer fields are stored using indirect allocation. The declaration

**DCL (R(M), DI(N), RI(N), W) FIXED BIN, D(M) CHAR (10) VARYING;**

is given. Here W gives the address of the root of the tree. D(J) gives the value of a node $k$; R(J) gives the first address in the chain of addresses of successors of $k$, and this is stored in memory locations whose data field is given by DI and whose pointer field is given by RI. Write a program that prints the values of the nodes in (a) preorder, (b) postorder, (c) level-number representation, and (d) parenthetical representation.

**3.1.4**   Graphically represent a standard form for the tree in Fig. 3.1.10 using indirect storage of the pointer fields.

**3 1.5**   A tree of degree 3 whose nodes have character strings as values is given in standard form. Write a program segment that prints the values of the nodes as a two-dimensional representation of a tree.

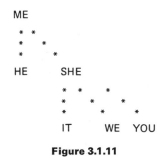

**Figure 3.1.11**

*Hint:* A two-dimensional representation of the tree in Fig. 3.1.2(a) might look something like Fig. 3.1.11.

**3.1.6** Why is condition c necessary in Def. 3.1.1?

**3.1.7** Is it possible that, in the level-number representation of a tree, $vk = vk'$ even though k and k' are not successors of the same node?

## Section 3.2  Binary Trees

Ordered trees of degree 2 play a particularly important role in the applications of tree structures. For one thing, many algorithms for tree handling become very simple when applied to ordered trees of degree 2. Also trees of arbitrary degree can be reduced in a simple way to trees of degree 2.

**Definition 3.2.1** (Binary Tree) A *binary tree* is an ordered tree of degree 2. A node is specifically allowed to have a second successor and no first successor.

When dealing with binary trees, instead of "first" and "second" successors or subtrees, we often speak of *left* and *right* successors or subtrees. In the standard form of a binary tree it is convenient to use two pointer fields with one component each instead of a single pointer field with two components.

The transformation of a general tree of arbitrary degree into a binary tree is accomplished by replacing a node k having n successors $k_1, k_2, \ldots, k_n$ by the node k with left successor $k_1$ and using $k_{i+1}$ as the right successor of $k_i$ for $i = 1, 2, \ldots,$ $n - 1$. A general definition of a binary tree corresponding to a sequence of $n \geqslant 0$ trees follows.

**Definition 3.2.2** (Corresponding Binary Tree) Let $B = (B_1, B_2, \ldots, B_n)$ be a sequence of $n \geqslant 0$ trees. A *corresponding binary tree* $\beta(B)$ is obtained as follows:

(a)  If $n = 0$, then $\beta(B)$ is empty.
(b)  If $n > 0$, then the root of $\beta(B)$ is the root of $B_1$; the left subtree of $\beta(B)$ is $\beta(A_1, A_2, \ldots, A_m)$, where $A_1, A_2, \ldots, A_m$ are the subtrees of $B_1$; and the right subtree of $\beta(B)$ is $\beta(B_2, B_3, \ldots, B_n)$.

If we begin with a sequence of ordered trees, then a unique corresponding binary tree is obtained.

**Example 3.2.1** (Transformation of a General Tree into a Binary Tree) Consider the ordered tree in Fig. 3.2.1. We wish to find the corresponding binary tree.

If we begin by following the intuitive definition given above, we obtain Fig. 3.2.2 in which the newly formed successor relation in the binary tree is indicated with dotted lines and the as yet unchanged successor relation in the original tree is denoted by solid lines.

Through repeated application of the technique to the subtrees of the original tree with roots B and F the corresponding binary tree shown in Fig. 3.2.3 is obtained.

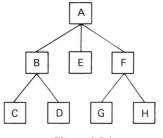

**Figure 3.2.1**

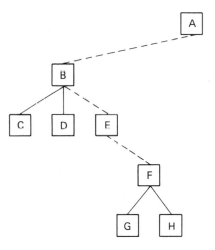

**Figure 3.2.2**

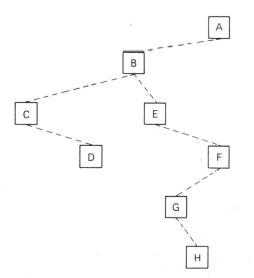

**Figure 3.2.3**

If we apply Def. 3.2.2 systematically and write the symbol $\boxed{\text{X}}$ for each subtree of the given tree with root X, then we obtain

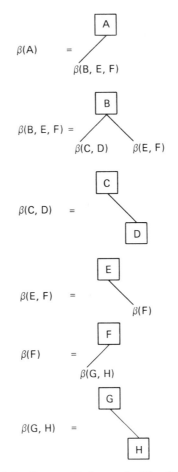

Combining these we obtain the result shown in Fig. 3.2.3.

**Example 3.2.2** (Transformation of a General Tree into a Binary Tree) Suppose there is a tree B of degree 3 given in standard form and the values of the nodes are character strings. The following program segment yields a binary tree B′ corresponding to B in standard form with a top pointer WNEW, for which the declaration **DCL WNEW FIXED BIN**; is used. Additional declarations for the program segment are **DCL (R11(M), R12(M), R13(M)) FIXED BIN**; for the pointer field, **DCL D(M) CHAR (10) VARYING**; for the data field, and **DCL W FIXED BIN**; for the top pointer W of the given tree.

Assume there is also given a free storage stack S of memory locations with two pointer fields, each having one component, for the corresponding binary tree. The appropriate declarations for this are **DCL** S(M) **CHAR** (10) **VARYING**; for the data field and **DCL** (R1(M), R2(M)) **FIXED BIN**; for the two pointer fields. In the free storage stack, we use linked storage (R1 as the pointer) with start pointer a; this corresponds to the declaration **DCL A FIXED BIN**;.

As often is the case in working with trees, a recursive solution proves to be the simplest (here the recursive solution is based on the recursive Def. 3.2.2). This can easily be converted into a nonrecursive program by using Sec. 2.3.

```
BETA: PROCEDURE (P, Q, R) RETURNS (FIXED BIN) RECURSIVE;
      DCL (P, Q, R, RES) FIXED BIN; /* BETA(P, Q, R)
          PRODUCES THE BINARY TREE CORRESPONDING TO UP TO
          3 TREES WHOSE ROOTS ARE GIVEN BY P, Q, R, AND
          GIVES THE ADDRESS OF THE ROOT OF THIS BINARY TREE */
      IF P ¬ = 0 THEN DO;
                        RES = A; A = R1(A);
                        S(RES) = D(P);
                        R1(RES) = BETA(+R11(P), +R12(P),
                                            +R13(P));
                        R2(RES) = BETA(+Q, +R, 0);
                   END;
             ELSE RES = 0;
        RETURN (RES);
   END BETA;
   WNEW = BETA(+W, 0, 0);
```

Work through this program segment by hand using the storage method given in Fig. 3.1.8 of the tree in Fig. 3.1.3(a) having degree 3 and W = 1; notice how the binary tree of Fig. 3.2.4 is formed.

In addition to preorder and postorder of nodes, for binary trees we also define *symmetric order*.

**Definition 3.2.3** (Symmetric Order) Let B = (K, R) be a binary tree. The nodes of B are traversed in *symmetric order* by first traversing the nodes of the left subtree, next processing the root, and then traversing the nodes of the right subtree.

The nodes of the binary tree of Fig. 3.2.5 in symmetric order are W, U, B, V, A, R, X, S, T.

If a binary tree is drawn so that the left subtree of a node k lies completely to the left of k and so that the right subtree of a node k lies completely to the right of k, then the symmetric order of the nodes can be read off by using the "projection" indicated in Fig. 3.2.5.

**Example 3.2.3** (Symmetric Order) Let there be given in standard form a binary tree B with character strings as nodes. Appropriate declarations for a program segment are **DCL** D(M) **CHAR** (1); for the data field, **DCL** (R1(M), R2(M)) **FIXED BIN**; for the two pointer fields, and **DCL** W **FIXED BIN**; for the top pointer.

The following two program segments illustrate two techniques for printing the nodes of the tree in symmetric order. Program segment A uses a procedure F recur-

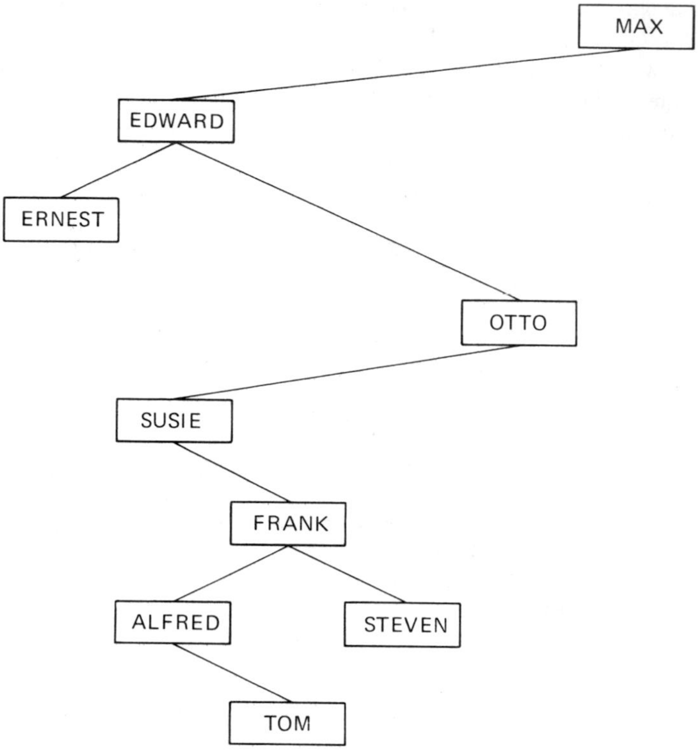

MAX
EDWARD
ERNEST
OTTO
SUSIE
FRANK
ALFRED
STEVEN
TOM

**Figure 3.2.4**

A
B
X
U
V
R
S
W
T
W U B V A R X S T

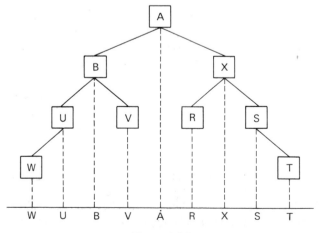

**Figure 3.2.5**

sively. In program segment B a stack S, similar to the one in program segment B of Example 3.1.5, is used in which a negative address on the top of the stack indicates that the value of the node in question should now be printed.

```
A: BEGIN;
   F: PROCEDURE (P) RECURSIVE;
      DCL P FIXED BIN;
      IF R1(P) ¬= 0 THEN CALL F(+R1(P));
      PUT LIST (D(P));
      IF R2(P) ¬= 0 THEN CALL F(+R2(P));
   END F;
   CALL F(+W);
END;

B: BEGIN;
   DCL (S(M), P, Q) FIXED BIN; /* M SUITABLE */
   Q = 1; S(1) = W; /* INITIALLY THE STACK CONTAINS ONLY
                        THE ADDRESS OF THE ROOT */
   DO WHILE (Q ¬ = 0);
      P = S(Q); Q = Q − 1;
      IF P > = 0 THEN DO;
                       IF R2(P) ¬ = 0 THEN DO;
                                           Q = Q + 1,
                                           S(Q) = R2(P);
                                           END;
                       Q = Q + 1;
                       S(Q) = −P;
                       IF R1(P) ¬= 0 THEN DO;
                                           Q = Q + 1;
                                           S(Q) = R1(P);
                                           END;
                       END;
                 ELSE PUT LIST (D(−P));
   END;
END;
```

Work through program segments A and B using the tree in Fig. 3.2.5.

The possibility of representing arithmetic expressions by means of ordered trees was mentioned in Sec. 3.1. Simple arithmetic expressions can indeed be represented using binary trees, where an operator O with left operand a and right operand b is viewed as a binary tree with root O and subtrees a and b. Using this mode of representation, the nodes taken in symmetric order correspond to the order of the operands and operators in the given simple arithmetic expression. The nodes in postorder give the corresponding parenthesis-free expression.

As an example, the simple arithmetic expression $((3. \times (5. - 2.)) + 7.)$ is represented with a binary tree in Fig. 3.1.6(a). The values of the nodes in symmetric order are $3. \times 5. - 2. + 7.$; whereas in postorder they are $3. 5. 2. - \times 7. +$.

Thus, as an alternative to the algorithm in Example 2.2.5 for finding the parenthesis-free expression corresponding to a given arithmetic expression, we could first construct the corresponding binary tree and then print the nodes of the tree in post-order.

**Example 3.2.4** (Generating a Binary Tree for a Given Simple Arithmetic Expression) A simple arithmetic expression separated into elements (as described in the explanation for Example 2.2.4) is available as input. The following program stores the corresponding tree in standard form.

For the nodes of the tree, arrays E (for the data field) and R1, R2 (for the pointer fields) are declared. The program is a variation of the program from Example 2.2.5 for converting an expression into postfix notation and makes use of the fact that the construction of the desired tree is trivial once the expression is in postfix form.

An auxiliary stack X is maintained for the addresses of operands. Whenever a number is printed in the program for Example 2.2.5, the number will be stored as a node of the tree and its address will be added to the operand stack. Whenever an operator is printed in the program for Example 2.2.5, the operator will be stored as a node of the tree, pointing to the top two operands of the operand stack, and then the top two entries of the operand stack are replaced by a single entry representing the address of the operator in question.

After executing the program, X(1) is the address of the root of the tree.

```
BEGIN;
    DCL (E(M), D(M), Z) CHAR (10) VARYING,
        (R1(M), R2(M), X(M), AE, AX, A) FIXED BIN;
    D(1) = '('; A = 1; AE = 0; AX = 0; GET LIST (Z);
    DO WHILE (Z ¬ = '#');
        IF NUMBER (Z) THEN DO; AE = AE + 1; E(AE) = Z;
            /* ADDS NUMBER TO TREE */
            AX = AX + 1; X(AX) = AE;
            /* ADDS ADDRESS OF NUMBER TO OPERAND STACK */
            END;
        ELSE IF Z = '(' THEN DO; A = A + 1; D(A) = '('; END;
        /* D AS IN PROGRAM FOR EXAMPLE 2.2.5 */
        ELSE IF Z = ')' THEN DO;
                        DO WHILE (D(A) ¬ = '(');
                                CALL ADDOP; A = A − 1;
                        END;
                        A = A − 1;
                END;
        ELSE IF (Z = '+')|(Z = '−') THEN DO;
                DO WHILE (D(A) ¬ = '(');
                        CALL ADDOP; A = A − 1;
                END;
                A = A + 1; D(A) = Z;
                        END;
        ELSE IF (Z = '*')|(Z = '/') THEN DO;
                DO WHILE ((D(A) = '*')|(D(A) = '/'));
                        CALL ADDOP; A = A − 1;
                END;
```

$$A = A + 1; \; D(A) = Z;$$
$$\textbf{END};$$

**GET LIST** (Z);
**END**; **DO WHILE** (D(A) $\neg = $ '('); **CALL** ADDOP; A = A − 1; **END**;
/* NOW THE TREE HAS BEEN CREATED */
ADDOP: **PROCEDURE**;

$$AE = AE + 1; \; E(AE) = D(A); \; /* \text{ ADDS OPERATOR TO}$$
$$\text{TREE } */$$

R2(AE) = X(AX); R1(AE) = X(AX − 1);
/* OPERATOR IS MADE TO POINT TO TWO OPERANDS */
AX = AX − 1; X(AX) = AE;
/* ADDRESS OF ROOT REPLACES TOP TWO ENTRIES IN
OPERAND STACK */

**END** ADDOP;
**END**;

Try to trace the program using an expression such as 3. × (5. − 2.) + 7..

In the standard form of a binary tree that we have now used several times, the pointer fields of many nodes have the value 0. It seems reasonable to try to make better use of these pointer fields.

One possibility is the use of *threading* (relative to the symmetric order), in which a pointer field that is not used in the standard form is used to point to the preceding or succeeding node.

**Definition 3.2.4** (Threading) A binary tree is called a *threaded tree* if standard form is used in both of the first two pointer fields, but then for each node k without a left (or right) successor we let $\rho_1 k = \alpha k'$ (or $\rho_2 k = \alpha k'$), where k' is the node immediately before (or immediately after) k in symmetric order. Each pointer field that is used for the threading has an indicator $\neq 0$, in order to be able to distinguish "actual" successors from successors or predecessors in symmetric order.

The case $\rho_1 k = 0$ (or $\rho_2 k = 0$) then arises in a threaded tree only if k is the first (or last) node in symmetric order. In all following programs involving threaded storage an indicator $\neq 0$ is designated by a negative value of the pointer field.

Figure 3.2.6(a) shows a binary tree with additional dashed lines to indicate the threading. The threaded form is portrayed graphically in Fig. 3.2.6(b) with a top pointer a, and the realization of a threaded form is shown in PL/I notation in Fig. 3.2.6(c).

The following example shows rather impressively that the nodes of a tree in symmetric order can be manipulated easily without stacks or inverse form by using threaded storage.

It will be demonstrated in program segment B of Example 4.1.4 that even the threading is unnecessary.

**Example 3.2.5** (Applications of Threading) A binary tree with character strings as nodes is given in threaded form. Appropriate declarations for a program segment are **DCL** D(M) **CHAR** (1); for the data field, **DCL** (R1(M), R2(M)) **FIXED BIN**;

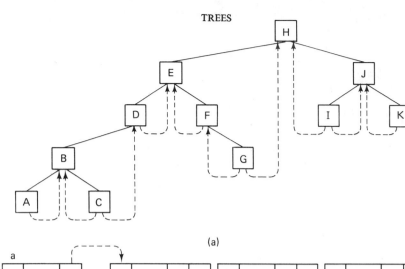

(a)

(b)

| M | D(M) | R1(M) | R2(M) |
|---|------|-------|-------|
| 1 | A | 0 | − 2 |
| 2 | B | 1 | 3 |
| 3 | C | − 2 | − 4 |
| 4 | D | 2 | − 5 |
| 5 | E | 4 | 6 |
| 6 | F | − 5 | 7 |
| 7 | G | − 6 | − 8 |
| 8 | H | 5 | 10 |
| 9 | I | − 8 | − 10 |
| 10 | J | 8 | 10 |
| 11 | K | − 10 | 0 |

(c)

**Figure 3.2.6**

for the two pointer fields, each having one component, and **DCL W FIXED BIN**; for the top pointer W.

(a)   If P has the address of a node k as its value, then the following program segment produces the address of the node immediately following k in symmetric order or zero if no such successor exists.

```
SUCC: PROCEDURE (P) RETURNS (FIXED BIN);
       DCL (P, Q) FIXED BIN;
       Q = R2(P);
       IF Q = 0 THEN RETURN (Q);
       /* THEN THE GIVEN NODE IS LAST IN SYMMETRIC ORDER */
       IF Q < 0 THEN RETURN (−Q);
       /* THEN THE THREADING POINTS TO THE SUCCESSOR IN
          SYMMETRIC ORDER. OTHERWISE LEFT SUCCESSORS MUST
          BE DETERMINED UNTIL THE LAST ONE IS REACHED:
          CONSIDER THE SITUATION IN FIG. 3.2.6(A) BY TAKING
          THE SUCCESSOR OF H IN SYMMETRIC ORDER, NAMELY I */
       DO WHILE (R1(Q) > 0);
           Q = R1(Q);
       END;
       RETURN (Q);
    END SUCC;
```

(b)  If P gives the address of the first node in symmetric order, then the following program segment prints the values of all the nodes in symmetric order.

```
DO WHILE (P ¬ = 0);
    PUT LIST (D(P));
    P = SUCC(P);
END;
```

(c)  If P gives the address of a node k, the following program segment produces the address of the predecessor of k in symmetric order.

```
PRED: PROCEDURE (P) RETURNS (FIXED BIN);
       DCL (P, Q) FIXED BIN;
       Q = R1(P); IF Q > 0 THEN DO;
           DO WHILE (R2(Q) > 0);
               Q = R2(Q);
           END; END;
       RETURN (ABS(Q));
    END PRED;
```

The next example is an application of threading in binary trees and shows that when changes are made in a binary tree, it is simple to adjust the threading accordingly.

**Example 3.2.6** (Sorting Using Threading) Let $T = a_1, a_2, \ldots, a_n$ be a sequence of values on which the order relation r is defined. If from the n values we build a binary tree with n nodes so that for every node k and every node k′ in the left subtree of k the relation $(\omega k', \omega k) \in r$ holds and for every node k″ in the right subtree of k the relation $(\omega k'', \omega k) \notin r$ holds, then the values $a_1', a_2', \ldots, a_n'$ of the nodes of the binary tree obtained, taken in symmetric order, represent the values T sorted (relative to r). This fact can be used in constructing an efficient sorting technique.

As an example, if the given sequence is a sequence of numbers $T = 13, 7, 8, 20,$ 18, 9, 5, 6, 11, 3 with the usual $\leqslant$ relation as the order relation, then using the technique described we obtain the binary tree in Fig. 3.2.7 whose nodes in symmetric order are 3, 5, 6, 7, 8, 9, 11, 13, 18, 20, that is, a sequence sorted relative to $\leqslant$.

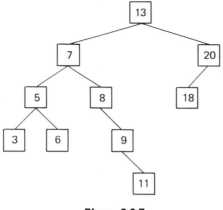

**Figure 3.2.7**

In the following program, a number n is given as input, followed by n whole numbers $T = a_1, a_2, \ldots, a_n$. From T a binary tree is built, as described, in standard form. Threading is used so that the nodes of the tree can easily be printed in symmetric order.

```
SORT: PROC OPTIONS (MAIN);
    DCL N FIXED BIN;
    GET LIST (N);
    BEGIN;
    DCL (D(N), R1(N), R2(N), I, P, THREAD) FIXED BIN;
    SUCC: PROCEDURE (P1) RETURNS (FIXED BIN);
        DCL (P1, Q) FIXED BIN;
        Q = R2(P1);
        IF Q > 0 THEN DO;
                        DO WHILE (R1(Q) > 0);
                            Q = R1(Q);
                        END;
                    END;
        RETURN (ABS(Q));
    END SUCC;
    /* THE PROCEDURE ABOVE IS LIKE EXAMPLE 3.2.5 */
    GET LIST (D(1)); R1(1), R2(1) = 0;
    THREAD = 1;
    /* THE ROOT OF THE TREE IS DETERMINED. "THREAD" REFERS
       TO THE FIRST NODE IN SYMMETRIC ORDER */
    DO I = 2 TO N;
        GET LIST (D(I)); P = 1;
        W: IF D(I) < = D(P) THEN DO;
                IF R1(P) > 0 THEN DO;
                                P = R1(P);
                                GOTO W;
                            END;
                R1(I) = R1(P); R2(I) = -P; R1(P) = I;
                IF R1(I) = 0 THEN THREAD = I;
                            END;
```

```
        ELSE DO;
            IF R2(P) > 0 THEN DO;
                                    P = R2(P);
                                    GOTO W;
                    END;
                R2(I) = R2(P); R1(I) = -P; R2(P) = I;
            END;
        END; /* NOW PRINT */
        P = THREAD;
        DO WHILE (P ¬ = 0);
            PUT LIST (D(P)); P = SUCC(P);
        END;
    END;
END;
```

Work through the program by hand using the input n = 10, T = 13, 7, 8, 20, 18, 9, 5, 6, 11, 3 (as in Fig. 3.2.7).

It is easily seen that the sorting technique obtained corresponds exactly to the Quicksort technique of Sec. 2.6. For example, if we apply the Quicksort technique to T = 13, 7, 8, 20, 18, 9, 5, 6, 11, 3, we successively find

$$
\begin{array}{llllllllll}
7, & 8, & 9, & 5, & 6, & 3, & \underline{13}, & 20, & 18 \\
5, & 6, & 3, & 7, & 8, & 9, & \underline{13}, & 18, & \underline{20} \\
3, & \underline{5}, & 6, & \underline{7}, & \underline{8}, & 9, & \underline{13}, & 18, & \underline{20}
\end{array}
$$

where the underlined numbers are those whose final position in the sorted sequence is already determined. These numbers correspond precisely to the roots of the subtrees of the tree in Fig. 3.2.7.

In the techniques discussed so far for storing binary trees, the addresses of the individual nodes give no information: with appropriate changes in the pointer fields, each node could be stored in any memory location with arbitrary address. While this allows considerable flexibility that may be advantageous, particularly if nodes frequently are removed from the tree or added to the tree, this flexibility is not always necessary. It actually may be possible to get by with very few pointer fields. For example, in the standard form of a binary tree, the need for pointer fields for the left successor can be eliminated simply by always storing a node and its left successor in adjacent memory locations. To determine whether a node does in fact have a left successor, an indicator is used.

**Definition 3.2.5** (Sequential Storage) A binary tree is said to be *sequentially stored* if memory locations with one pointer field having one component are used and conditions a through c are satisfied.

(a)  If k′ is the successor of k in preorder, then $\alpha k' = \alpha k + 1$.
(b)  If k′ is the right successor of k, then $\rho k = \alpha k'$.
(c)  If k has no left successor, then the indicator in the first pointer field $\neq 0$.

In the PL/I programs using sequential storage, if a is the value of the pointer field, an indicator = 0 is denoted by the value a + 1 and an indicator $\neq 0$ is denoted by the value $-a - 1$.[2] The value 0 is chosen for the pointer field of the last node in preorder, however, in order to mark the end of the occupied storage area.

Figure 3.2.8(a) shows the sequential form with top pointer a of the tree in Fig. 3.2.6(a); Fig. 3.2.8(b) shows a realization of a sequential form in PL/I notation.

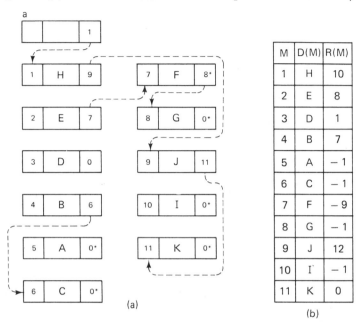

| M | D(M) | R(M) |
|---|------|------|
| 1 | H | 10 |
| 2 | E | 8 |
| 3 | D | 1 |
| 4 | B | 7 |
| 5 | A | − 1 |
| 6 | C | − 1 |
| 7 | F | − 9 |
| 8 | G | − 1 |
| 9 | J | 12 |
| 10 | I˙ | − 1 |
| 11 | K | 0 |

(b)

(a)

**Figure 3.2.8**

**Example 3.2.7** (Working with Sequentially Stored Binary Trees) A binary tree with character strings as nodes is stored sequentially with top pointer w. Appropriate declarations for a program segment are **DCL DA(M) CHAR** (1); for the data field, **DCL R(M) FIXED BIN**; for the pointer field, and **DCL (W, P, P1, Q) FIXED BIN**; for the top pointer W, a variable P whose value gives the address of a node k, and auxiliary variables P1 and Q.

The following program segment prints the value of the node k′ (or * if k′ does not exist), where, in program segment A, k′ is the left successor of k; in B, k′ is the right successor of k; in C, k′ is the successor of k in preorder; in D, k′ is the predecessor k in preorder; and in E, k′ is the predecessor of k.

```
A: IF R(P) > 0 THEN PUT LIST (DA(P + 1));
            ELSE PUT LIST ('*');
B: IF ABS(R(P)) > 1 THEN PUT LIST (DA(ABS(R(P)) − 1));
            ELSE PUT LIST ('*');
C: IF R(P) = 0 THEN PUT LIST ('*');
            ELSE PUT LIST (DA(P + 1));
```

---

[2]The "shifting" of the address by 1 is necessary since even in the absence of a right successor (if the pointer field had the value 0) it must also be determined whether a left successor exists or not.

```
    D: IF P = W THEN PUT LIST ('*');
            ELSE PUT LIST (DA(P − 1));
    E: IF P = W THEN PUT LIST ('*');
            ELSE DO; P1 = P; P = P − 1;
                    DO WHILE ((R(P) < = 0) | (P ¬ = P1 − 1));
                        Q = ABS(R(P)) − 1;
                        IF (Q > 0) & (Q = P1) THEN GOTO Z;
                        P = P − 1;
                    END;
                    Z: PUT LIST (DA(P));
            END;
```

*Remarks and References*

The idea of *threading* originated with Perlis [1].


**Exercises**

3.2.1   Consider the tree in Exercise 3.1.1 as an ordered tree.
(a)   Graphically represent the binary tree B′ corresponding to the tree B.
(b)   Write the values of the nodes of B′ in preorder, postorder, and symmetric order.

3.2.2   Given as input is a binary tree in standard form whose n nodes have whole numbers as values, which in symmetric order yield a sequence that is sorted in ascending order. Write a program which prints the values of all those nodes lying on a branch which leads to a node with a given value.

3.2.3   A binary tree B whose nodes have positive whole numbers as values is given as input in the following way: let B′ be the complete binary tree obtained from B by putting the value 0 in place of missing nodes. The values of the nodes of B′ are given in level-number representation. Write a program that stores B using threading.

3.2.4   Replace the program in Example 3.2.2 by a nonrecursive program.

3.2.5   Let B be an ordered tree with whole-number nodes and B′ be the corresponding binary tree. Let B′ be given in standard form. Write a program segment that
(a)   Prints the nodes of B in preorder.
(b)   Prints the nodes of B in postorder.
(c)   Determines the yield of B.
(d)   Determines the degree of B.
(e)   Stores the tree B in standard form using indirect storage for the pointer fields.

3.2.6   As input there is a binary tree B with whole-number nodes stored sequentially. Write a program that prints the nodes of B
(a)   in postorder and   (b)   in symmetric order.

3.2.7   A supply of memory locations with two pointer fields and one whole-number data field is available for use as a free storage stack with start pointer sp and is linked using the first pointer field. (Assume declaration **DCL** (D(M), R1(M), R2(M), SP) **FIXED BIN**;.) Write several procedures for manipulating binary trees whose nodes have positive whole numbers as values, such as

BUILD: **PROCEDURE** (WV, LEFT, RIGHT);

which constructs a binary tree whose root has the value WV, where the addresses of the roots of the subtrees are designated by LEFT and RIGHT, and which gives as a result the address of the root of the constructed tree. For example,

BUILD(15, BUILD(4, 0, 0), BUILD(20, BUILD(18, 0, 0), 0))

establishes the binary tree in Fig. 3.2.9. LEFT: **PROCEDURE** (W); produces a copy of the left subtree of the tree determined by the root having address W.

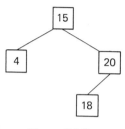

**Figure 3.2.9**

Use these routines for the solution of various tree manipulation problems. For example, use BUILD to construct a complete binary tree from a given parenthetical form by interpreting each subexpression i[j, k] in parenthetical form as BUILD (i, j, k).

**3.2.8**   Prove that if B is a tree and B′ is the corresponding binary tree, then the nodes of B and B′ in preorder are the same.

## Section 3.3   Tree Searching

The binary search described in Sec. 2.7 is particularly well-suited for locating a node with a given key v in a sorted sequence of nodes $F = k_1, k_2, \ldots, k_n$. Of course, to apply the binary search, F must be stored sequentially, which would be quite a disadvantage if the nodes in F are to be removed, added, or rearranged frequently. Through the use of *sorted trees*, techniques can be developed which combine the advantages of linked storage with the efficiency of the binary search and which do not require F to be sorted.

**Definition 3.3.1** (Sorted Tree) A binary tree is said to be *sorted* if its nodes in symmetric order represent a sorted sequence of nodes. If F is a sequence of nodes and B is a sorted binary tree consisting of exactly the nodes of F, then B is called a sorted tree *for* F or *of* F.

Among the sorted trees for a sequence F, the *natural tree* is distinguished in that it can be constructed very easily given the sequence F, which need not even be sorted.

**Definition 3.3.2** (Natural Tree) Let $F = k_1, k_2, \ldots, k_n$ be a sequence of nodes. The sorted tree B of F obtained by starting with an initially empty tree B and performing the following *extension step* for $i = 1, 2, \ldots, n$, is called the *natural tree for* F or *of* F.

*Extension step:* The node $k_i$ is added to B as an additional leaf in such a way that B remains a sorted tree.

The construction outlined in Def. 3.3.2 of a natural and therefore sorted tree for a given sequence F has already been used in Example 3.2.6 to sort a sequence of nodes. The importance of sorted trees in search problems is based on the ease with which a node having a given key can be found in a sorted tree.

**Definition 3.3.3** (Searching by Partitioning) To locate a node with a given key v in a sorted tree by *partitioning* we perform the following *search step* repeatedly:

*Search step:* Let w be the key of the root W of a given tree. If $v = w$, then W is the desired node and the process terminates. Otherwise, seek the node with key v by partitioning, namely in the left subtree of W for $v < w$ and in the right subtree of W for $v > w$.

Since the number of search steps necessary to locate a node k in a sorted tree B with n nodes is one more[3] than the length $\lambda k$ of the branch to k, we obtain

$$\text{Max (search by partitioning)} = \max \{1 + \lambda k \mid k \text{ in } B\}$$

$$\text{Avg (search by partitioning)} = \sum_{k \text{ in } B} p(k)(1 + \lambda k),$$

where p(k), as used already in Sec. 2.7, is the relative usage frequency of the node k.

If we first consider only the case of equal relative usage frequencies $p(k) = 1/n$ for all k, then

$$\text{Avg (search by partitioning)} = \frac{1}{n} \sum_{k \text{ in } B} (1 + \lambda k)$$

clearly becomes minimal if the tree has the most possible nodes with the shortest possible branches, i.e., if the tree is a *full tree*.

**Definition 3.3.4** (Full Tree) A binary tree B is called a *full tree* if for any two nodes with branch lengths s and t, having fewer than two successors, the relation abs $(s - t) \leqslant 1$ holds.

A full sorted tree can be constructed for any sequence of n nodes.

**Definition 3.3.5** (Constructing a Full Sorted Tree by Bisecting) From a sequence of nodes that can be assumed (without loss of generality) to be sorted, a full sorted

---

[3]One larger than $\lambda k$ since the length of the branch to the root of the tree is zero according to Def. 3.1.2.

tree can be obtained by *bisecting* as follows:

(a)   If the sequence is empty, take the empty tree.
(b)   If the sequence consists of $n \geqslant 1$ nodes $k_1, k_2, \ldots, k_n$, then let $m = (n + 1) \div 2$ and take the tree consisting of root $k_m$, left subtree $B_1$, and right subtree $B_2$, where $B_1$ and $B_2$ are full sorted trees obtained by bisecting the sequence $k_1, k_2, \ldots, k_{m-1}$ or $k_{m+1}, k_{m+2}, \ldots, k_n$.

It is easily seen by applying induction on n that the given construction actually produces a full tree for any n.

**Example 3.3.1**  Consider the linear array with 15 nodes as shown in Fig. 2.7.1(a). The full sorted tree represented in Fig. 3.3.1 is generated using bisecting.

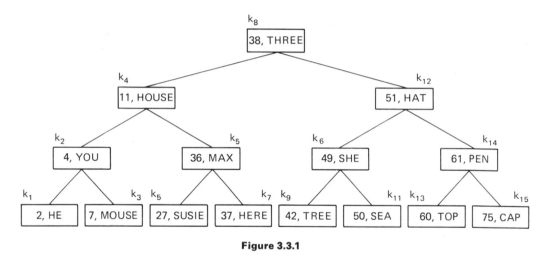

**Figure 3.3.1**

If we wish to find the node with key $v = 27$ using the technique of searching by partitioning, the desired node $k_5$ is found in four steps after examining the nodes $k_8, k_4, k_6$; this corresponds exactly to the bisecting steps for the binary search (Def. 2.7.3).

In general, the binary search may be performed in a sorted sequence F in the same number of steps as the search by partitioning in full sorted trees of F.

It therefore holds for full sorted trees with n nodes, as for the binary search, that

$$\text{Avg (search by partitioning)} \approx -1 + \log_2 n.$$

Since on the other hand for a sorted tree that is degenerated to a linear list

$$\text{Avg (search by partitioning)} = \frac{1}{n} \sum_{k \text{ in } B} (1 + \lambda k)$$

$$= \frac{1}{n} \sum_{i=0}^{n-1} (1 + i) \approx \frac{n}{2},$$

the number of search steps in a sorted tree with n nodes varies (corresponding to the lengths of the branches of the tree) between $\log_2 n$ and n.

If we consider all binary trees with n nodes as equally likely, then we can show that the average length of a branch is $\sqrt{n}$. On the other hand if we consider all possible sequences of n nodes with keys 1, 2, . . . , n as equally likely, and take the corresponding natural trees, then it can be demonstrated that the average length of a branch is $\log_2 n$.[4]

The big advantage in using sorted trees and searching by partitioning as contrasted with using the binary search with sequential storage is that it is easy to insert additional nodes into sorted trees or to remove nodes from such trees.

To insert an additional node, an extension step, like the one in Def. 3.3.2, is performed. The removal of a leaf is trivial. When removing an inner node k with left successor k', the right subtree $B_2$ of k' is modified so that the right subtree of k is used as right successor of the last node of $B_2$ in symmetric order and then k is replaced by k'. For the removal of an inner node k without a left successor and with a right successor k'', k can simply be replaced by k''.

**Example 3.3.2** If we remove the nodes with values 1, then 2, 3, 4, and finally 12 from the sorted tree in Fig. 3.3.2(a), we obtain the ordered trees shown in Fig. 3.3.2(b), (c), and (d) in this order.

As explained, full trees are most useful for searching by partitioning. By using the modifications described above on sorted trees, of course, nonfull trees can be easily produced from full trees. In actual practice it is often wise either to consider only full trees (by restructuring) or to ignore whether a tree is full or not and to work with trees that are "nearly" full. In this way, the number of search steps for searching by partitioning is still small. On the other hand, either trees seldom arise in which a restructuring is necessary or the restructuring is less time-consuming. Of the several suggestions for explaining the concept of "nearly" full trees, the concept of the *balanced tree* is particularly elegant.

**Definition 3.3.6** (Height, Balance, Balanced Tree) Let B be a binary tree. The *height* of B, written symbolically h(B) or h(W), where W is the root of B, is the length of the longest branch of B. The *balance* of a node k in a tree, symbolically $\beta k$, is defined by $\beta k = h(B_r) - h(B_l)$, where $B_l$ is the left subtree of k and $B_r$ is the right subtree of k. A tree is said to be *balanced* if, for every node k, abs $(\beta k) \leqslant 1$, i.e., if the heights of the left and right subtrees of every node differ from one another by at most 1. Every full tree is balanced but not vice versa.

**Example 3.3.3** The tree in Fig. 3.3.1 is full and balanced. The tree in Fig. 3.3.3(a) is balanced but not full. The tree in Fig. 3.3.3(b) is neither full nor balanced. In Fig. 3.3.3(a) and (b) the balance is written beside each node.

---

[4]The difference lies in the fact that in the case of natural trees for all possible sequences of n nodes many trees occur more than once. There are only about $\dfrac{4^n}{n} \sqrt{\pi n}$ different binary trees with n nodes but n! different sequences with n nodes.

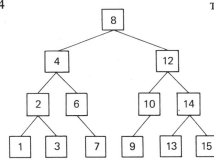

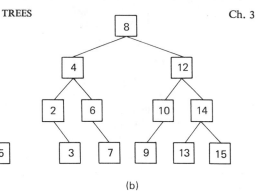

(a)                                                              (b)

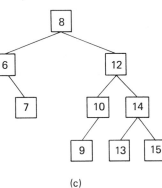

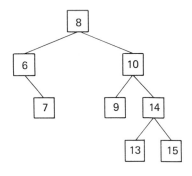

(c)                                                              (d)

**Figure 3.3.2**

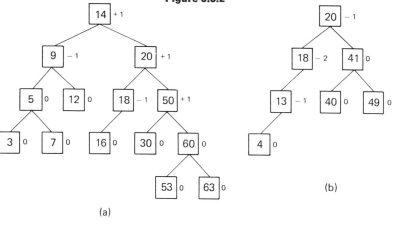

(a)                                                              (b)

**Figure 3.3.3**

In the following it will be assumed that in the storage of a balanced tree the balance of each node is always stored along with each node.

Since it can be shown that in a balanced tree with n nodes the maximum length of a branch is less than $\frac{3}{2} \log_2 n$, balanced sorted trees are almost as well-suited for searching by partitioning as full trees.

The principal advantage of a balanced sorted tree with n nodes over a full sorted tree lies in the fact that a node can be deleted or added in $\log_2$ n steps in such a way that the resulting tree is still sorted and balanced. A technique called *Adelson's method* for adding a node is given below; however, the rather complicated process of deleting a node is not discussed.

**Definition 3.3.7** (Adelson's Method) Let B be a balanced sorted tree and k a new node that is to be added to B. The new tree obtained will be balanced and sorted.

Adelson's method consists of three processes: *inserting*, *balancing*, and *restructuring*, which are performed consecutively. The balance of each node is considered to be a part of the node and is carried along with it.

*Inserting:*  The node k is inserted without regard to balance using an *extension step* as in Def. 3.3.2. A balance $\beta k = 0$ is assigned to the new node.

*Balancing:*  Now let $k_0, k_1, \ldots, k_m = k$ be a branch from the root $k_0$ to the node k. Follow this branch from k toward the root to adjust the balances until either the root $k_0$ of the tree is reached or a node $k_i$ is reached with $\beta k_i \neq 0$. If a node $k_j$ is reached from the left (or right) [i.e., $k_{j+1}$ is the left (or right) successor of $k_j$], this means that the height of the left (or right) subtree of $k_j$ has increased by 1. All nodes $k_j$ between k and $k_i$ (for $m > j > i$) that are reached in the tracing process initially have a balance of 0; their balance is changed to $-1$ or $+1$ if $k_j$ is reached from the left or right, respectively. The increase in the height of the left (or right) subtree of $k_j$ is thus produced.

*Restructuring:*  In the *balancing* process, $k_i$ is the root with $\beta k_i = 0$ and we are finished, or $\beta k_i \neq 0$. If $\beta k_i = -1$ and $k_i$ has been reached from the right (or if $\beta k_i = +1$ and $k_i$ has been reached from the left), then the heights of the left and right subtrees of $k_i$ are the same. We set $\beta k_i = 0$ and we are done. If, on the other hand, $k_i$ with $\beta k_i = -1$ is reached from the left, then now the height of the left subtree of $k_i$ is 2 more than that of the right and a restructuring as described in the process *Left* is necessary. An analogous restructuring process *Right* is necessary if $k_i$ is reached from the right and $\beta k_i = +1$.

*Left:*  The node $k_i$ with $\beta k_i = -1$ is reached from the left. If we let $A_s^t$ for arbitrary s denote a tree of height t, then the subtree of B with the root $k_i$ must have one of the forms given in Fig. 3.3.4(a) through (d). Thus in Fig. 3.3.4(a), $\beta k_{i+1} = -1$; in the others, $\beta k_{i+1} = +1$.

The (unbalanced) trees in Fig. 3.3.4(a) through (d) are replaced by the trees in Fig. 3.3.5(a) through (d).

The trees in Fig. 3.3.5 are balanced; their roots have balance 0. In Fig. 3.3.5(b), $\beta k_i = +1$; in the others, $\beta k_i = 0$. In Fig. 3.3.5(c), $\beta k_{i+1} = -1$; in the others, $\beta k_{i+1} = 0$.

*Right:*  Analogous to *Left*.

**Example 3.3.4** Follow the process of adding the nodes with values 100, 80, 52, 40, 83 to the balanced tree in Fig. 3.3.6(a); the result is the balanced and sorted trees

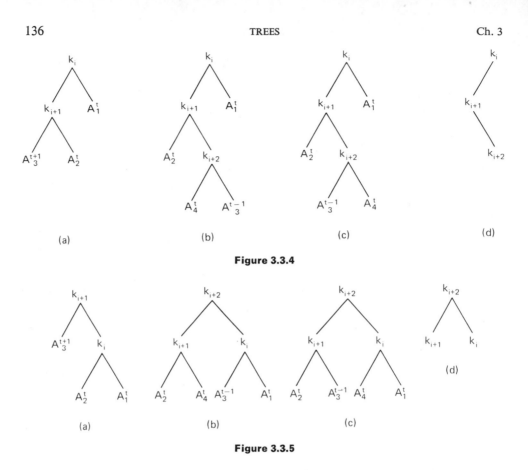

Figure 3.3.4

Figure 3.3.5

represented in Fig. 3.3.6(b) through (f). The balance of each node is given beside the node.

The restructuring of Fig. 3.3.6(b) to (c) corresponds to the transition from Fig. 3.3.4(a) to 3.3.5(a); the restructuring of Fig. 3.3.6(e) to (f) corresponds to the transition from Fig. 3.3.4(c) to 3.3.5(c).

**Example 3.3.5** (Adelson's Method) As input there is a number n followed by n different whole numbers $a_1, a_2, \ldots, a_n$. A sorted and balanced tree whose n nodes have the values $a_1, a_2, \ldots, a_n$ is to be constructed using Adelson's method.

One possible approach to programming the technique of inserting the node k consists of storing in a stack the addresses of the nodes on the branch leading to k so that in the balancing process the necessary path tracing of the branch can be accomplished. Actually a stack is not necessary.

Instead, in the following program a pointer PKI ("position of $k_i$") is carried along during the insertion, which points to that node in the tree where a restructuring may be potentially necessary. There is also a pointer PPKI ("position of the predecessor of $k_i$"), which points to the predecessor of the node determined by PKI. So that the special case of PKI pointing to the root of the tree does not have to be handled

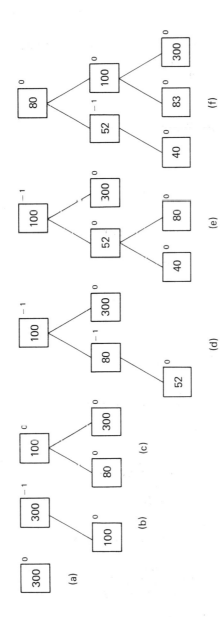

**Figure 3.3.6**

separately, the top pointer of the tree will be treated like a tree node, to which PPKI can point. The pointer PKI is carried along so that before the beginning of the balancing process only nodes with a balance 0 occur between k and the node determined by PKI.

In the following program, the tree is stored in standard form using the declarations **DCL** $(A(N + 1), B(N + 1), R1(N + 1), R2(N + 1))$ **FIXED BIN**;. The values of the nodes are given by A; the balance, by B; and the pointer fields, by R1 and R2. The top pointer R1(1) gives the address of the root of the tree.

```
ADELSON: PROC OPTIONS (MAIN);
    DCL N FIXED BIN;
    GET LIST (N);
    BEGIN;
        DCL (A(N + 1), B(N + 1), R1(N + 1), R2(N + 1), FREE,
            PKI, PPKI, P, Q, PKI1, PKI2, AUX, U1, U2, U3, U4)
            FIXED BIN;
        GET LIST (A(2)); R1(2), R2(2), B(2) = 0; R1(1) = 2;
        /*  THE (CURRENT) ROOT OT THE TREE IS STORED; NOW COMF
            THE OTHER NODES */
        DO FREE = 3 TO N + 1;
            GET LIST (A(FREE));
            R1(FREE), R2(FREE), B(FREE) = 0;
            /* THE NODE K WITH VALUE A(FREE) IS NOW READ AND
                STORED; IT MUST NOW BE INSERTED IN THE PROPER
                PLACE */
            INSERT: PKI = R1(1); PPKI = 1; P = R1(1);
            /* P TRACES THROUGH THE TREE */
            SEARCH: IF A(FREE) < A(P) THEN Q = R1(P);
                                        ELSE Q = R2(P);
                    DO WHILE (Q ¬ = 0);
                        IF B(Q) ¬ = 0 THEN DO;
                                            PKI = Q;
                                            PPKI = P;
                                        END;
                        /* IF B(Q) ≠ 0 THEN A RESTRUCTURING
                            IS CONSIDERED FOR Q */
                        P = Q;
                        IF A(FREE) < A(P) THEN Q = R1(P);
                                            ELSE Q = R2(P);
                    END;
                    IF A(FREE) < A(P) THEN Q, R1(P) = FREE;
                                        ELSE Q, R2(P) = FREE;
            BALANCE: /* THE BALANCE OF THE NODES BETWEEN
                PKI AND K IS NOW ADJUSTED */
                IF A(FREE) < A(PKI) THEN P, PKI1 = R1(PKI);
                                        ELSE P, PKI1 = R2(PKI);
                /* PKI1 IS USED LATER AND POINTS TO THE
                    SUCCESSOR K(I + 1) OF K(I) IN THE BRANCH
                    CONSIDERED, THUS TO K(I + 1) IN FIG. 3.3.4 */
                DO WHILE (P ¬ = Q);
```

```
                    IF A(FREE) < A(P) THEN DO;
                                        B(P) = −1;
                                        P = R1(P);
                                    END;
                                ELSE DO;
                                        B(P) = +1;
                                        P = R2(P);
                                    END;
            END;
RESTRUCTURE: /* PKI POINTS EITHER TO THE ROOT OF
                THE TREE OR TO A NODE K(I) WITH
                βK(I) ≠ 0, PPKI POINTS TO THE
                PREDECESSOR OF K(I), AND PKI1
                POINTS TO THE SUCCESSOR OF K(I)
                IN THE BRANCH CONSIDERED */
            IF A(FREE) < A(PKI) THEN AUX = −1;
                            ELSE AUX = +1;
            IF B(PKI) = 0 THEN DO,
                                B(PKI) = AUX;
                                GOTO FIN;
                            END;
            /* THEN K(I) WAS THE ROOT AND THE
                HEIGHT OF THE LEFT OR RIGHT
                SUBTREE HAS BEEN INCREASED BY 1 */
            IF B(PKI) = −AUX THEN DO;
                                B(PKI) = 0;
                                GOTO FIN;
                            END;
            /* THEN THE HEIGHTS OF BOTH SUBTREES
                OF K(I) ARE BALANCED. IN THE
                REMAINING CASE B(PKI) = AUX A
                RESTRUCTURING IS NECESSARY. THUS
                THE PROCESS LEFT OR RIGHT MUST BE
                PERFORMED */
            IF AUX = −1 THEN GOTO LEFT;
                        ELSE GOTO RIGHT;
LEFT: /* FIRST IT MUST BE DETERMINED WHETHER WE
        HAVE THE CASE SHOWN IN FIG. 3.3.4(A) OR ONE
        OF THE CASES IN FIG. 3.3.4(B) THROUGH (D)
        THAT CAN BE HANDLED TOGETHER */
    IF B(PKI1) = −1 THEN GOTO FIG334A;
                    ELSE GOTO FIG334BCD;
FIG334A: IF R1(PPKI) = PKI THEN R1(PPKI) = PKI1;
                        ELSE R2(PPKI) = PKI1;
    U2 = R2(PKI1); R2(PKI1) = PKI; R1(PKI) = U2;
    B(PKI), B(PKI1) = 0; GOTO FIN;
    /* FIG. 3.3.4(A) HAS BEEN TRANSFORMED TO
        FIG. 3.3.5(A). THE AUXILIARY VALUE U2
        IS A POINTER TO A(2) IN FIG. 3.3.4(A) */
FIG334BCD: PKI2 = R2(PKI1); /* PKI2 POINTS IN
        FIG. 3.3.4(B) AND (C) TO THE NODE
        K(I + 2) */
```

```
                    U1 = R2(PKI);  U2 = R1(PKI1);
                    U3 = R2(PKI2);  U4 = R1(PKI2);
                    /* U1, U2, U3, U4 POINT TO A(1), A(2),
                        A(3), A(4) IN FIG. 3.3.4(B), (C), (D) */
                    IF R1(PPKI) = PKI THEN R1(PPKI) = PKI2;
                                        ELSE R2(PPKI) = PKI2;
                    R1(PKI2) = PKI1;  R2(PKI2) = PKI;
                    R2(PKI1) = U4;  R1(PKI) = U3;
                    /* FOR INTRODUCING THE BALANCES, SEVERAL
                        CASES MUST BE DISTINGUISHED */
                    B(PKI1), B(PKI) = 0;
                    IF B(PKI2) < 0 THEN B(PKI) = +1;
                    IF B(PKI2) > 0 THEN B(PKI1) = −1;
                    B(PKI2) = 0;  GOTO FIN;
                    /* THUS FIG. 3.3.4(B), (C), (D) HAVE BEEN
                        TRANSFORMED TO FIG. 3.3.5(B), (C), (D) */
        RIGHT:  /* ANALOGOUS TO LEFT */
                IF B(PKI1) = 1 THEN GOTO CASEA;
                               ELSE GOTO CASEBCD;
        CASEA:  /* LIKE FIG334A ABOVE */
                IF R1(PPKI) = PKI THEN R1(PPKI) = PKI1;
                                  ELSE R2(PPKI) = PKI1;
                U2 = R1(PKI1);  R1(PKI1) = PKI;  R2(PKI) = U2;
                B(PKI), B(PKI1) = 0;  GOTO FIN;
        CASEBCD:  /* LIKE FIG334BCD ABOVE */
                    PKI2 = R1(PKI1);
                    U1 = R1(PKI);  U2 = R2(PKI1);  U3 = R1(PKI2);
                    U2 = R2(PKI2);
                    IF R1(PPKI) = PKI THEN R1(PPKI) = PKI2;
                                      ELSE R2(PPKI) = PKI2;
                    R2(PKI2) = PKI1;  R1(PKI2) = PKI;
                    R1(PKI1) = U4;  R2(PKI) = U3;
                    B(PKI1), B(PKI) = 0;
                    IF B(PKI2) > 0 THEN B(PKI) = −1;
                    IF B(PKI2) < 0 THEN B(PKI1) = +1;
                    B(PKI2) = 0;
        FIN: END;
    END;
  END;
```

For a better understanding of the program above, follow it using the input n = 6, followed by the numbers 300, 100, 80, 52, 40, 83, which yields the trees shown successively in Fig. 3.3.6.

Sorted trees are useful not only for handling sorted sequences of nodes $F = k_1$, $k_2, \ldots, k_n$, where nodes with given key values are to be found, but also for finding a node $k_i$ with a given position i in F.

*Method 1:*   The ith node of B in symmetric order is determined by going through the nodes in symmetric order. This is the desired node.

*Method 2:* The initial position of the nodes is carried along; i.e., a sequence $F' = k'_1, k'_2, \ldots, k'_n$ with $\omega k'_i = (i, \omega k_i)$ is considered. Then the ith node can be found easily using searching by partitioning. The principal disadvantage of this technique is that, when adding or deleting nodes, on the average n/2 nodes must have their first components changed.

*Method 3:* Each node k in a sorted tree B is associated with a number $\gamma k$, which gives the number of nodes in the left subtree of k. By using this number $\gamma k$, the ith node can be determined just as quickly as with Method 2; however, the process of adding or deleting k necessitates only the change of the $\gamma k$ along the branch to the node k.

Of the methods described, therefore, Method 3 is almost always the most practical. If we use Method 3 and balanced trees in standard form, then we have a technique for storing linear lists with n nodes in which not only the ith node for a given i but also a node with a given key v can be found, added, or deleted in $\log_2$ n steps. This method combines the advantages of linked and sequential storage of trees without having the disadvantages and is therefore effective in many situations.

**Example 3.3.6** Let there be given a sorted tree B meeting the specifications of Method 3 for a sequence of whole number nodes $F = k_1, k_2, \ldots, k_m$. Such a tree is given in Fig. 3.3.7 for 10 nodes with values 18, 20, 22, 24, 30, 36, 50, 70, 72, 80, and the value $\gamma k$ is written beside each node k.

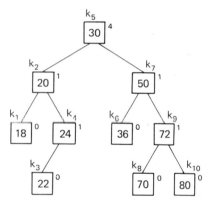

**Figure 3.3.7**

Let B be stored in standard form using the declaration **DCL** (D(M), G(M), R1(M), R2(M)) **FIXED BIN**; (for a suitable M), where D represents the value of a node k; G, the value $\gamma k$; and R1 and R2, the pointer fields for the standard form. Let W be a variable that gives the address of the root of the tree.

The following program segment searches for and prints the ith node of F, without checking the validity of i or the storage of B.

```
DCL (J, P) FIXED BIN;
P = W; J = I;
DO WHILE (G(P) ¬ = J − 1);
    IF G(P) > J − 1 THEN P = R1(P);
                    ELSE DO;
                            J = J − G(P) − 1;
                            P = R2(P);
                    END;
END;
PUT LIST ('THE ITH NODE HAS THE VALUE', D(P));
```

When searching by partitioning in a sorted tree B with n nodes, we have the following relation that was derived at the beginning of this section:

$$\text{Avg (searching by partitioning)} = \sum_{k \text{ in } B} p(k)(1 + \lambda k),$$

where $p(k)$ is the relative usage frequency of k. In attempting to minimize the Avg (searching by partitioning) we have thus far considered only the case $p(k) = 1/n$ of equal relative usage frequencies. The general case will now be handled using a somewhat modified formulation.

**Definition 3.3.8** (Optimal Search Tree) Let $K = \{k_1, k_2, \ldots, k_n\}$ be n nodes with which arbitrary positive numbers $f(k_1), f(k_2), \ldots, f(k_n)$ have been associated as *frequencies*.[5] A binary tree B with nodes K is called an *optimal search tree* if $\sum_{k \text{ in } B} f(k)\lambda k$ is minimal.

A binary tree B with leaves K is called an *optimal leaf*[6] *search tree*, if $\sum_{k \in K} f(k)\lambda k$ is minimal.

We speak analogously of an *optimal sorted search tree* or an *optimal leaf sorted search tree* if the tree (in a leaf tree the sequence of yield nodes) is sorted and the minimum is considered only over sorted trees.

The optimal search tree is quite simple to obtain. To do this we take a full tree with n nodes and arrange the nodes so that those with high frequencies are most probable near the root.

Huffmann's algorithm is used to produce the optimal leaf search tree.

**Definition 3.3.9** (Huffmann's Algorithm) Let there be given a sequence of nodes $F = k_1, k_2, \ldots, k_n$ with frequencies $f(k_i)$ (for $1 \leqslant i \leqslant n$). Huffmann's algorithm for determining an optimal leaf search tree is based on a sequence A of nodes. Initially $A = F$. The following *construction step* is performed for $t = 1, 2, \ldots, n − 1$.

---

[5]The numbers

$$p(k_i) = \frac{f(k_i)}{\sum_j f(k_j)}$$

can be regarded as relative usage frequencies.

[6]"Leaf tree" or "hollow tree," since the nodes sought for occur as leaves; all inner nodes contain only information useful to "point the way."

*Construction step:* Let $A = a_1, a_2, \ldots, a_m$. Let $a_i$ and $a_j$ be nodes with the smallest and second smallest frequencies, respectively. Replace in A the $a_i$ by a node $b_t$ with $f(b_t) = f(a_i) + f(a_j)$, remove $a_j$ from A, and construct the tree (Fig. 3.3.8) from the already existing trees with roots $a_i$ and $a_j$ and the new node $b_t$.

Frequencies here and in later examples will be written to the right of the nodes. The frequencies generated in the course of the algorithm are underlined to distinguish them from the frequencies specified initially.

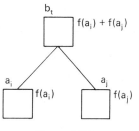

**Figure 3.3.8**

**Example 3.3.7** Let there be given five nodes $F = k_1, k_2, \ldots, k_5$ with frequencies $f(k_1) = 16$, $f(k_2) = 2$, $f(k_3) = 18$, $f(k_4) = 16$, $f(k_5) = 23$.

By applying Huffmann's algorithm, the sequence A of nodes is changed as shown in Fig. 3.3.9(a) and the corresponding optimal leaf search tree is given in Fig. 3.3.9(b).

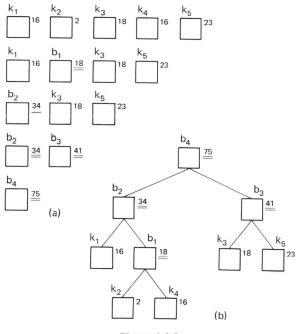

**Figure 3.3.9**

Optimal leaf search trees are in general not sorted and thus cannot be used to find a node with a given key;[7] however, for every subset T of nodes there is a test to determine whether a node with key v occurs in T or not. Such an exceptional case is described here: five nodes $k_1, k_2, k_3, k_4, k_5$ with frequencies 2, 16, 16, 18, 23 and values $\omega k_1 = (2, HE), \omega k_2 = (3, SHE), \omega k_3 = (5, IT), \omega k_4 = (7, WE), \omega k_5 = (11, US)$ are given. Since in this case the keys of the nodes are different prime numbers, for each subset T of nodes, the product p of their keys can be considered. A node with key v then occurs in T if and only if v divides the number p without a remainder. Therefore we store the five given nodes in the leaves of the optimal tree in Fig. 3.3.9(b). In each node k that is not a leaf, the product of the keys of all leaves of the left subtree of k is stored, as shown in Fig. 3.3.10. By inquiring whether a key v divides the value of an inner node k without a remainder or not, it can be determined whether the node with key v appears in the left or right subtree of k.

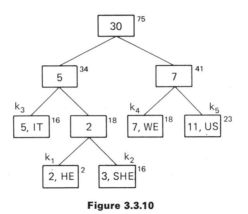

**Figure 3.3.10**

Optimal leaf search trees prove most useful in coding problems. Consider the following situation: words are given that consist only of the five letters A, B, C, D, E. The frequencies of the five letters in these words are (on the average) 23, 2, 16, 18, and 16 in this order. Each of the given letters is to be encoded as a bit string[8] so that bit strings can be uniquely decoded and the bit strings necessary for encoding are (on the average) as short as possible.

If we associate the letters C, B, E, D, A from left to right in the optimal search tree in Fig. 3.3.9(b) with the leaves (according to the frequencies) and if we interpret each branching in the tree to the left as 0 and each to the right as 1, then we obtain an encoding as desired with C . . . 00, B . . . 010, E . . . 011, D . . . 10, A . . . 11. Notice that certainly not every bit string is a valid encoding; however, every valid encoding can be easily and uniquely decoded using the tree in Fig. 3.3.9(b); for example, 010011111011 is decoded to BEADA.

In order to be able to perform the technique of searching by partitioning in

---

[7]Thus the name *search tree* is not really deserved but is used in the literature.
[8]That is, a word (a string) of zeros and ones.

a binary tree, the tree must be sorted. For this reason, the optimal sorted search trees and optimal leaf sorted search trees are particularly important.

For simplicity, in the following we shall consider only complete binary trees. It is easy to see that these always consist of n inner nodes and n + 1 leaves and that in symmetric order every other node is a leaf.

Now assume we are given a sorted sequence $F = k_1, k_2, \ldots, k_{2n+1}$ of nodes with frequencies $f_1, g_1, f_2, g_2, \ldots, f_n, g_n, f_{n+1}$. If we notice that in an optimal sorted search tree each subtree is in turn an optimal sorted search tree, then an optimal sorted search tree for F can be obtained by systematically constructing larger and larger optimal sorted search trees. Based on this fact, *Knuth's algorithm* produces the optimal sorted search tree for a sequence F as given above in $n^2$ steps.

Since in every complete sorted tree the nodes $k_2, k_4, \ldots, k_{2n}$ are inner nodes, the technique mentioned contains as a special case for $g_1 = g_2 = \cdots = g_n = 0$ the construction of an optimal complete sorted leaf search tree for the sequence $k_1, k_3, \ldots, k_{2n+1}$ with frequencies $f_1, f_2, \ldots, f_{n+1}$.

Another elegant technique that determines an optimal complete sorted leaf search tree (abbreviated H-tree) for n frequencies in $n \log_2 n$ steps is the *Hu and Tucker algorithm* defined below.

**Definition 3.3.10** (Hu and Tucker Algorithm) There is given a sorted sequence of *initial nodes* $F = k_1, k_2, \ldots, k_n$ with frequencies $f(k_i)$ where $1 \leqslant i \leqslant n$. The Hu and Tucker algorithm consists of three phases: a *construction phase*, a *marking phase*, and a *building phase*. In the marking phase, on the basis of the tree obtained in the construction phase, each node $k \in F$ is assigned a *level*, level (k); then in the building phase the desired H-tree is produced by using only the nodes $k_1, k_2, \ldots, k_n$ and their levels.

*Construction phase:* In this phase, we work with a sequence A of *initial nodes* and *inner nodes*. Initially $A = F$, and A consists only of initial nodes. The following *construction step* is performed for $t = 1, 2, \ldots, n - 1$.

*Construction step:* Let $A = a_1, a_2, \ldots, a_m$. A pair $(a_i, a_j)$ where $1 \leqslant i < j \leqslant m$ is said to be *good* if no initial nodes between $a_i$ and $a_j$ occur in A. Let $\mu = \min \{f(a_i) + f(a_j) | (a_i, a_j) \text{ is good}\}$. Among the good pairs $(a_i, a_j)$ with $f(a_i) + f(a_j) = \mu$ we consider those with the smallest i and from among these we take the one with the smallest j. Call this $(a_i, a_j)$. Now replace the node $a_i$ by an inner node $b_t$ where $f(b_t) = f(a_i) + f(a_j)$, remove $a_j$ from A, and construct the tree (Fig. 3.3.11) out of the already existing trees with roots $a_i$ and $a_j$ and the new node $b_t$.

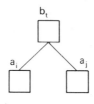

**Figure 3.3.11**

*Marking phase:* Let B be the tree finally obtained in the construction phase. To each node $k \in F$, assign as level (k) the length of the branch to k in the tree B.

*Building phase:* In this phase we always work with a sequence A of nodes having certain levels. Initially $A = F$. The following *building step* is performed for $t = 1$, $2, \ldots, n - 1$.

*Building step:* Let $A = a_1, a_2, \ldots, a_m$ and $\mu = \max \{\text{level } (a_i) | 1 \leqslant i \leqslant m\}$. Let $(a_i, a_{i+1})$ be the first pair in A with level $(a_i)$ = level $(a_{i+1})$ = $\mu$. Replace $a_i$ and $a_j$ in A by a node $c_t$ where level $(c_t)$ = $\mu - 1$ and construct the tree (Fig. 3.3.12) from the already existing trees with roots $a_i$ and $a_{i+1}$ and the new node $c_t$. The tree obtained at the end of the building phase is the desired H-tree.

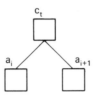

**Figure 3.3.12**

**Example 3.3.8** Let $k_1, k_2, k_3, k_4, k_5$ be a sorted sequence of nodes with frequencies 23, 18, 2, 16, 16, respectively. The modifications of the sequence A during the construction phase are represented in Fig. 3.3.13(a) and the resulting tree is shown in Fig. 3.3.13(b). The frequencies of inner nodes are underlined.

In the tree obtained, the yield is the sequence of nodes $k_1, k_3, k_4, k_2, k_5$ and, therefore, not the given sorted sequence $k_1, k_2, k_3, k_4, k_5$ of nodes. In the marking phase, we obtain level $(k_1)$ = level $(k_2)$ = level $(k_5)$ = 2, level $(k_3)$ = level $(k_4)$ = 3. From that the building step produces the desired H-tree shown in Fig. 3.3.13(c). The numbering of the nodes $c_i$ illustrates the order of the building. The levels are written to the left of the nodes.

The proof that the Hu and Tucker algorithm always works is complicated and will not be given here.

In programming this technique, the construction step is of critical importance. If the t initial nodes $a_{i_1}, a_{i_2}, \ldots, a_{i_t}$ occur exactly in the sequence $A = a_1, a_2, \ldots, a_m$ and if we write $A = D_1, a_{i_1}, D_2, a_{i_2}, \ldots, D_t, a_{i_t}, D_{t+1}$, then we must determine the minimal pair in the sequences $E_1 = D_1, a_{i_1}; E_2 = a_{i_1}, D_2, a_{i_2}; E_3 = a_{i_2}, D_3, a_{i_3}; \ldots;$ $E_{t+1} = a_{i_t}, D_{t+1}$ and then if necessary combine two sequences into one (if in using an initial node a further "barrier" is removed). Consequently, in order to be able to perform a construction step in $\log_2 n$ steps, we merely need to solve the following *modification problem*, which also occurs repeatedly in other situations.

**Definition 3.3.11** (Modification Problem) Let there be given sets $E_1, E_2, \ldots$ of at most n whole-number nodes. The nodes are stored so that a *modification* can be

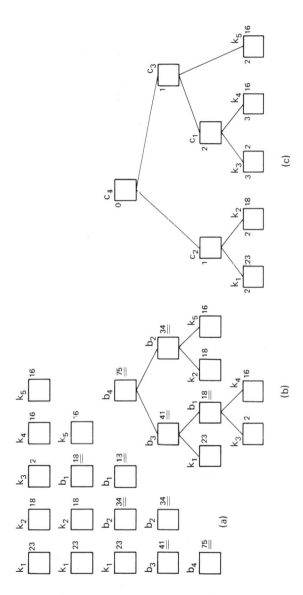

**Figure 3.3.13**

performed in $\log_2$ n steps. A *modification* is one of the following tasks a through d:

(a)   Determine the smallest node in $E_i$ for a given i.
(b)   Remove the smallest node of $E_i$ for a given i.
(c)   Insert a given node k in $E_i$ for a given i.
(d)   Combine the nodes of $E_i$ and $E_j$ into one set for a given i, j.

A solution of the modification problem is possible for example using *leftist trees*. It is worthwhile to make clear first just how difficult the solution of the modification problem seems to be: if we store the sets $E_i$ linked as nonsorted linear arrays, then for tasks c and d only one step is necessary, but for tasks a and b up to n steps are necessary; however, if we store the sets $E_i$ as sorted linear arrays, then for tasks a and b only one step is necessary, but for tasks c and d up to n steps are necessary. If we try using balanced trees for the sets $E_i$, then for tasks a, b, and c only $\log_2$ n steps are necessary, but for task d again n steps are necessary, and so on.

**Definition 3.3.12** (Leftist Tree) Let B be a binary tree. For every node k of B, let there be defined a value $\epsilon k$ (which is one more than the shortest "distance" from k to a node with less than two successors) as follows: if k has less than two successors, then $\epsilon k = 1$; otherwise $\epsilon k = 1 + \min \{\epsilon k', \epsilon k''\}$, where k', k'' are the two successors of k. The tree B is called a *leftist tree* if, for every node k, conditions a and b are satisfied.

(a)   For each successor k' of k, $\omega_1 k \leqslant \omega_1 k'$; i.e., of all the nodes of a subtree, the smallest is the root.
(b)   If k has a left successor k' and a right successor k'', then $\epsilon k' \geqslant \epsilon k''$. If k has no left successor, then k also has no right successor.

Figure 3.3.14(a) and (b) illustrate two leftist trees. The values $\epsilon k$ here and in later diagrams are written below the nodes. Notice that in a leftist tree with n nodes and root k it is always true that $\epsilon k \leqslant \log_2 (n + 1)$ and every subtree of a leftist tree is again a leftist tree. In storing a leftist tree, the value $\epsilon k$ is carried along with each node.

Tasks a through d mentioned in the modification problem (Def. 3.3.11) can be performed in a leftist tree with n nodes in $\log_2$ n steps:

(a)   Because the smallest node is the root.
(b)   Because the root can be removed by combining the two subtrees of the root into a leftist tree.
(c)   Because the insertion of a node can be interpreted as the combining of two leftist trees, one of which consists of just a single node.
(d)   Because the combination of two leftist trees A and B with right subtrees $A_r$ and $B_r$, respectively, can be accomplished in $\log_2$ n steps, as follows:
        If one of the two trees is empty, then the other tree is the desired result; otherwise if the root of A is smaller than the root of B, then in A the subtree $A_r$ is replaced by the combination of leftist trees $A_r$ and B; otherwise, in B,

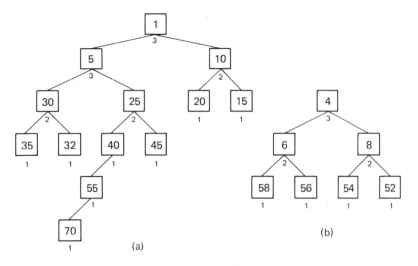

(a)

(b)

**Figure 3.3.14**

$B_r$ is replaced by the combination of leftist trees $B_r$ and A. Call the resulting tree C. If C is not a leftist tree, then we obtain a leftist tree from C by "changing sides," i.e., by interchanging the left and right subtrees of C.

To combine the leftist trees in Fig. 3.3.14, according to the technique above, first the trees in Fig. 3.3.14(b) and 3.3.15(a) must be combined. To do this, first the trees in Fig. 3.3.15(a) and (b) must be combined, and this in turn requires that first the trees in Fig. 3.3.15(a) and (c) be combined; therefore first the trees in Fig. 3.3.15(c) and (d)

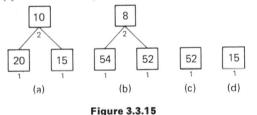

(a)              (b)              (c)      (d)

**Figure 3.3.15**

must be combined. Then going backward we obtain first Fig. 3.3.16(a); by changing sides we obtain Fig. 3.3.16(a'); from there we obtain Fig. 3.3.16(b), and then Fig. 3.3.16(c). By changing sides we obtain Fig. 3.3.16(c'), then Fig. 3.3.16(d), and finally the result shown in Fig. 3.3.16(e).

**Example 3.3.9** (Leftist Trees) Two leftist trees A and B with whole-number nodes are given in standard form with start pointers aa and ab, respectively. A program segment is to be written that combines A and B into a new leftist tree C with start pointer ac.

As declarations we use **DCL** (D(0 : M), E(0 : M), R1(0 : M), R2(0 : M), AA, AB, AC) **FIXED BIN**;, where D(I) is used for the whole-number value of a node k, E(I)

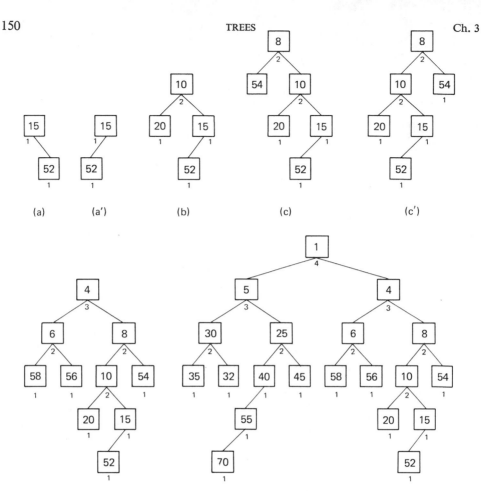

**Figure 3.3.16**

is used for the value $\epsilon k$; R1(I) and R2(I) are the pointer fields $(I \geqslant 1)$; and AA, AB, AC are the start pointers. We let $E(0) = 0$ so that even in the absence of a left or right successor of a node k with address p, we can apply the formula $\epsilon k = \min \{E(R1(p)), E(R2(p))\} + 1$.

```
COMBINE: PROCEDURE (AA, AB)  RETURNS (FIXED BIN) RECURSIVE;
        DCL (AA, AB, P) FIXED BIN;
        /* IF AA AND AB ARE TWO START POINTERS OF THE LEFTIST TREES
           A AND B, THEN BY COMBINING A AND B, COMBINE (AA, AB)
           PRODUCES A LEFTIST TREE C WHERE THE ADDRESS OF THE ROOT
           OF C IS THE VALUE OF THE PROCEDURE */
        IF AA = 0 THEN RETURN (AB);
        IF AB = 0 THEN RETURN (AA);
        /* IF ONE OF THE GIVEN TREES IS EMPTY, THEN THE
           COMBINATION OF THE TWO TREES IS THE OTHER TREE */
```

```
        IF D(AA) <= D(AB) THEN DO;
                        R2(AA) = COMBINE (+R2(AA), +AB);
                        IF E(R1(AA)) >= E(R2(AA))
                            THEN E(AA) = E(R2(AA)) + 1;
                            ELSE DO; /* AN INTERCHANGE
                                       IS NECESSARY */
                            E(AA) = E(R1(AA)) + 1;
                            P = R1(AA);
                            R1(AA) = R2(AA);
                            R2(AA) = P;
                            END;
                        RETURN (AA);
                    END;
                ELSE DO;
                        R2(AB) = COMBINE (+R2(AB), +AA);
                        IF E(R1(AB)) >= E(R2(AB));
                        THEN E(AB) = E(R2(AB)) + 1;
                        ELSE DO:
                            E(AB) = E(R1(AB)) + 1;
                            P = R1(AB);
                            R1(AB) = R2(AB);
                            R2(AB) = P;
                            END;
                        RETURN (AB);
                    END;
        END COMBINE;
        /* THE ACTUAL PROCEDURE CALL FOLLOWS */
        AC = COMBINE (+AA, +AB);
```

For better understanding, work through the program first combining only two nodes $\boxed{52}$ and $\boxed{15}$ and then combining the two trees in Fig. 3.3.14.

If we have a sequence $F = k_1, k_2, \ldots, k_n$ of nodes and a key v and if we wish to locate the node in F with given key v, then a sorted tree can be used for F and the technique of searching by partitioning can be applied to find k, using the methods already explained in this section. Other types of trees and other search techniques may also be of interest, however.

**Definition 3.3.13** (Key Tree) Let $F = k_1, k_2, \ldots, k_n$ be a sequence of nodes and $s_1, s_2, \ldots, s_t$ be a sequence of functions that are defined for the keys of F in such a way that different nodes k', k'' correspond to different sequences $s_1(\omega_1 k'), s_2(\omega_1 k'), \ldots,$ $s_t(\omega_1 k')$ and $s_1(\omega_1 k''), s_2(\omega_1 k''), \ldots, s_t(\omega_1 k'')$. A *key tree* B *of* F or *for* F is obtained by starting with a tree B that initially consists of only a root W (without a value) and performing the following *building process* for $k_i$ (where $i = 1, 2, \ldots, n$):

*Building process:* Let the root W be the *current* node. Perform the *building step* described below for $j = 1, 2, \ldots, t - 1$ and then the *final step*.

*Building step:* If the current node has a successor k with value $s_j(\omega_1 k_i)$, then let k be the current node; otherwise insert a new node k with value $s_j(\omega_1 k_i)$ as successor of the current node in the tree B and then denote this node k as the current node.

*Final step:* The node $k_i$ is inserted as successor of the current node in the tree B and thus the key of $k_i$ as well as the value $s_t(\omega_1 k_i)$ may be taken.

Thus in a key tree B of F, a node k is associated with a branch as in Fig. 3.3.17 according to the building process described above and k is modified if necessary by replacing the first component by $s_t(\omega_1 k)$ since it is not always necessary to carry along the entire key.

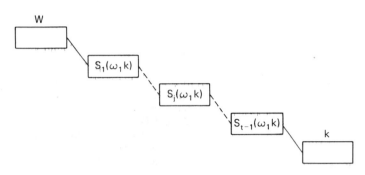

**Figure 3.3.17**

The process of finding a node with a given key in a key tree is just like the building process except that in the final step the node being searched for is taken.

**Example 3.3.10** Let $F = k_1, k_2, \ldots, k_{10}$ be a sequence of nodes with $\omega k_1, \omega k_2, \ldots,$ $\omega k_{10} = (338, Z), (145, A), (136, H), (214, I), (146, C), (334, Y), (333, P), (127, G),$ $(310, O), (322, X)$, and let $s_1(n) = n \div 100, s_2(n) = \mathrm{mod}\,(n \div 10, 10)$ and $s_3(n) = \mathrm{mod}\,(n, 10)$. We then obtain the tree in Fig. 3.3.18.

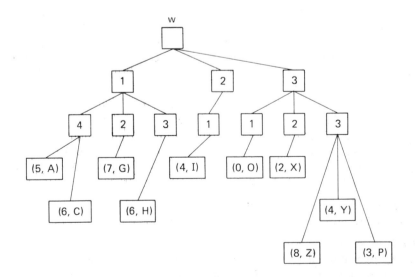

**Figure 3.3.18**

Let B be a key tree with n nodes, and let h be its height, i.e., the length of the longest branch to a leaf. The cost of searching for a node with a given key v depends on h and the number of successors of the node. If every inner node has exactly t successors (i.e., if B is a complete tree of degree t), then to determine the "correct" successor of a node k (assuming equal relative usage frequencies), an average of

$$\frac{1}{t}[1 + 2 + \cdots + (t - 1) + (t - 1)] = \frac{t + 1}{2} - \frac{1}{t}$$

comparisons are required, assuming that the node with key v does in fact occur in B. Therefore

$$\text{Avg (search in key tree)} = h\left(\frac{t + 1}{2} - \frac{1}{t}\right)$$

and

$$\text{Max (search in key tree)} = h(t - 1),$$

where $h = \log_t n = (\ln n)/(\ln t)$. Therefore, for searching in a key tree, the cost is $\log_2 n$ if $t \geqslant 2$. For $t = 2$,

$$\text{Avg (search in key tree)} = \text{Max (search in key tree)} = h.$$

For $t = 3$ and $t = 4$ the result is about 10% more; for $t = 8$, about 60% more; for $t = 16$, around 110% more. So searching in a key tree is advisable if the nodes do not have "too many" successors.

For storing key trees, it is common to use the corresponding binary tree. A standard form of the binary tree corresponding to the tree in Fig. 3.3.18 is shown in Fig. 3.3.19. Notice that this method of storage is very similar to that given in Fig. 2.4.4.

To find a node with key v, begin with the address $p = \rho_1 W$ and perform the process *Search* for $t = 1, 2, 3$:

*Search:* Of the memory locations with addresses $a_1 = p, a_2 = \rho_2 a_1, a_3 = \rho_2 a_2, \ldots$, let z be the first with $\delta_1 z = s_t(v)$. If $t < 3$, set $p = \rho_1 z$.

At the end of the process *Search*, z is the location in memory of the desired node.

In this section, as in the sections on sorting and merging and on searching in linear lists, nodes with whole numbers as keys have always been used. It must be stressed that in actual practice other keys, such as character strings, also occur very frequently. The techniques discussed here can be adapted without great difficulty to the use of keys with values that are not whole numbers.

In sorted "alphabetical" trees, a natural order relation would be, for example, alphabetical order; in "alphabetical" search trees the functions $s_i$ (for $i = 1, 2, \ldots$) are often used where $s_i(v) =$ the ith character from the left in the word v, or the symbol * if v consists of less than i symbols. An "alphabetical" key tree with several German words and their English equivalents is given in Fig. 3.3.20 using the functions just mentioned.

In contrast to the key tree defined in Def. 3.3.13, a modification has been made so that the building process or the search process for a given key v is terminated as soon as $s_i(v) = *$ (i.e., as soon as the end of the key v is found).

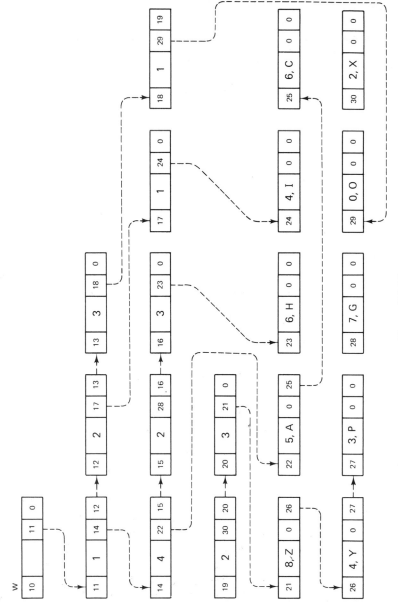

**Figure 3.3.19**

154

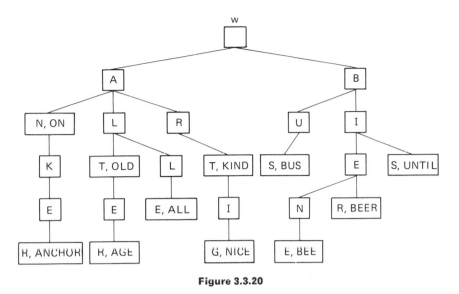

**Figure 3.3.20**

*Remarks and References*

For the average branch length in trees, see Knuth [1] for the result $\sqrt{n}$ ; for the result $\log_2 n$, see the analysis of Quicksort in Sec. 2.6. *Balanced trees* were introduced in Adelson [1]. Other popular treatments of the subject are Landauer [1], Nievergelt [1] and C. C. Foster [1]. Related to the balanced trees are the *B-trees* described in Bayer [1]. For changing *natural trees* to *full trees*, see Martin [2].

The technique for determining optimal leaf trees for searching originated with Huffmann [1]. Knuth's algorithm is found in Knuth [2], and the Hu and Tucker algorithm is taken from Hu [1]. *Leftist trees* were introduced in Crane [1]. The first work with key trees was done in Sussenguth [1]. Further research and additional references may be found in Stanfel [1].

## Exercises

**3.3.1**  Given as input is a sequence $a_1, a_2, \ldots, a_n$ of whole numbers. Write a program to modify a (initially empty) sorted binary tree B, with whole-number nodes, for $i = 1, 2, \ldots, n$ as follows: if $a_i > 0$, then $a_i$ is added to the tree B so that B remains sorted; if $a_i < 0$ and $-a_i$ does not occur in B, then an error message must be printed, but if $-a_i$ does occur in B, then $-a_i$ should be removed from B so that a sorted tree remains; if $a_i = 0$, the program stops.

**3.3.2**  A natural tree is given in standard form. Write a program to produce a balanced, sorted tree with the same nodes and print it in level-number representation.

**3.3.3**  Given as input is a sequence $a_1, a_2, \ldots, a_n$ of whole numbers. Write a program to produce a sorted tree whose nodes have the values $a_1, a_2, \ldots, a_n$ in standard form.

**3.3.4**  A binary tree is given in standard form. Write a program segment that prints the nodes in level-number representation and also along with each node k prints out its balance $\beta(k)$.

**3.3.5**  Given as input is a sequence F of pairs $(f_1, a_1)$, $(f_2, a_2)$, ..., $(f_n, a_n)$, where $f_i \in \{0, 1, 2, 3, 4, 5, 6\}$ and $a_i$ (for $1 \leqslant i \leqslant n$) is a whole number. Develop a program using Method 3 in Sec. 3.3 that modifies a (initially empty) sorted sequence A of numbers for i = 1, 2, ..., n as follows: if $f_i = 0$, then $a_i$ is inserted in the sorted sequence A; if $f_i = 1$, then the sorted sequence A is printed; if $f_i = 2$, then the $a_i$th number is removed from A and if $f_i = 3$, it is also printed; if $f_i = 4$, then the number $a_i$ is removed from A and if $f_i = 5$, it is also printed; if $f_i = 6$, the program stops.

**3.3.6**  Given as input is a sequence of positive whole numbers $f_1, f_2, \ldots, f_n$ that represent the frequencies of n nodes $k_1, k_2, \ldots, k_n$. Write a program that produces an optimal leaf tree for searching with leaves $k_1, k_2, \ldots, k_n$. *Hint*: Use Huffmann's algorithm.

**3.3.7**  Input is given as described in Exercise 3.3.6. Design a program that produces an optimal leaf tree for searching, called B, with leaves $k_1, k_2, \ldots, k_n$, where the yield of B consists exactly of the nodes $k_1, k_2, \ldots, k_n$ in this order.
(a)  Write the program to do the work in $n^2$ steps.
(b)  Write the program to do the work in $n \log_2 n$ steps.

*Hint*:  Use the Hu and Tucker algorithm and for b also use leftist trees.

**3.3.8**  A leftist tree B with whole-number nodes is given, stored as in Example 3.3.9.
(a)  Write a program that prints the values of the nodes of B as a sorted sequence.
(b)  Define the procedure "COMBINE" from Example 3.3.9 without using recursion.

## Section 3.4  Searching Solution Trees

Problems frequently arise in which all possible solutions can be determined by a systematic examination of finitely many possibilities. Often the possibilities in question may be interpreted as nodes of a tree, called a *solution tree*. A systematic evaluation of all possibilities then corresponds to a systematic search through the solution tree. In this section several important practical methods for searching solution trees will be presented using two concrete examples. The methods considered are called *backtracking*, *bounded searching* or *branch and bound*, *heuristic searching*, and combinations of these methods.

It is sometimes useful to consider the solution of a problem as a special case of the following general formulation.

**Definition 3.4.1**  (Problem Solving Using a Solution Tree) Let there be given a set S of *situations* and a set R of *rules*. For each situation $s \in S$, let R define a finite set of *successor situations* $s_1, s_2, \ldots, s_t$, for which we write $R(s) = \{s_1, s_2, \ldots, s_t\}$. Among the situations S, let one be designated as an *initial situation* A and several as *end* *situations* E. If we let P denote the set of situations that can be obtained from starting with A and applying the rules R, then often the solution to a given problem can be found by determining among the end situations of P that particular *solution situation* that satisfies certain specified conditions.

If P is a finite set, then the set P corresponds in a natural way to a tree called the *solution tree*. It consists of a root that corresponds to the initial situation A. If a node k corresponds to the situation s, then k has $t \geqslant 0$ successors $k_1, k_2, \ldots, k_t$ that correspond to the successor situations $R(s) = \{s_1, s_2, \ldots, s_t\}$.

To find the solution situation we can essentially

(1) Produce the solution tree B.
(2) Systematically examine the nodes of the solution tree B to see if they represent a solution situation or not.

To speed up the examination of the nodes in step 2 it can often be stipulated that any subtree whose root does not satisfy the condition cannot contain a solution situation and therefore need not be considered further. In this case, when creating the solution tree in step 1, it is reasonable not to produce subtrees that because of the condition would not be considered anyway.

Due to the size of the solution trees that generally arise, often the examination of the nodes in step 2 and the production of the tree in step 1 are done simultaneously. In such a step-by-step production and examination of the solution tree, nodes that have already been handled and are not to be used further need no longer be carried along.

If the step-by-step production and examination of a solution tree proceeds branch by branch from left to right, then it usually suffices in the examination of a branch T of length n to carry along n nodes. All nodes to the "left" of T will have already been inspected; all nodes to the "right" of T have yet to be produced. If a branch T to a leaf is obtained in this way, then the next branch to the right of T is obtained by backtracking through T to the first not yet "used" offshoot to the right (thus the name *backtracking*) and from there one step right and then again to the left until a leaf is reached.

If the step-by-step production and examination of a solution tree is not done branch by branch, then at each step we continue with the production of that branch which because of certain secondary factors is considered most likely to lead to a solution situation. This technique is called *branch and bound*. (The secondary factors mentioned are often restrictions on certain components of the tree nodes.)

The technique of *heuristic searching* is similar to the branch and bound technique, except that a branch that was once chosen because of some secondary factor continues to be used until it leads to an end situation or until it is certain that it cannot lead to a solution situation.

The three methods mentioned will now be demonstrated using the *knapsack problem.*

**Definition 3.4.2** (Knapsack Problem) Assume there are n *objects* called $d_1, d_2, \ldots,$ $d_n$ and associated with each $d_i$ (for $1 \leqslant i \leqslant n$) there is a whole-number *weight* $w_i > 0$ and a whole-number *value* $v_i > 0$.

The problem is to fill a knapsack with a subset of these n objects in such a way that the total weight does not exceed a given amount called TOT and the value of the objects in the knapsack is as large as possible.

The filling of the knapsack can be accomplished by considering successively for $i = 1, 2, \ldots, n$ the object $d_i$ and either putting it into the knapsack or not. If this is done, the contents of the knapsack can be described by a number triple (weight, value, m), where weight gives the current weight of the contents, value gives the current value, and m indicates that objects $d_1, d_2, \ldots, d_m$ have been considered.

For simplification in the following, it will be assumed that the *relative values*

$$\frac{v_1}{w_1}, \frac{v_2}{w_2}, \ldots, \frac{v_n}{w_n}$$

are sorted in descending order, i.e.,

$$\frac{v_1}{w_1} \geqslant \frac{v_2}{w_2} \geqslant \cdots \geqslant \frac{v_n}{w_n}$$

and that the *degenerate cases*

$$\sum_{i=1}^{n} w_i \leqslant \text{TOT} \quad \text{and} \quad \min \{w_i \mid 1 \leqslant i \leqslant n\} \geqslant \text{TOT}$$

do not occur.

In accordance with Def. 3.4.1, let a situation be a triple of numbers, the initial situation A the triple (0, 0, 0), and the end situation any triple (weight, value, n), and let the rule for determining the successor of a given situation s = (weight, value, m) be the following rule:

If m = n, then s has no successor and is an end situation. Otherwise s has the successor $s_2$ = (weight, value, m + 1) and as long as weight + $w_{m+1} \leqslant$ TOT (i.e., as long as $d_{m+1}$ can still be packed in the knapsack), there is also the successor $s_1$ = (weight + $w_{m+1}$, value + $v_{m+1}$, m + 1).

If from among all the end situations (weight, value, n) that can be derived from A we wish to determine that one with maximum "value" (i.e., a knapsack filled with maximum value), then we have exactly the problem described in Def. 3.4.1. In the corresponding solution tree, the desired solution can be determined by one of the methods backtracking, branch and bound, or heuristic searching.

**Example 3.4.1** The solution tree for the knapsack problem, whose values $w_i$, $v_i$, n, and TOT are given in Fig. 3.4.1, is shown in Fig. 3.4.2.

| i     | 1 | 2  | 3  | 4  | 5· |
|-------|---|----|----|----|----|
| $w_i$ | 8 | 16 | 21 | 17 | 12 |
| $v_i$ | 8 | 14 | 16 | 11 | 7  |

n = 5

TOT = 37

**Figure 3.4.1**

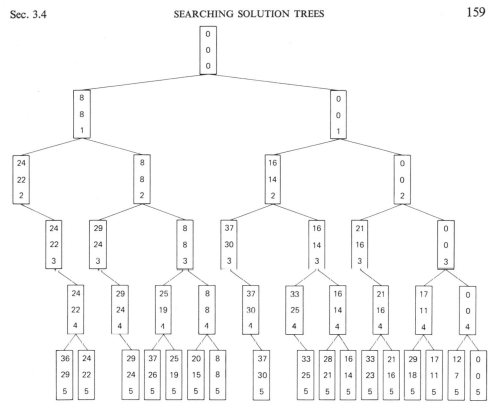

**Figure 3.4.2**

Each node is represented by a rectangle of the form

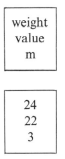

The node

$$\boxed{\begin{array}{c} 24 \\ 22 \\ 3 \end{array}}$$

in the leftmost branch in Fig. 3.4.2, for example, indicates that objects $d_1, d_2, d_3$ have already been considered, and the current weight of the knapsack is 24 and its value is 22.

In solution trees for knapsack problems such as the one in Fig. 3.4.2, a node $k'$ with $\omega k' = $ (weight', value', $m + 1$) is considered to be a left successor of the node $k$ where $\omega k = $ (weight, value, $m$) if it is produced by the inclusion of the object $d_{m+1}$; otherwise it is interpreted as a right successor.

An upper bound $f(t, m)$ (where $0 \leqslant t \leqslant TOT$, $1 \leqslant m \leqslant n$) for the value that can be obtained with the $n - m$ objects $d_{m+1}, d_{m+2}, \ldots, d_n$ using a weight limit of $t$ is clearly

$$f(t, m) = \begin{cases} 0, & \text{if } m = n \text{ or if } t = 0, \\ f(t - w_{m+1}, m + 1) + v_{m+1}, & \text{if } t \geqslant w_{m+1}, \\ \text{floor}\left(\dfrac{t \times v_{m+1}}{w_{m+1}}\right) & \text{if } t < w_{m+1}, \end{cases}$$

where the most valuable objects are used first. Then finally if necessary an object is "cut up" so that all together exactly $t$ units of weight are included. Therefore, if $k$ is a node with $\omega k = (\text{weight, value, } m)$, then $u(k) = \text{value} + f(TOT - \text{weight}, m)$ indicates that starting with $k$ there is no way to fill the knapsack with value $> u(k)$.

Consequently if $y$ is the value of a certain known way of filling a knapsack, then the examination of the nodes of the solution tree can be greatly expedited since for each node $k$ with $u(k) < y + 1$ no further successor of $k$ need be examined.

Since $f(t, m)$ is needed so often, it is appropriate when producing efficient programs to store $f(t, m)$ in a table so that the value $f(t, m)$ can be determined in a single step.

In the program given here such a table is not used since the construction of the table might impair the clarity of the procedure. As input for the knapsack problem, there is a sequence of numbers $n, w_1, v_1, w_2, v_2, \ldots, w_n, v_n, TOT$ that are not checked for validity.

**Example 3.4.2** (Backtracking) The program "Backtrack1" represents a solution of the knapsack problem using backtracking. The branches of the solution tree are examined from left to right and, as explained, $f(t, m)$ is used to eliminate unnecessary nodes.

The nodes of the solution tree are examined in preorder, as in Example 3.1.5, program segment B. The declaration **DCL** (WEIGHT($N + 1$), VAL($N + 1$), M($N + 1$)) **FIXED BIN**; corresponds to a sequentially stored stack in which the roots of those subtrees of the solution tree that are still to be considered are always stored.

```
BACKTRACK1: PROC OPTIONS (MAIN);
    DCL (N, I, TOT, Y, AUX) FIXED BIN; GET LIST (N);
    BEGIN;
        DCL (W(N), V(N), WEIGHT(N + 1), VAL(N + 1), M(N + 1))
            FIXED BIN:
        F:  PROCEDURE (T, M) RETURNS (FIXED BIN) RECURSIVE;
            DCL (T, M) FIXED BIN;
            IF (N = M)|(T = 0) THEN RETURN (0);
            ELSE IF T > = W(M + 1) THEN RETURN (F(T - W(M + 1),
                M + 1)+ V(M + 1));
            RETURN (FLOOR((T * V(M + 1))/W(M + 1) + 0.05));
            /* 0.05 AS A PRECAUTION AGAINST EQUALITY DUE TO
                ROUNDOFF ERROR */
        END F;
```

```
DO I = 1 TO N;
    GET LIST (W(I), V(I));
END;
GET LIST (TOT);
Y = 0; /* NO KNAPSACK FILLING FOUND YET. AS THE
            FIRST STEP, THE SUCCESSOR OF THE SITUATION
            (0, 0, 0) IS INSERTED IN THE STACK */
WEIGHT(1), VAL(1) = 0; M(1) = 1;
WEIGHT(2) = W(1); VAL(2) = V(1); M(2) = 1; I = 2;
DO WHILE (I ¬ = 0); /* THEN THE WHOLE SOLUTION TREE
                        IS SEARCHED */
    IF M(I) = N THEN DO; /* THEN A NEW KNAPSACK FILLING
                            HAS BEEN FOUND */
            IF VAL(I) > Y THEN Y = VAL(I);
            I = I − 1;
        END;
        /* FIRST CHECK WHETHER THE SUBTREE
        WITH THE GIVEN NODE CAN GIVE A
        BETTER KNAPSACK FILLING */
    ELSE DO;
            IF VAL(I) + F(TOT − WEIGHT(I),
                +M(I)) > = Y + 1 THEN DO;
            /* THEN THE CURRENT NODE IS
            REPLACED BY ITS RIGHT
            SUCCESSOR */
                M(I) = M(I) + 1;
                /* AND IF NECESSARY A LEFT
                SUCCESSOR IS INSERTED */
                IF WEIGHT(I) + W(M(I)) < = TOT
                THEN DO;
                    AUX = M(I);
                    WEIGHT(I + 1) = WEIGHT(I) +
                        W(AUX);
                    VAL(I + 1) = VAL(I) + V(AUX);
                    M(I + 1) = AUX; I = I + 1,
                END;
            END; ELSE I = I − 1;
        END;
END;
PUT LIST ('THE BEST KNAPSACK FILLING HAS THE VALUE', Y);
END;
END BACKTRACK1;
```

Work through the program with the input shown in Fig. 3.4.1. The stack changes as shown in Fig. 3.4.3.

Of the tree in Fig. 3.4.2, only the part shown in Fig. 3.4.4 is examined. The number written to the upper right of the nodes indicates the order in which the nodes will be examined (i.e., in which they occur at the top of the stack, see Fig. 3.4.3). The numbers to the lower right give the value u(k) for each node k.

The program "Backtrack1" determines the value of the optimal filling of the knapsack but not how this is obtained. In "Backtrack2" the entire branch to the node

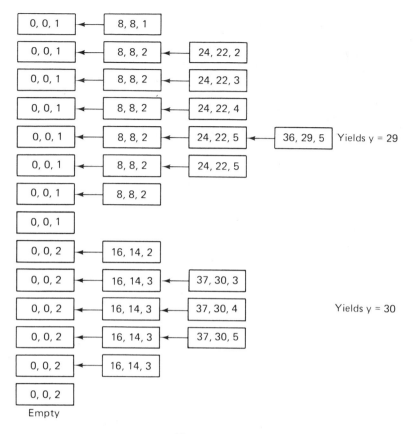

**Figure 3.4.3**

currently being considered is also carried along. The additional nodes allow information to be printed that shows how the optimal filling is obtained. In the additional nodes, the third component is taken to be negative, in order to distinguish this node from the nodes necessary for the search process.

```
BACKTRACK2: PROC OPTIONS (MAIN);
    DCL N FIXED BIN; GET LIST (N);
    BEGIN;
        DCL (W(N), V(N), WEIGHT(2 * N), VAL(2 * N), M(2 * N),
            I, TOT, Y, AUX, J) FIXED BIN;
        /* PROCEDURE F AS IN BACKTRACK1 */
        DO I = 1 TO N;
            GET LIST (W(I), V(I));
        END;
        GET LIST (TOT);
        WEIGHT(1), VAL(1) = 0; M(1) = 1;
        WEIGHT(2) = W(1); VAL(2) = V(1); M(2) = 1; I = 2;
```

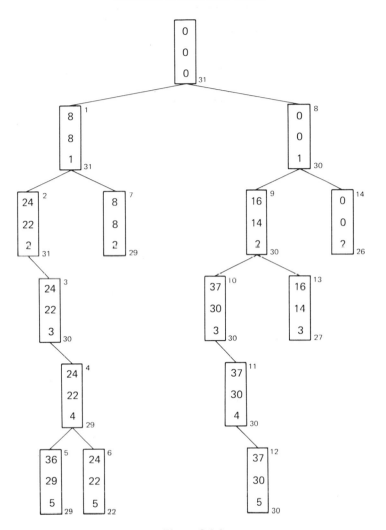

**Figure 3.4.4**

```
DO  WHILE  (I ¬ = 0);
   IF  M(I) = N  THEN  DO;
      IF  VAL(I) > Y  THEN  DO;
         Y = VAL(I);
         /* A NEW KNAPSACK FILLING HAS BEEN FOUND;
            NOW THE CORRESPONDING BRANCH IS PRINTED */
         M(I) = −M(I); PUT LIST ('THE BEST FILLING SO
             FAR IS');
         DO J = 1 TO I;
            IF  M(J) < 0  THEN PUT LIST (WEIGHT(J),
                VAL(J),  −M(J)) SKIP;
         END;
      END;
```

```
                        I = I - 1;
                    END;
                ELSE DO;
                    IF M(I) >= 0 THEN DO;
                        IF VAL(I) + F(TOT - WEIGHT(I),
                            +M(I)) < Y + 1 THEN I = I - 1;
                        ELSE DO;
                                WEIGHT(I + 1) = WEIGHT(I);
                                VAL(I + 1) = VAL(I);
                                M(I + 1) = M(I) + 1;
                                M(I) = -M(I); I = I + 1;
                                IF WEIGHT(I) + W(M(I)) <= TOT
                                THEN DO;
                                    AUX = M(I);
                                    WEIGHT(I + 1) = WEIGHT
                                    (I) + W(AUX);
                                    VAL(I + 1) = VAL(I) +
                                    V(AUX);
                                    M(I + 1) = AUX;
                                    I = I + 1;
                                        END;
                            END;
                            END;
                        ELSE I = I - 1;
                END;
            END; END;
        END BACKTRACK2;
```

For the input given in Fig. 3.4.1, "Backtrack2" proceeds just like "Backtrack1" but also prints

```
THE BEST FILLING SO FAR IS
(8, 8, 1) (24, 22, 2) (24, 27, 3) (24, 22, 4) (36, 29, 5)
THE BEST FILLING SO FAR IS
(0, 0, 1) (16, 14, 2) (37, 30, 3) (37, 30, 4) (37, 30, 5)
```

which corresponds to the "successful" branches in Fig. 3.4.4.

**Example 3.4.3** (Bounded Searching) The program "Bounded" represents a solution of the knapsack problem using a bounded search. The nodes of the solution tree that still must be examined are called *active* nodes. The solution tree is constructed beginning with an active node with value $(0, 0, 0)$ so that at any given time we work with that active node for which $u(k)$ is maximum. In order to distinguish the active nodes from the others, to speed the process of finding the active node $k$ with maximum $u(k)$, and to facilitate the removal of an active node $k$ with $u(k) < y + 1$ (which could not yield a better filling) from the set of active nodes, in the program "Bounded" the active nodes are stored as a chain with start pointer AK so that they occur in the chain with values decreasing to the value $u(k)$. It is clear that a still more efficient way of manipulating the active nodes would be to treat them as a sorted binary tree with a special pointer to the largest element in the tree, allowing immediate access to the largest element and permitting a considerably faster addition and deletion of nodes. To keep the program simple, however, a linear list is used instead. Upon obtaining a new, best yet, knapsack filling in order to be able to print how this filling was achieved, inverse storage is used for the solution tree, in which each node points to its predecessor in the solution tree. As the declaration for storage of the nodes of the solution tree we use **DCL** (TW(S), TV(S), M(S), U(0 : S), RC(0 : S), RI(S)) **FIXED BIN**;. For a node k, TW, TV, and M give the total weight, total value, and the number of objects already considered; U is the number u(k) = total value + f(TOT — total weight, m) and is carried along in order to avoid frequently calculating f; RC and RI serve as pointer fields for the chaining of active nodes and for the inverse storage to state the predecessor of k.

The choice of S is difficult since the number of nodes to occur in the tree of solutions is hard to predict. In the following program the choice of S = N * N + 1 is used. All storage locations not currently needed for nodes of the tree are chained together with start pointer AS and end pointer ES. RC is used for this purpose and thus plays a dual role.

```
BOUNDED: PROC OPTIONS (MAIN);
        DCL (N, S) FIXED BIN; GET LIST (N); S = N * N + 1;
        BEGIN; DCL (TW(S), TV(S), M(S), U(O:S), RC(O:S),
                RI(S)) FIXED BIN;
            DCL (W(N), V(N), TOT, I, Y, AS, ES, AC, P, Q, POS,
                    AUX) FIXED BIN;
            FIND: PROCEDURE (T) RETURNS (FIXED BIN);
                /* THIS PROCEDURE DELIVERS THE ADDRESS OF THE LAST
                    NODE K IN THE CHAIN OF ACTIVE NODES WITH U(K)
                    >= T > 0 AND DELIVERS 0 IF NO SUCH ACTIVE
                    NODE EXISTS */
                DCL (T, POS) FIXED BIN;
                IF U(AC) < T THEN RETURN (0);
                        ELSE DO;
                                POS = AC;
                                DO WHILE (U(RC(POS)) >= T);
                                POS = RC(POS);
                                END; RETURN (POS);
                        END;
            END FIND;
            /* NOTE THAT U(0) = 0 THROUGHOUT PROGRAM EXECUTION */
            /* HERE THE DECLARATION OF THE PROCEDURE F(T, M) AS
                DEFINED IN BACKTRACK1 IS REQUIRED */
            DCL ERROR ENTRY (FIXED DEC(1));
            DO I = 1 TO N: GET LIST (W(I), V(I)); END; GET LIST (TOT);
            DO I = 1 TO S - 1; RC(I) = I + 1; END;
            AS = 1; ES = S; Y, U(0), RC(0), RC(S) = 0;
            /* NOW THE INPUT HAS BEEN READ AND A LIST OF AVAILABLE
                SPACE HAS BEEN CREATED. SINCE SO FAR NO FILLING
                OF THE KNAPSACK HAS BEEN FOUND THE BOUND Y IS 0.
                NOW THE ROOT OF THE SOLUTION TREE IS ESTABLISHED */
```

```
P = AS; AS = RC(AS);
TW(P), TV(P), M(P), RC(P), RI(P) = 0;
U(P) = F(+TOT, 0); AC = P;
/* THE CHAIN OF ACTIVE NODES AT THIS POINT CONSISTS
   OF A SINGLE ELEMENT; IT WILL BE EXAMINED NOW
   UNTIL IT IS EMPTY */
DO WHILE (AC ¬ = 0);
     Q = AC; /* NOW TEST WHETHER NEW FILLING IS OBTAINED;
                 IF THIS IS THE CASE IT IS THE BEST
                 FILLING SO FAR AND SUITABLE INFORMATION
                 IS PRINTED */
   IF M(Q) = N THEN DO;
     Y = TV(Q); /* NEW BOUND */ PUT LIST (Y);
     DO WHILE (Q ¬ = 0);
        PUT LIST (TW(Q), TV(Q), M(Q)); Q = RI(Q);
     END;
     /* NOW ALL NODES K WITH U(K) < Y + 1 ARE
        REMOVED FROM CHAIN OF ACTIVE NODES AND THE
        CORRESPONDING MEMORY LOCATIONS ARE ADDED TO
        THE LIST OF AVAILABLE SPACE */
     POS = FIND (Y + 1);
     RC(ES) = RC(POS);
     IF POS = 0 THEN AC = 0; ELSE RC(POS) = 0;
                     END;
                 ELSE DO;
     /* THE FIRST NODE IS REMOVED FROM LIST OF ACTIVE
        NODES AND ITS UP TO TWO SUCCESSORS ARE ADDED
        TO THE LIST OF ACTIVE NODES */
   AC = RC(AC); RC(ES) = Q; RC(Q) = 0;
   IF TW(Q) + W(M(Q) + 1) < = TOT THEN DO;
   /* THEN THE LEFT SUCCESSOR CAN BE ADDED TO ACTIVE
      LIST */
   P = AS; AS = RC(AS); IF AS = ES THEN CALL ERROR (1);
   TW(P) = TW(Q) + W(M(Q) + 1);
   TV(P) = TV(Q) + V(M(Q) + 1);
   M(P) = M(Q) + 1;
   RI(P) = Q; U(P) = U(Q);
   /* THE NEW NODE CAN BE ADDED AS FIRST ELEMENT
      TO ACTIVE LIST */ RC(P) = AC; AC = P; END;
   /* NOW THE RIGHT SUCCESSOR IS CONSIDERED */
   AUX = TV(Q) + F(TOT − TW(Q), M(Q) + 1);
   IF AUX > = Y + 1 THEN DO;
      /* THEN THE RIGHT SUCCESSOR COULD LEAD TO
         AN OPTIMUM */
      P = AS; AS = RC(AS); IF AS = ES THEN CALL
         ERROR (1);
      TW(P) = TW(Q); TV(P) = TV(Q); M(P) = M(Q) + 1;
      RI(P) = Q; U(P) = AUX; RC(P) = 0;
      POS = FIND (+AUX);
      IF POS = 0 THEN DO; RC(P) = AC; AC = P; END;
                 ELSE DO; RC(P) = RC(POS); RC(POS) = P;
                 END; END; END;
        END;
     END;
END BOUNDED;
```

Given input corresponding to Fig. 3.4.1, the program "Bounded" produces nodes of the solution tree shown in Fig. 3.4.5. The number written at the upper right of the nodes gives the order in which the nodes are produced; the number at the lower right is the value u(k) as in Fig. 3.4.4.

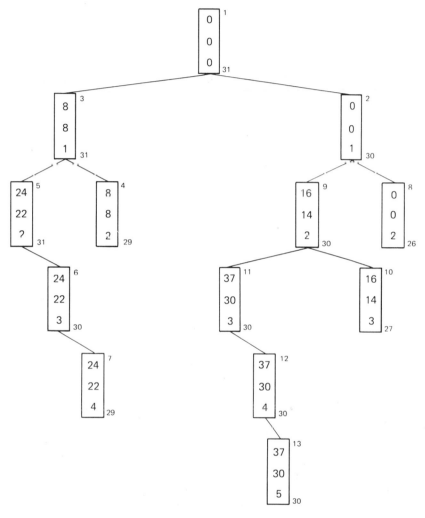

**Figure 3.4.5**

Compare Fig. 3.4.5 carefully with Fig. 3.4.4. Nodes 5 and 6 of Fig. 3.4.4 do not appear in Fig. 3.4.5. As soon as node 7 of Fig. 3.4.5 is reached, we go on to node 2 whose u(k) is greater and which is now therefore "more promising" (more likely to lead to success). The bounded search proves in many cases to be significantly better than the backtracking method for large n.

**Example 3.4.4** (Heuristic Search) For the definition of heuristic search we consider a generalized knapsack problem. Let there be given as input a sequence of numbers n, $w_1$, $v_1$, $w'_1$, $v'_1$, . . . , $w_n$, $v_n$, $w'_n$, $v'_n$, TOT. The values n, TOT, $w_i$, and $v_i$ have the same meaning as before; however, $w'_i$, $v'_i$ represent *alternatives* $d'_i$ for the object $d_i$ as follows: at the ith step of filling the knapsack either the object $d_i$ with value $v_i$ and weight $w_i$ or the object $d'_i$ with value $v'_i$ and weight $w'_i$ should be put into the knapsack.[9]

For simplicity we assume

$$\frac{v_1}{w_1} \geqslant \frac{v_2}{w_2} \geqslant \cdots \geqslant \frac{v_n}{w_n} \text{ and } \frac{v'_1}{w'_1} \geqslant \frac{v'_2}{w'_2} \geqslant \cdots \geqslant \frac{v'_n}{w'_n}.$$

Just like the knapsack problem, this problem can be approached using a solution tree. The root has the value (0, 0, 0) and a node with value (weight, value, m) has a potential left successor (weight $+ w_{m+1}$, value $+ v_{m+1}$, m $+$ 1) and a potential right successor (weight $+ w'_{m+1}$, value $+ v'_{m+1}$, m $+$ 1).

For the function f(t, m) to eliminate nodes that are no longer relevant, we use

$$f(t, m) = \begin{cases} 0 & \text{if } m = n \text{ or if } t = 0 \\ \text{floor}\left(\max\left\{\frac{t \times v_{m+1}}{w_{m+1}}, \frac{t \times v'_{m+1}}{w'_{m+1}}\right\}\right) & \text{otherwise.} \end{cases}$$

The bound u(k) is defined as before but now uses the new definition of f.

The solution tree for the values shown in Fig. 3.4.6 is given in Fig. 3.4.7. The numbers at the lower right of the nodes again give u(k).

| i | 1 | 2 | 3 | 4 | |
|---|---|---|---|---|---|
| $w_i$ | 10 | 30 | 10 | 15 | |
| $v_i$ | 25 | 60 | 18 | 25 | n = 4, TOT = 65 |
| $w'_i$ | 25 | 10 | 5 | 10 | |
| $v'_i$ | 65 | 25 | 5 | 8 | |

**Figure 3.4.6**

In backtracking, the solution tree is searched branch by branch from left to right, and in the bounded search the active node with maximum u(k) is always used as the next node. When using the heuristic search we proceed branch by branch but do not search the branches left to right; rather, if k' and k'' are successors of the current node, we proceed next to k' if u(k') $\geqslant$ u(k'') and to k'' if u(k') $<$ u(k'').

The numbering of the nodes in Fig. 3.4.7 shows the order in which they are considered in the heuristic search. The maximum value y = 133 is already found in node 5. The programming of the heuristic search is analogous to that for backtracking.

**Example 3.4.5** (Queens Problem) An *n-chessboard* is a square arrangement of $n^2$ squares in n rows and n columns. A queen is attacking another queen if they are both on the same row, column, or diagonal on an n-chessboard. Figure 3.4.8(a) shows a 5-chessboard, in which queen 1 is attacking queen 2 and queen 3 but queen 2 and queen 3 are not attacking each other.

---

[9]For $w'_i = v'_i = 0$ we have the original knapsack problem.

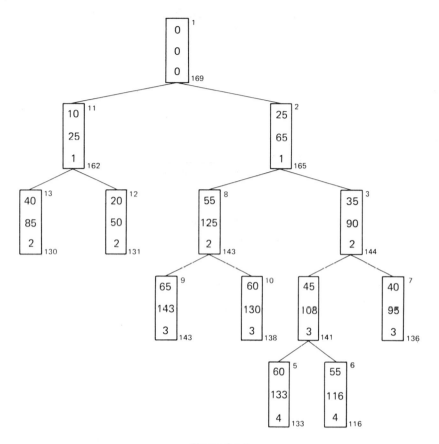

**Figure 3.4.7**

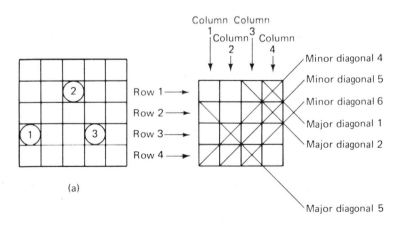

**Figure 3.4.8**

In an n-chessboard the n rows are numbered from top to bottom; the n columns, left to right; the $(2n - 1)$ *major diagonals*, from top right to bottom left; and the *minor diagonals*, from top left to bottom right. In Fig. 3.4.8(a) we find, for example, queen 1 in row 4, column 1, major diagonal 8, and minor diagonal 4. The numbering of rows, columns, and diagonals of a 4-chessboard is indicated in Fig. 3.4.8(b).

The queens problem for an n-chessboard is to find an arrangement (if such exists) of n queens on the chessboard so that no queen is attacking any other queen.

This problem falls in the general case described in Def. 3.4.1. We consider $(0, 0)$ to be the initial situation. Each situation is of the form $(R, C)$, where $1 \leqslant R, C \leqslant n$, and signifies that in row R and column C a (additional) queen is placed. Any situation $(n, C)$ is an end situation. Any situation $(R, C)$ with $R < n$ has the n successor situations $(R + 1, i)$ for $i = 1, 2, \ldots, n$. The solution of the queens problem consists of finding an end situation attainable from $(0, 0)$ that together with its predecessor situations in the solution tree defines an arrangement of n queens on the chessboard in which no queen is attacking another. A part of a solution tree for $n = 4$ is shown in Fig. 3.4.9(a).

The heavily drawn branch of Fig. 3.4.9(a) defines the arrangement of four queens shown in Fig. 3.4.9(b), which gives a solution to the queens problem for $n = 4$.

In the following program the queens problem is solved by backtracking. The branches of the solution tree are examined from left to right (in preorder).

A sequentially stored stack, corresponding to the declaration **DCL** (R(N * N), C(N * N)) **FIXED BIN**;,[10] contains all roots of the subtrees still to be processed; it also

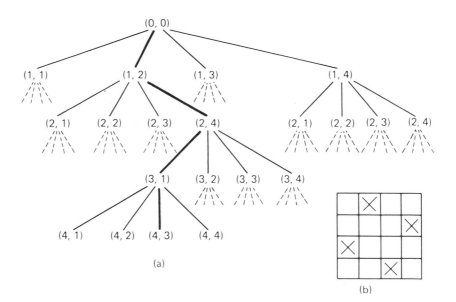

Figure 3.4.9

---

[10] Since the technique is only useful for small n anyway, the N * N storage requirement is not unreasonable.

contains all nodes of the branch leading to the node currently under consideration. (In order to distinguish this node, the first component is taken to be negative.)

For a node k at the top of the stack with $\omega k = (R, C)$ before additional n successors are added to the stack, it is necessary to check whether the queen represented by k is already attacking another queen, i.e., whether in column C or in the major diagonal through C (with number $R - C + n$) or in the minor diagonal through C (with number $R + C - 1$) there is already a queen. For this only three steps are necessary if we use auxiliary arrays declared by **DCL** (S(N), MD(2 * N — 1), SD (2 * N — 1)) **FIXED BIN**;, where S(I), MD(I), SD(I) indicate with the value 0 an unoccupied column, major diagonal, or minor diagonal and with the value 1 an already occupied column, major diagonal, or minor diagonal.

```
QUEENS: PROC OPTIONS (MAIN);
    DCL N FIXED BIN; GET LIST (N);
    BEGIN;
        DCL (R(N * N), C(N * N), S(N), MD(2 * N — 1),
            SD(2 * N — 1), I, P, ROW) FIXED BIN;
        S, MD, SD = 0;
        /* INITIALLY THE N NODES IN THE STACK GIVE THE N
           POSSIBLE POSITIONS OF A QUEEN IN ROW 1 */
        DO I = 1 TO N;
            R(I) = 1; C(I) = N + 1 — I;
        END;
        P = N;
        DO WHILE (P ¬ = 0);
            IF R(P) < 0 THEN DO;
                        /* THE NODES ALREADY CONSIDERED
                           ARE REMOVED FROM THE STACK.
                           S, MD, SD ARE ADJUSTED */
                        ROW = —R(P); S(C(P)) = 0;
                        MD(ROW — C(P) + N) = 0;
                        SD(ROW + C(P) — 1) = 0;
                        P = P — 1;
                END;
                /* NOW A TEST IS MADE WHETHER
                   THE NODE AT THE TOP OF THE
                   STACK REPRESENTS A POSSIBLE
                   POSITION FOR THE QUEEN */
            ELSE IF (S(C(P)) = 1) | (MD(R(P) — C(P)
                + N) = 1) | (SD(R(P) + C(P) — 1)
                = 1) THEN P = P — 1;
                /* IF THE NODE REPRESENTS A VALID
                   POSITION THEN S, MD, AND SD
                   ARE ADJUSTED ACCORDINGLY */
            ELSE DO;
                S(C(P)) = 1; MD(R(P) — C(P) +
                N) = 1; SD(R(P) + C(P) — 1) = 1;
                /* ALSO THE NODE IS MARKED
                   "CONSIDERED" */
                R(P) = —R(P);
                /* A CHECK IS MADE WHETHER THIS
                   IS A SOLUTION */
```

```
                                    IF −R(P) = N THEN DO;
                                       DO I = 1 TO P;
                                          IF R(I) < 0 THEN PUT LIST
                                          (−R(I), C(I));
                                       END;
                                       GOTO FIN;
                                    END;
                                    /*  N SUCCESSOR NODES ARE ADDED
                                        TO THE STACK */
                                    DO I = 1 TO N;
                                       R(P + I) = −R(P) + 1;
                                       C(P + I) = N + 1 − I;
                                    END;
                                    P = P + N;
                           END;
                    END;
                    PUT LIST ('NO SOLUTION FOR N =', N);
             END;
         FIN: END;
```

*Remarks and References*

*Backtracking* and *heuristic searching* are illustrated with examples in Maurer [2]. For *bounded searching*, see Weinberg [1]; for the knapsack problem, see Kolesar [1].

## Exercises

**3.4.1**   Write a program for the heuristic search in Example 3.4.4.

**3.4.2**   Modify the program for solving the queens problem in Example 3.4.5 so that a stack of n elements (instead of $n^2$ elements) is used.

**3.4.3**   Given as input is a number n. Write a program using the backtracking technique which prints all permutations $i_1, i_2, \ldots, i_n$ of the n numbers $1, 2, \ldots, n$ which can be obtained with three stacks A, B, C as explained in Exercise 2.2.2.

**3.4.4**   Let the operation $X \longrightarrow Y$ for arbitrary stacks X, Y be defined as in Exercise 2.2.2. As input, let there be given three numbers n, m, and t. Four stacks A, B, C, D are given, B, C, and D are initially empty, and A contains the numbers $1, 2, \ldots, n$ with 1 at the top of the stack. Write a program which determines all permutations of numbers $i_1, i_2, \ldots, i_m$ in the stack D which can be obtained by a total of t of the operations $A \longrightarrow B, A \longrightarrow C, B \longrightarrow D, C \longrightarrow D$.

**3.4.5**   Consider the two functions $f_0(j) = 2j + 1$ and $f_1(j) = 3j − 1$. Two whole numbers $m_1$ and n where $0 < m_1 < n$ are given. Write a program that determines whether there exists a sequence $x_1, x_2, \ldots, x_t$ ($x_i = 0$ or $x_i = 1$) such that

(a)   $\sum_{i=1}^{k} x_i \leqslant \dfrac{k}{2}$      for every $k \leqslant t$

(b)   For $m_{i+1} = f_{x_i}(m_i)$ $(1 \leqslant i \leqslant t)$ the equality $m_{t+1} = n$ holds.

**Example:** For $m_1 = 1$, $n = 89$ we have the solution $x_1 = 0$, $x_2 = 0$, $x_3 = 0$, $x_4 = 1$, $x_5 = 0$ since $f_0(1) = 3$, $f_0(3) = 7$, $f_0(7) = 15$, $f_1(15) = 44$, and $f_0(44) = 89$.

**3.4.6** Given as input are two whole numbers n and m followed by m number pairs $(i_1, j_1)$, $(i_2, j_2)$, ..., $(i_m, j_m)$ where $1 \leqslant i_k$, $j_k \leqslant n$. Each pair $(i_k, j_k)$ specifies that there exists a direct road connection (i.e., with no city in between) between cities $i_k$ and $j_k$. Write a program to determine a route that passes through every city exactly once and returns to the city from which the tour was begun. (Such a route is called a *Hamiltonian circuit*.) There are several possible algorithms for the solution to this problem. A systematic search of all possibilities using backtracking is often sufficient if only a "suitable" choice of the next city is always made. Such a suitable choice can be made as follows: let x be an arbitrary city. $A_1(x)$ denotes the number of cities which have not yet been visited which can be reached directly from x; $A_2(x)$ denotes the number of not yet visited cities which can be reached from x by passing through exactly one other not yet visited city. For each city y, we always choose as the next city that city x for which $A_1(x)$ is minimal. If there are several cities x and x' with $A_1(x) = A_1(x')$, then we choose a city x for which $A_2(x)$ is minimal. Test the program using a small example ($n \leqslant 8$) for which it is known that a Hamiltonian circuit actually does exist.

**3.4.7** Use the program developed in Exercise 3.4.6 to determine a "knight's tour" on a chessboard. In a knight's tour, the knight begins on any arbitrary square, visits every other square exactly once, and then returns to the starting point.

## Section 3.5   Trees and Backus Systems

In this section it will be shown that certain transformations on character strings, called *translations*, can be defined and applied in a natural and systematic way by using Backus systems.

**Definition 3.5.1** (Simple Backus System) A word w consists of variables and terminal symbols. Let L(w) denote the total number of terminal symbols and variables in a word w. A Backus system is said to be *simple* if conditions a through c are satisfied:

(a)   No alternative of any variable contains a variable more than once.
(b)   For each alternative a, $L(a) \geqslant 1$.
(c)   For no variable A can any substitutions of variables be made and obtain the word consisting only of A.

Condition a is necessary so that later we can easily combine two parallel substitution processes; condition b assures that beginning with a word w we shall never obtain from the substitution process a word w' with $L(w') < L(w)$; and condition c guarantees that in the substitution process the same word will not arise more than once.

A *Backus pair* consists of two simple Backus systems in which a combination of the substitution processes is defined.

**Definition 3.5.2** (Backus Pair) Two simple Backus systems B and $\bar{B}$ are called a *Backus pair* $P = (B, \bar{B})$ if the productions of B are written as

$$v_1 ::= w_{11} | w_{12} | \cdots | w_{1n_1}$$
$$v_2 ::= w_{21} | w_{22} | \cdots | w_{2n_2}$$
$$\cdot$$
$$\cdot$$
$$\cdot$$
$$v_m ::= w_{m1} | w_{m2} | \cdots | w_{mn_m}$$

and the productions of $\bar{B}$ are written as

$$\overline{v_1} ::= \overline{w_{11}} | \overline{w_{12}} | \cdots | \overline{w_{1n_1}}$$
$$\overline{v_2} ::= \overline{w_{21}} | \overline{w_{22}} | \cdots | \overline{w_{2n_2}}$$
$$\cdot$$
$$\cdot$$
$$\cdot$$
$$\overline{v_m} ::= \overline{w_{m1}} | \overline{w_{m2}} | \cdots | \overline{w_{mn_m}}$$

so that for each i, j $(1 \leqslant i \leqslant m, 1 \leqslant j \leqslant n_i)$ the variables in $\overline{w_{ij}}$ can be obtained from the variables in $w_{ij}$ by replacing each variable $v_t$ by the *corresponding* variable $\overline{v_t}$.

In a Backus system B a variable X defines a set of words B(X). Similarly in a Backus pair $P = (B, \bar{B})$, a variable pair $(X, \bar{X})$ (where X belongs to B, $\bar{X}$ to $\bar{B}$) defines a set of word pairs $P(X, \bar{X})$. To define $P(X, \bar{X})$ an auxiliary set M of word pairs is needed. Each word of the first or second component of a pair of M consists of terminal symbols and variables that are *marked* with one of the numbers 0, 1, 2, .... The marking of a variable is written at the upper right of the variable so that for example $v_i^t$ denotes the variable $v_i$ marked t.

The set of word pairs $P(X, \bar{X})$ is defined by a, b, and c:

(a)   M contains the word pair $(X^0, \bar{X}^0)$.

(b)   If M contains the word pair $(w, \bar{w})$ and if the first variable from the left in w is $v_i^t$, then M also contains each pair $(z, \bar{z})$ that is obtained from $(w, \bar{w})$ by replacing $v_i^t$ in w by $w_{ij}$ and replacing $\overline{v_i^t}$ in $\overline{w}$ by $\overline{w_{ij}}$ $(1 \leqslant j \leqslant n_i)$, where the variables in $w_{ij}$ and $\overline{w_{ij}}$ are marked with s and s is a number different from any other marking already used. (The marking intuitively serves to unite variables added in the same "substitution step.")

(c)   $P(X, \bar{X})$ consists of all word pairs of M that contain no variables.

**Definition 3.5.3** (Translation) If we let $\sum^*$ denote the set of all words built up of terminal symbols, then the relation T over $\sum^* \times \sum^*$ is called a *translation* since each word y in the domain of T is associated with (at least) one[11] word $\bar{y}$ in the range of T because of the relation $(y, \bar{y}) \in T$. Every such word y is said to be *translated* into a word $\bar{y}$.

---

[11] An interesting case arises when T is a function and each y is associated with exactly one $\bar{y} = T(y)$.

Notice that a Backus pair $P = (B, \bar{B})$ and a variable pair $(X, \bar{X})$ define a translation $P(X, \bar{X})$.

**Example 3.5.1** Consider the Backus system B with productions

$\langle SAE \rangle \quad ::= \langle Term \rangle \,|\, \langle Term \rangle \langle Addop \rangle \langle SAE \rangle$

$\langle Addop \rangle \quad ::= + \,|\, -$

$\langle Term \rangle \quad ::= \langle Factor \rangle \,|\, \langle Factor \rangle \langle Multop \rangle \langle Term \rangle$

$\langle Multop \rangle \quad ::= * \,|\, \div$

$\langle Factor \rangle \quad ::= \langle Num \rangle \,|\, (\langle SAE \rangle)$

$\langle Num \rangle \quad ::= \langle Dig \rangle . \,|\, \langle Dig \rangle \langle Num \rangle$

$\langle Dig \rangle \quad ::= 0 \,|\, 1 \,|\, 2 \,|\, 3 \,|\, 4 \,|\, 5 \,|\, 6 \,|\, 7 \,|\, 8 \,|\, 9$

and the Backus system $\bar{B}$ with the productions

$\langle PFE \rangle \quad ::= \langle Term \rangle \,|\, \langle Term \rangle \langle PFE \rangle \langle Addop \rangle$

$\langle Addop \rangle \quad ::= + \,|\, -$

$\langle Term \rangle \quad ::= \langle Factor \rangle \,|\, \langle Factor \rangle \langle Term \rangle \langle Multop \rangle$

$\langle Multop \rangle \quad ::= * \,|\, \div$

$\langle Factor \rangle \quad ::= \langle Num \rangle \,|\, \langle PFE \rangle$

$\langle Num \rangle \quad ::= \langle Dig \rangle . \,|\, \langle Dig \rangle \langle Num \rangle$

$\langle Dig \rangle \quad ::= 0 \,|\, 1 \,|\, 2 \,|\, 3 \,|\, 4 \,|\, 5 \,|\, 6 \,|\, 7 \,|\, 8 \,|\, 9$

The systems B and $\bar{B}$ are simple and $P = (B, \bar{B})$ is a Backus pair. The set M of pairs of words defined as in Def. 3.5.2(a) and (b) contains, for example, the following pairs of words:

$(\langle SAE \rangle^0, \langle PFE \rangle^0)$

$(\langle Term \rangle^1 \langle Addop \rangle^1 \langle SAE \rangle^1, \langle Term \rangle^1 \langle PFE \rangle^1 \langle Addop \rangle^1)$

$(\langle Factor \rangle^2 \langle Multop \rangle^2 \langle Term \rangle^2 \langle Addop \rangle^1 \langle SAE \rangle^1,$
$\quad \langle Factor \rangle^2 \langle Term \rangle^2 \langle Multop \rangle^2 \langle PFE \rangle^1 \langle Addop \rangle^1)$

$(\langle Dig \rangle^4 . \langle Multop \rangle^2 \langle Term \rangle^2 \langle Addop \rangle^1 \langle SAE \rangle^1,$
$\quad \langle Dig \rangle^4 . \langle Term \rangle^2 \langle Multop \rangle^2 \langle PFE \rangle^1 \langle Addop \rangle^1)$

$(3. * 2. + 1., 3. 2. * 1. +)$

The set $P(\langle SAE \rangle, \langle PFE \rangle)$ of pairs of words contains, for example,

$(3. * 2. + 1., 3. 2. * 1. +)$

$(3. + (2. + 6.), 3. 2. 6. + +)$

$((2. + 3.) * (1. + 2.), 2. 3. + 1. 2. + *),$

etc. Note that the translation $T = P(\langle SAE \rangle, \langle PFE \rangle)$ consists of exactly those pairs of words $(y, \bar{y})$ for which y is a simple arithmetic expression and $\bar{y}$ is the corresponding parenthesis-free expression. To determine for a given simple arithmetic expression y the corresponding parenthesis-free expression it thus suffices to determine that $\bar{y}$ for which $(y, \bar{y}) \in P(\langle SAE \rangle, \langle PFE \rangle)$.

This is a special case of a general principle.

**Definition 3.5.4** (Translation Problem) Let T be a translation. The *translation problem* is, for given $y \in$ domain $(T)$, to determine a $\bar{y} \in$ range $(T)$ such that $(y, \bar{y}) \in T$.

If the translation can be defined by a Backus pair, i.e., if there is a Backus pair $P = (B, \bar{B})$ and a variable pair $(X, \bar{X})$ as in Def. 3.5.2 with $T = P(X, \bar{X})$, then the translation problem can be handled by searching a solution tree (see Def. 3.4.1). Consider $(X, \bar{X})$ as the initial situation and each situation $(z, \bar{z})$ with $L(z) \geqslant L(y)$ as an end situation. For each situation $(w, \bar{w})$ we obtain several successor situations by the process of substituting variables as described in Def. 3.5.2(b).

In solving the translation problem it suffices to start with $(X, \bar{X})$ and find an end situation with first component y. The second component then represents the desired translation $\bar{y}$ of y.

In the following discussion the solution tree will be manipulated using backtracking.

The following considerations may be made to accelerate the search of the solution tree:

*Consideration 1:*   A node k with $\omega k = (w, \bar{w})$ is eliminated if the beginning of w, which consists of terminal symbols, does not agree with the beginning of y.

*Consideration 2:*   If k is a node with $\omega k = (w, \bar{w}) = (w_1 v_i^t w_2, \bar{w})$, where $v_i^t$ is the first variable (from the left) in w, and if $y = w_1 a_1 y_2$, where $a_1$ is a terminal symbol, then we consider as successor nodes of k only those nodes that correspond to the alternatives of $v_i$ with the following property: by the substitution of variables at least one word is obtained from $v_i$ with first symbol $a_1$.[12]

**Example 3.5.2** (Translation of Expressions) For the Backus pair of Example 3.5.1 using consideration 2, the nodes of the solution tree will be examined from left to right as shown in Fig. 3.5.1.

A node k with $\omega k = (w, \bar{w})$ is represented by $\boxed{\dfrac{w}{\bar{w}}}$ .

**Example 3.5.3** (Translation Using a Backus Pair) A program is to be constructed that when supplied with a Backus pair $P = (B, \bar{B})$ and a pair of variables $(X, \bar{X})$ will

---

[12]The idea stated here is the basis of the introduction of LL(1) systems. In the LL(t) systems not just one symbol $a_1$ but t symbols $a_1, a_2, \ldots, a_t$ are considered. One can easily give an algorithm that for given $a_1$ and $v_i$ determines whether from $v_i$ a word with first symbol $a_1$ can be obtained.

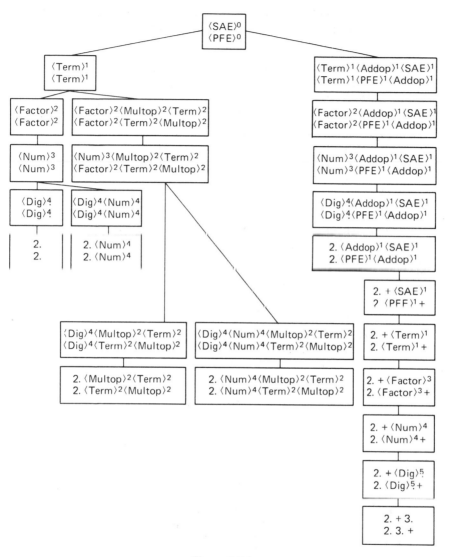

**Figure 3.5.1**

determine for each y in B(X) a $\bar{y}$ such that $(y, \bar{y}) \in P(X, \bar{X})$. Thus, the program can be used to solve an arbitrary translation problem if such a problem can be formulated by means of a Backus pair.

All sequences of symbols used in the program will be considered data of type **CHARACTER**. Anything between angular brackets will be considered a variable (unmarked or marked) of the Backus pair. Thus $\langle SAE \rangle$ and $\langle SAE, 1 \rangle$ will both denote the variable $\langle SAE \rangle$ of the Backus pair of Example 3.5.1, the second construction indicating $\langle SAE \rangle^1$ i.e., the variable $\langle SAE \rangle$ marked with the number 1.

It is assumed that the Backus pair has already been stored appropriately and that a number of function procedures as follows have already been defined.

L: **PROCEDURE** (W) **FIXED BIN**; /* W of type **CHAR** */
/* delivers total number of terminal symbols and
variables in W; e.g., L('39 ⟨X, 2⟩ $ ⟨Y, 3⟩ ') = 5, since
there are two variables ⟨X, 2⟩ and ⟨Y, 3⟩ and three
terminal symbols 3, 9, and $ */
FIRSTVAR: **PROCEDURE** (W) **CHAR** (*); /* W of type **CHAR** */
/* delivers first variable in W, e.g., FIRSTVAR('39 ⟨X, 2⟩
$ ⟨Y, 3⟩ ') = ' ⟨X, 2⟩ ' */
VAR: **PROCEDURE** (W) **CHAR** (*); /* W of type **CHAR** */
/* W must be a marked variable; delivers unmarked
version of that variable; e.g., VAR(' ⟨X, 2⟩ ') =
' ⟨X⟩ ' */
MAR: **PROCEDURE** (W) **FIXED BIN**; /* W of type **CHAR** */
/* W is a marked variable; delivers marking, e.g.,
MAR(' ⟨X, 2⟩ ') = 2 */
MARK: **PROCEDURE** (W, I) **CHAR** (*);
/* W of type **CHAR**, I of type **FIXED BIN**; delivers a
sequence of symbols obtained from W by marking all
variables of W with the number I; e.g., MARK('39 ⟨X⟩
$ ⟨Y⟩', 2) = '39 ⟨X, 2⟩ $ ⟨Y, 2⟩ ' */
CORR: **PROCEDURE** (W) **CHAR** (*); /* W of type **CHAR** */
/* W must be an unmarked variable of B; delivers
corresponding variable of $\overline{B}$; e.g., CORR(' ⟨SAE⟩ ') =
' ⟨PFE⟩ ' for Example 3.5.1 */
TERMINALS: **PROCEDURE** (W) **CHAR** (*); /* W of type **CHAR** */
/* delivers that part of W up to but excluding the
first variable in W; e.g., TERMINALS ('39 ⟨X, 2⟩ $
⟨Y, 2⟩ ') = '39' */
INITIAL: **PROCEDURE** (W, Z) **BIT** (1); /* W, Z of type **CHAR** */
/* delivers '1'B if Z begins with W, '0'B otherwise */
NALT: **PROCEDURE** (W) **FIXED BIN**; /* W of type **CHAR** */
/* delivers number of alternatives for variable W;
e.g., NALT(' ⟨Dig⟩ ') = 10 in Example 3.5.1 */
ALT: **PROCEDURE** (W, I) **CHAR** (*); /* W of type **CHAR**, I of type
**FIXED BIN** */    /* delivers ith alternative for
variable W of B; e.g., ALT(' ⟨SAE⟩',2) = ' ⟨Term⟩
⟨Addop⟩ ⟨SAE⟩ ' in Example 3.5.1 */
ALTQ: **PROCEDURE** (W, I) **CHAR** (*); /* analogous to ALT, but for
W variable of $\overline{B}$, e.g., ALTQ('⟨PFE⟩', 2) = '⟨Term⟩
⟨PFE⟩ ⟨Addop⟩' in Example 3.5.1 */
POSS: **PROCEDURE** (B, W) **BIT** (1);
/* B of type **CHAR** (1), W of type **CHAR** (*); delivers
'1' B if starting with W and by replacing variables,
a sequence of symbols can be obtained starting with
terminal symbol B, e.g.,
POSS('*', '⟨Dig⟩') = '0'B and
POSS('(', '⟨SAE⟩') = '1'B for Example 3.5.1 */

```
REPL: PROCEDURE (W, V, Z) CHAR (*); /* W, V, Z of type CHAR */
      /* delivers the sequence of symbols obtained from
      W by replacing the marked variable V by the sequence
      of symbols Z, e.g., REPL('39⟨X, 2⟩ $ ⟨Y, 4⟩', '⟨X, 2⟩',
      '4⟨A, 6⟩ 5') = '394 ⟨A, 6⟩ 5$ ⟨Y, 4⟩' */
X: PROCEDURE CHAR (*); /* delivers starting variable of B, e.g.,
      X = '⟨SAE⟩' for Example 3.5.1 */
XQ: PROCEDURE CHAR (*); /* delivers starting variable of B̄ */
```

In the following program the solution tree of the given translation problem will be searched systematically branch by branch from left to right. A stack declared by **DCL** (D(M), DQ(M)) **CHAR** (K) **VARYING**; will be used. A pair (D(I), DQ(I)) represents a currently obtained situation, starting with a pair of variables (X, X̄). The roots of all subtrees of the solution tree that still have to be dealt with will be deposited in the stack.

```
DCL (D(M), DQ(M)) CHAR (K) VARYING; /* M AND K SUITABLE */
DCL (Y, VA, VAQ, AUX, AUX1, AUX2, AUXQ, A, Z, ZQ) CHAR
    (K) VARYING; DCL (P, I, MA, N, S) FIXED BIN;
GET LIST (Y); S = 1; /* S FOR MARKING THROUGHOUT */
D(1) = MARK(X, 0); DQ(1) = MARK(XQ, 0); P = 1;
/* NOW THE STACK CONTAINS THE ROOT OF THE SOLUTION TREE */
DO WHILE (P ¬ = 0);
    IF D(P) = Y THEN DO;
        PUT LIST ('THE TRANSLATION OF', Y, 'IS', DQ(P));
        STOP;    END;
    IF L(D(P)) = LENGTH(D(P)) /* THEN D(P) CONTAINS NO
        VARIABLES */ THEN DO; P = P − 1; END;
    ELSE DO;
        /*  D(P), DQ(P) REPRESENT A NODE OF THE SOLUTION
            TREE AND POSSIBLE SUCCESSORS HAVE TO BE ADDED;
            TO ELIMINATE SOME POSSIBILITIES A COMBINATION
            OF CONSIDERATIONS 1 AND 2 IS USED */
        A = FIRSTVAR(D(P)); VA = VAR(A); MA = MAR(A);
        /*  THE FIRST VARIABLE IN W (I.E., THE ONE TO BE
            REPLACED) IS VA WITH MARKING MA */
        Z  = D(P); ZQ = DQ(P); P = P − 1; N = NALT(VA);
        /*  THUS THERE ARE N POTENTIAL SUCCESSORS */
        DO I = N BY −1 TO 1;
            AUX = REPL(Z, A, MARK(ALT(VA, I), S));
            /* THIS IS FIRST COMPONENT OF POTENTIAL SUCCESSOR
                OF THE NODE (Z, ZQ); NOW IT IS TESTED WHETHER
                AUX CAN LEAD TO Y */
            IF (L(AUX) <= LENGTH(Y)) & (INITIAL(TERMINALS
                (AUX), Y)) THEN DO;
                IF L(AUX) = LENGTH(Y) THEN CALL STACK;
                ELSE IF POSS(SUBSTR(Y, LENGTH(TERMINALS(AUX))
                        + 1, 1), VAR(FIRSTVAR(AUX)))
                    THEN CALL STACK;
```

```
STACK: PROCEDURE;
       VAQ = CORR(VA);
       AUXQ = REPL(ZQ, MARK(VAQ, MA),
                   MARK(ALTQ(VAQ, I), S));
       P = P + 1; D(P) = AUX; DQ(P) = AUXQ;
END STACK;
     END;
END; S = S + 1;
   END; END;
PUT LIST (Y, 'HAS NO TRANSLATION');
```

**Example 3.5.4** (File Transformation) The Backus pair P = (B, B̄) described below defines the translation of *segments* of a *hierarchical file* into segments of a *linear file*. Intuitively a segment of a hierarchical file consists of a *segment name*, none or arbitrarily many additional segments, a *segment information item*, and a *segment number* in this order.[13] A corresponding segment in a linear file differs only in that the segments contained in a segment A are replaced by a *marking* (an asterisk in the following discussion) but are themselves placed after the segment number of A.

If in a segment X the abbreviations Nam X, Inf X, Num X denote the name, the information item, and the number of the segment X, respectively, then A, B, and C are segments of the hierarchical file and Ā, B̄, and C̄ are the corresponding (translated) segments of the linear file, where segments are enclosed by the symbol $\#$.

A = #Nam A, Inf A, Num A#
Ā = #Nam A, Inf A, Num A#
B = #Nam B, #Nam A, Inf A, Num A#, Inf B, Num B#
B̄ = #Nam B, *, Inf B, Num B##Nam A, Inf A, Num A#
C = #Nam C, #Nam B, #Nam A, Inf A, Num A#, #Nam D, Inf D, Num D#,
    Inf B, Num B#, #Nam E, Inf E, Num E#, Inf C, Num C#
C̄ = #Nam C, *, *, Inf C, Num C##Nam E, Inf E, Num E##Nam B, *,
    #Nam D, Inf D, Num D#, Inf B, Num B##Nam A, Inf A, Num A#

Thus, for example, C consists of the name Nam C, two segments B and E, the information item Inf C, and the number Num C. The segment B itself consists of the name Nam B, two segments A and D, the information item Inf B, and the number Num B. The segment E consists of the name Nam E, the information item Inf E, and the number Num E, etc.

The Backus system B defines the set of all segments of the hierarchical file by B(⟨s⟩); the Backus system B̄ defines the set of all segments of the linear file by B̄(⟨s⟩). The Backus pair P = (B, B̄) defines the translation of the hierarchical segments into the linear segments, while the Backus pair P′ = (B̄, B) defines the translation of the linear into the hierarchical segments.

B consists of the productions

⟨s⟩  ::= #⟨heading⟩, ⟨v⟩

⟨v⟩  ::= ⟨s⟩, ⟨v⟩|⟨Information⟩, ⟨number⟩#

---

[13]The designation *hierarchical* is based on the fact that a segment may contain further segments.

⟨Information⟩ ::= ⟨symbol⟩|⟨symbol⟩⟨Information⟩

⟨heading⟩ ::= ⟨alpha⟩|⟨alpha⟩⟨heading⟩

⟨number⟩ ::= ⟨Dig⟩|⟨Dig⟩⟨number⟩

⟨symbol⟩ ::= ⟨alpha⟩|⟨Dig⟩|⟨special symbol⟩

⟨alpha⟩ ::= A|B|C|D|E|F|G|H|I|J|K|L|M|N|O|P|Q|R|S|T|U|
V|W|X|Y|Z

⟨Dig⟩ ::= 0|1|2|3|4|5|6|7|8|9

⟨special symbol⟩ ::= .|:|+|−|×|÷|/|%|$|¢|!|?

$\bar{B}$ consists of exactly the same productions except instead of

⟨v⟩ ::= ⟨s⟩, ⟨v⟩|⟨Information⟩, ⟨number⟩#

$\bar{B}$ contains the production

⟨v⟩ ::= *, ⟨v⟩⟨s⟩|⟨Information⟩, ⟨number⟩#.

As an example, let $P(⟨s⟩, ⟨s⟩)$ contain the word pairs $(y, \bar{y})$, $(z, \bar{z})$, and $(w, \bar{w})$, where

$y =$ #AUSTRALIA, CONTINENT, 12300000#

$\bar{y} =$ #AUSTRALIA, CONTINENT, 12300000#

$z =$ #AUSTRALIA, #CANBERRA, CITY, 94000#, CONTINENT,
12300000#

$\bar{z} =$ #AUSTRALIA, *, CONTINENT, 12300000##CANBERRA, CITY,
94000#

$w =$ #NORTH AMERICA, #CANADA, #OTTAWA, CITY, 530000#,
COUNTRY, 22000000#, #USA, #WASHINGTON, CITY, 760000#,
COUNTRY, 204000000#, #MEXICO, #MEXICO CITY, CITY,
3500000#, COUNTRY, 49000000#, CONTINENT, 275000000#

$\bar{w} =$ #NORTH AMERICA, *, *, *, CONTINENT, 275000000##MEXICO,
*, COUNTRY, 49000000##MEXICO CITY, CITY, 3500000##USA,
*, COUNTRY, 204000000##WASHINGTON, CITY, 760000#
#CANADA, *, COUNTRY, 22000000##OTTAWA, CITY, 530000#

**Example 3.5.5** (Language Translation) The Backus pair $P = (B, \bar{B})$ in Fig. 3.5.2 defines a compiler for very simple Algol-60 programs into very simple assembler programs. For every Algol-60 program $y \in B(⟨Prog⟩)$, $\bar{y}$ with $(y, \bar{y}) \in P(⟨Prog⟩, ⟨Prog⟩)$ is the corresponding assembler program.

Productions of B

⟨Prog⟩ ::= **begin** ⟨Declarations⟩; ⟨Commands⟩ **end**
⟨Declarations⟩ ::= ⟨Dec⟩ | ⟨Dec⟩; ⟨Declarations⟩
⟨Dec⟩ ::= **integer** ⟨Name⟩
⟨Name⟩ ::= ⟨Alph⟩ | ⟨Alph⟩⟨Name⟩
⟨Alph⟩ ::= a|b|c|d|e|f|g|h|i|j|k|l|m|n|o|p|q|r|s|
 t|u|v|w|x|y|z|

⟨Commands⟩ ::= ⟨Command⟩ | ⟨Command⟩; ⟨Commands⟩
⟨Command⟩ ::= ⟨Name⟩: ⟨Com⟩
⟨Com⟩ ::= ⟨Assignment⟩ | ⟨If⟩ | ⟨Read⟩ | ⟨Print⟩
⟨Assignment⟩ ::= ⟨Name⟩ := ⟨Expression⟩
⟨Expression⟩ ::= ⟨Term⟩ | ⟨Term⟩⟨Addop⟩⟨Expression⟩
⟨Addop⟩ ::= + | −
⟨Term⟩ ::= ⟨Factor⟩ | ⟨Factor⟩⟨Multop⟩⟨Term⟩
⟨Multop⟩ ::= × | ÷
⟨Factor⟩ ::= ⟨Number⟩ | ⟨Name⟩ | (⟨Expression⟩)
⟨Number⟩ ::= ⟨Digit⟩ | ⟨Digit⟩⟨Number⟩
⟨Digit⟩ ::= 0|1|2|3|4|5|6|7|8|9
⟨If⟩ ::= **if** ⟨Expression⟩⟨Comp⟩⟨Exp⟩ **then goto** ⟨Name⟩
⟨Exp⟩ ::= ⟨Expression⟩
⟨Comp⟩ ::= < | = | > | ≤ | ≥ | ≠
⟨Read⟩ ::= **read** (⟨Name⟩)
⟨Print⟩ ::= **print** (⟨Expression⟩)

Corresponding Productions of B̄

⟨Prog⟩ ::= ⟨Commands⟩ ↓ ⊔ STP ↓ ⟨Declarations⟩ ↓ ⊔ END
⟨Declarations⟩ ::= ⟨Dec⟩ | ⟨Dec⟩ ↓ ⟨Declarations⟩
⟨Dec⟩ ::= ⟨Name⟩ ⊔ RES
⟨Name⟩ ::= ⟨Alph⟩ | ⟨Alph⟩⟨Name⟩
⟨Alph⟩ ::= a|b|c|d|e|f|g|h|i|j|k|l|m|n|o|p|q|r|s|
 t|u|v|w|x|y|z|

⟨Commands⟩ ::= ⟨Command⟩ | ⟨Command⟩ ↓ ⟨Commands⟩
⟨Command⟩ ::= ⟨Name⟩⟨Com⟩ | ⟨Com⟩
⟨Com⟩ ::= ⟨Assignment⟩ | ⟨If⟩ | ⟨Read⟩ | ⟨Print⟩
⟨Assignment⟩ ::= ⟨Expression⟩ ↓ ⊔ STR ⊔ ⟨Name⟩
⟨Expression⟩ ::= ⟨Term⟩ | ⟨Term⟩ ↓ ⟨Expression⟩ ↓ ⟨Addop⟩
⟨Addop⟩ ::= ⊔ ADD | ⊔ SUB
⟨Term⟩ ::= ⟨Factor⟩ | ⟨Factor⟩ ↓ ⟨Term⟩ ↓ ⟨Multop⟩
⟨Multop⟩ ::= ⊔ MUL | ⊔ DIV
⟨Factor⟩ ::= ⊔ LNS ⊔ ⟨Number⟩ | ⊔ LSS ⊔ ⟨Name⟩ | ⟨Expression⟩
⟨Number⟩ ::= ⟨Digit⟩ | ⟨Digit⟩⟨Number⟩
⟨Digit⟩ ::= 0|1|2|3|4|5|6|7|8|9
⟨If⟩ ::= ⟨Expression⟩ ↓ ⟨Exp⟩ ↓ ⊔ ⟨Comp⟩ ⊔ ⟨Name⟩
⟨Exp⟩ ::= ⟨Expression⟩
⟨Comp⟩ ::= BLT | BEQ | BGT | BGE | BLE | BNE
⟨Read⟩ ::= ⊔ RED ↓ ⊔ STR ⊔ ⟨Name⟩
⟨Print⟩ ::= ⟨Expression⟩ ↓ ⊔ PRT

**Figure 3.5.2**

The computer on which the assembler is based makes use of a built-in stack. The commands ADD, SUB, MUL, and DIV add, subtract, multiply, and divide the first two numbers in the stack and replace the two first numbers by the result.

LSS X copies the number in the memory location with name X into the stack, LNS n copies the number n into the stack. STR X removes the first number from the stack and stores it in the memory location with name X. STP stops the running of the program. BLT, BEQ, BGT, BGE, BLE, BNE are branch commands: they compare the two first numbers in the stack using the relations less than (LT), equal (EQ), greater than (GT), greater than or equal (GE), less than or equal (LE), and not equal (NE). If the condition holds, then a branch is made to the memory location named in the command; whether the condition is met or not, the two numbers compared are removed from the stack. RED reads in a number and stores it in the stack. PRT removes the first number from the stack and prints it.

RES and END are simply aids to the assembler. RES signals that a memory location is to be reserved and END signals that the end of the assembler program has been reached.

The symbol $\sqcup$ indicates a blank space. The symbol $\downarrow$ is suppressed in the following; it is interpreted as the beginning of a new line.

Consider, for example, the Algol-60 program

> **begin integer** m; **integer** n; **read** (m); n := 1;
>   h: n := n $\times$ n $+$ 3; print (n $-$ 6);
>     **if** n $<$ m **then goto** h
> **end**

Using the Backus pair $P = (B, \bar{B})$ it is translated into the assembler program

```
  ⊔ RED
  ⊔ STR ⊔ m
  ⊔ LNS ⊔ 1
  ⊔ STR ⊔ n
h ⊔ LSS ⊔ n
| | LSS ⊔ n
  ⊔ MUL
  ⊔ LNS ⊔ 3
  ⊔ ADD
  ⊔ STR ⊔ n
  ⊔ LSS ⊔ n
  ⊔ LNS ⊔ 6
  ⊔ SUB
  ⊔ PRT
  ⊔ LSS ⊔ n
  ⊔ LSS ⊔ m
  ⊔ BLT ⊔ h
  ⊔ STP
m ⊔ RES
n ⊔ RES
  ⊔ END
```

which for input value m $=$ 20 gives the output $-2$, 13, 358.

*Remarks and References*

*Backus pairs* are related to *syntax-directed translations*; see Aho [1], [2]. A good collection of results in the area of *lexical analysis* is also found in Aho [1], [2].

## Exercises

**3.5.1**   As in Example 3.5.2, determine all nodes of the solution tree that are searched through for y $= (((4. + 5.) \times 2.) - 7.)$ using consideration 2 and the Backus system of Example 3.5.1.

**3.5.2**   In the definition of Backus pairs, why are simple Backus systems used and not arbitrary Backus systems?

**3.5.3**   Using the standard procedures mentioned in Sec. 1.4, write program segments to define the procedures used in Example 3.5.3.
(a)   L(W)   (b)   FIRSTVAR(W)   (c)   VAR(V)   (d)   MAR(V)   (e)   MARK (W, I)   (f)   INITIAL(W, Z)   (g)   REPL(W, V, Z)

**3.5.4**   Write a program to perform the transformation (discussed in Example 3.5.4) of a hierarchical file into a linear file without using Backus systems.

**3.5.5**   Let B be an arbitrary complete tree with whole-number nodes. Determine a Backus pair that defines a translation that takes a parenthetical representation of the values of the nodes of B and delivers the values of the nodes in   (a)   preorder, (b)   postorder, and   (c)   symmetric order.

# 4 Complex Data Structures

## Section 4.1 Graphs and Lists

In this section we examine data structures $B = (K, R)$ in which $R$ consists of a single but arbitrary relation N. Such data structures are called *graphs*. If certain nodes are used only as pointers, then we have list structures called *Lists* (capital L), which are the underlying data structures in several programming languages.

**Definition 4.1.1** (Graph) Any data structure $B = (K, R)$ in which R consists of exactly one relation N, the *successor relation*, is called a *graph*. If for every pair $(k, k') \in N$ it is also true that $(k', k) \in N$, then B is an *undirected graph*.

In the following discussion, numbers are often assigned to the n nodes so that we can refer to the *number* of a node or to the *ith node*.

**Definition 4.1.2** (Notational Conventions) Let $B = (K, R)$, $R = \{N\}$, be a graph. Just as with trees the end nodes of B (if such exist) are the *leaves* of the graph, the *degree* of a node k is the number of successors of k, and the greatest degree of any node occurring in B is the *degree* of the graph. The number of predecessors and successors of a node k is called the *order* of k and the greatest order occurring in B is the *order* of the graph. A sequence $k = k_0, k_1, \ldots, k_n = k'$ of nodes with $(k_{i-1}, k_i) \in N$ for $i = 1, 2, \ldots, n$ (where $n \geqslant 1$) is called a *path* of *length* n from node k to node k', and we then say that k' *can be reached* from k. If $k = k'$, then the path is called a *circular path*. Each pair $(k, k') \in N$ is called an *edge* from k to k' with *beginning* k and *end* k'.

**Definition 4.1.3** (Rooted Graph, Connected Graph, Evaluated Graph) Let $B = (K, R)$, $R = \{N\}$, be a graph. The graph B is called a *rooted graph* if there is at least one node $W \in K$ called the *root* from which every node in K can be reached. A set

185

of nodes $\overline{K} \subseteq K$ is called *connected* if for any two nodes k, k' $\in \overline{K}$, k can be reached from k' and k' can be reached from k, and only nodes of $\overline{K}$ occur on the path. $\overline{K}$ is also called *maximal* if there is no proper subset of K containing $\overline{K}$ that is connected. The graph B is called *connected* if its set of nodes K is connected. The graph B is *evaluated* if, by using a so-called *evaluation function* f, each pair of nodes (k, k') $\in$ N is associated with exactly one value f(k, k').

Graphs and evaluated graphs are seen in the most diverse applications. Consider a group of cities for which direct public transportation connections are defined by a graph, and an evaluated graph is used to indicate their distances, costs, departure frequencies, etc. Other applications include a chemical formula whose structure is described in a graph, or a transport network, or a group of persons for which a graph shows which person plays another in a tennis tournament.

In the following discussion, rooted graphs are used first of all. Just as with trees, in the graphical representation of a rooted graph, a root is always designated as the top node. Also, as with trees, it is important when working with graphs to be able to search all nodes of a graph in a certain order.

**Definition 4.1.4** (Preorder) Let B $= (K, R)$ be a graph and k $\in$ K be a node. All nodes in K are initially *unmarked*. The nodes that can be reached from k may be obtained in a *preorder* by applying the process *Search* to k.

*Search:*   If k is marked, then the application of Search to the node k is finished. Otherwise let $k_1, k_2, \ldots, k_n$ (n $\geqslant 0$) be the successors of k (in any order); take the node k, mark k, and apply the process Search to $k_i$, i $= 1, 2, \ldots, n$.

Notice that the definition of preorder for nodes of trees (in Sec. 3.1) is a special case of the preorder defined here.

**Example 4.1.1** The nodes of the rooted graph in Fig. 4.1.1 in a preorder starting with $k_1$ are $k_1, k_2, k_4, k_5, k_7, k_8, k_9, k_{10}, k_{12}, k_{13}, k_{14}, k_{15}, k_{16}, k_{11}, k_6, k_3, k_{17}, k_{18}$.

The graph in Fig. 4.1.1 has only a single root $k_1$ and only one leaf $k_{16}$. There are several connected sets of nodes: $\{k_{18}\}, \{k_{14}, k_{15}\}, \{k_2, k_4, k_6\}, \{k_5, k_7, k_8, k_9, k_{10}, k_{11}, k_{12}, k_{13}\}$.

A rooted graph consisting of at least two nodes is completely determined[1] by the successor relation N; the graph in Fig. 4.1.1 is defined, for example, by

$$N = \{(k_1, k_2), (k_1, k_3), (k_2, k_4), (k_3, k_2), (k_3, k_6), (k_3, k_{17}), (k_4, k_5), (k_4, k_6),$$
$$(k_5, k_7), (k_6, k_2), (k_7, k_8), (k_8, k_5), (k_8, k_9), (k_9, k_{10}), (k_9, k_{11}), (k_{10}, k_{12}),$$
$$(k_{11}, k_{12}), (k_{11}, k_{14}), (k_{12}, k_{13}), (k_{13}, k_7), (k_{13}, k_{14}), (k_{14}, k_{15}), (k_{14}, k_{16}),$$
$$(k_{15}, k_{14}), (k_{17}, k_3), (k_{17}, k_{16}), (k_{17}, k_{18}), (k_{18}, k_{18})\}.$$

To avoid repetitions, for each node $k_i$ with $\mathfrak{t} \geqslant 1$ successors, these successors are put in a sequence $k_{i_1}, k_{i_2}, \ldots, k_{i_t}$ and written as $k_i [k_{i_1}, k_{i_2}, \ldots, k_{i_t}]$. The representa-

---

[1]This is not true for graphs in general since successorless and predecessorless nodes (*isolated nodes*) do not appear in N.

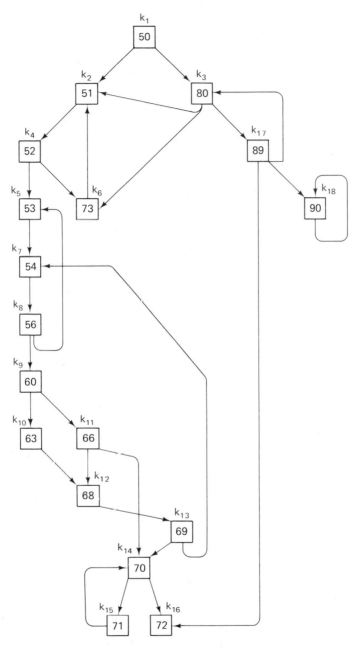

**Figure 4.1.1**

tion of all successors of a node $k_i$ obtained in this way is called a *successor image* of $k_i$. Then a graph with n nodes and m leaves can be represented by (n — m) successor images; the graph in Fig. 4.1.1 is represented by

$k_1$ [$k_2$, $k_3$], $k_2$ [$k_4$], $k_3$ [$k_2$, $k_6$, $k_{17}$], $k_4$ [$k_5$, $k_6$], $k_5$ [$k_7$], $k_6$ [$k_2$], $k_7$ [$k_8$],

$k_8$ [$k_5$, $k_9$], $k_9$ [$k_{10}$, $k_{11}$], $k_{10}$ [$k_{12}$], $k_{11}$ [$k_{12}$, $k_{14}$], $k_{12}$ [$k_{13}$], $k_{13}$ [$k_7$, $k_{14}$],

$k_{14}$ [$k_{15}$, $k_{16}$], $k_{15}$ [$k_{14}$], $k_{17}$ [$k_3$, $k_{16}$, $k_{18}$], $k_{18}$ [$k_{18}$].

From the successor images of nodes of a rooted graph there naturally arises the *parenthetical representation* of a rooted graph, which is a generalization of the parenthetical representation of a tree given in Def. 3.1.6.

**Definition 4.1.5** (Parenthetical Representation of a Rooted Graph) Let W be a root of a rooted graph B with n nodes and m leaves. A *parenthetical representation* of B *starting with* W is obtained by beginning with an *image* X, originally consisting only of the root W, and performing the following *replacement process* (n — m) times.

*Replacement process:*   The first node in X whose successor image has not yet been included is replaced by its successor image.

For the graph in Fig. 4.1.1 and the successor images written above we have the following replacement process:

$k_1$ [$k_2$, $k_3$]

$k_1$ [$k_2$ [$k_4$], $k_3$]

$k_1$ [$k_2$ [$k_4$ [$k_5$, $k_6$]], $k_3$]

$k_1$ [$k_2$ [$k_4$ [$k_5$ [$k_7$], $k_6$]], $k_3$]

.
.
.

$k_1$ [$k_2$ [$k_4$ [$k_5$ [$k_7$ [$k_8$ [$k_5$, $k_9$ [$k_{10}$ [$k_{12}$ [$k_{13}$ [$k_7$, $k_{14}$ [$k_{15}$ [$k_{14}$], $k_{16}$]]]], $k_{11}$ [$k_{12}$,

$k_{14}$]]]]], $k_6$ [$k_2$]]], $k_3$ [$k_2$, $k_6$, $k_{17}$ [$k_3$, $k_{16}$, $k_{18}$ [$k_{18}$]]]].

**Definition 4.1.6** (Standard Form) Let B = (K, R), R = {N}, be a rooted graph of degree n having order m. In the standard form of B the relation N is realized with linked allocation; i.e., each node k points using a pointer field (with n components) to its $\leqslant$ n successors. A start pointer (which points to a root of the graph) is often useful. For large n, the use of indirect storage is suggested for the pointer fields (see Sec. 1.4); this is called *indirect standard form*. In *extended standard form*, in addition to the linked realization of N, the inverse relation $N^{-1}$ is also realized linked, in such a way that each node k, by using an extended pointer field (with m — n components), points to its m — n predecessors.

Figure 4.1.2(a) shows the standard form; Fig. 4.1.2(b) shows the indirect standard form of the graph of Fig. 4.1.1. In both illustrations, $\alpha k_i = i$ for i = 1, 2, ... , 18.

The indirect standard form is particularly well-suited for the storage of evaluated graphs if for every node k with successor k' we store not only the address $\alpha k'$ of k' but also the evaluation f(k, k').

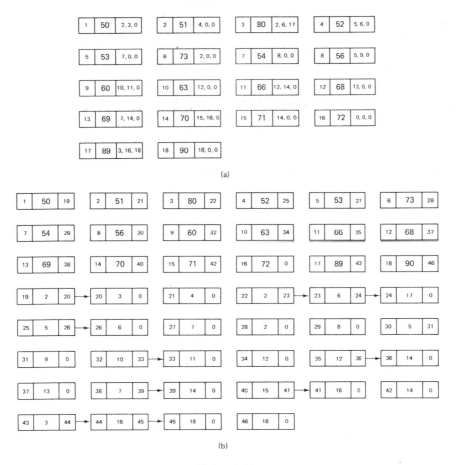

(a)

(b)

**Figure 4.1.2**

Notice that a variation of this storage technique has already been used in Example 2.5.2 to store the distance matrix given there. This close connection between several storage techniques for graphs and matrices is based on the fact that any graph can be associated in a natural way to various matrices.

**Definition 4.1.7** (Incidence Matrix, Evaluation Matrix) Let B be a graph with the n nodes $k_1, k_2, \ldots, k_n$, numbered arbitrarily. The *incidence matrix* is a rectangular array of order (n, n) in which the node in the ith row and jth column has the value 1 or 0 depending on whether there exists an edge from $k_i$ to $k_j$ or not. If f is an evaluation function of B, then the *evaluation matrix* is a rectangular array of order (n, n) in which the node $k_{ij}$ in the ith row and jth column has the value $\omega k_{ij} = f(k_i, k_j)$ if there is an edge from $k_i$ to $k_j$ and in which otherwise $\omega k_{ij}$ is different from all other values occurring as function values of the evaluation function.

The incidence matrix defines only the "structure" of a graph (its successor relation); whereas the evaluation matrix also gives the evaluation function. In many cases, as in Example 2.5.2, this information is all that is necessary. In general, however, for the complete storage of a graph not only the incidence matrix and the evaluation matrix but also the values of the nodes of the graph (i.e., the sequence $F = \omega k_1, \omega k_2, \ldots, \omega k_n$) must be stored.

**Example 4.1.2** Let M be the incidence matrix of a graph with nodes $k_1, k_2, \ldots, k_n$. Using M it is often quite convenient to obtain further information about the graph. For example, let $a_{ij}^t$ for $t \geqslant 1$ and $1 \leqslant i, j \leqslant n$, be the number of different paths of length t from $k_i$ to $k_j$ and let $M^t$ be that matrix of order (n, n) whose nodes in row i and column j have the value $a_{ij}^t$. Starting with the incidence matrix M, $M^t$ can be computed[2] for each t using the relation

$$M^1 = M, \qquad M^{s+t} = M^s M^t \qquad (s, t \geqslant 1),$$

where $M^s M^t$ represents the usual matrix product, i.e., where

$$a_{ij}^{s+t} = \sum_{r=1}^{n} a_{ir}^s a_{rj}^t.$$

The validity of the formula above is obvious since for every path of length $s + t$ from $k_i$ to $k_j$ there must be a node $k_r$ that can be reached from $k_i$ along a path of length s and from which a path of length t leads to $k_j$.

Although it may be simpler from the point of view of programming to work with incidence matrices that are stored in uncompressed form (e.g., sequentially row by row), this greatly increases the number of steps necessary for the solution of a problem. The following program solves a frequently occurring problem for a graph with n nodes and m edges in (n + m) steps; if uncompressed storage for the incidence matrix had been used, $n^2$ steps would have been required.

**Example 4.1.3** Given as input is a sequence of numbers

$$n, m; 1, w_1, t_1, a_{1,1}, a_{1,2}, \ldots, a_{1,t_1}; 2, w_2, t_2, a_{2,1}, a_{2,2}, \ldots, a_{2,t_2}; \ldots;$$

$$n, w_n, t_n, a_{n,1}, a_{n,2}, \ldots, a_{n,t_n};$$

that represent a rooted graph B with n positive whole-number nodes and $m = t_1 + t_2 + \cdots + t_n$ edges, where $i, w_i, t_i, a_{i,1}, a_{i,2}, \ldots, a_{i,t_i}$ (for $i = 1, 2, \ldots, n$) give the value $w_i$ of the ith node $k_i$ and the $t_i$ successors of the ith node $a_{i,1}, \ldots, a_{i,t_i}$. Let the node $k_1$ be the root of B.

As an example, the graph in Fig. 4.1.1 is defined by the sequence

18, 28; 1, 50, 2, 2, 3; 2, 51, 1, 4; 3, 80, 3, 2, 6, 17; 4, 52, 2, 5, 6; 5, 53, 1, 7;

6, 73, 1, 2; 7, 54, 1, 8; 8, 56, 2, 5, 9; 9, 60, 2, 10, 11; 10, 63, 1, 12; 11, 66, 2,

12, 14; 12, 68, 1, 13; 13, 69, 2, 7, 14; 14, 70, 2, 15, 16; 15, 71, 1, 14; 16, 72, 0;

17, 89, 3, 3, 16, 18; 18, 90, 1, 18.

We wish to develop a program that determines all maximal connected sets of nodes

---

[2]If we choose $s = t$, then we can obtain $M^m$ in $\log_2 m$ matrix multiplications by determining $M^1, M^2, M^4, M^8, \ldots$.

of B. The ability to make such a determination is useful in many cases, in order to be able to restrict the investigation of graphs to subgraphs.

The graph B is to be stored in indirect standard form, using the declaration **DCL** (D(N + M), R(N + M), NUM(N)) **FIXED BIN**;. The element D(I) (for $1 \leqslant i \leqslant n$) gives the value $w_i$ of the ith node $k_i$ and R(I) is the beginning address a (for $n + 1 \leqslant a \leqslant n + m$) of the linked addresses of successor nodes of $k_i$, as represented in Fig. 4.1.2(b) for the graph of Fig. 4.1.1. NUM(I) numbers the nodes in the order (we use a preorder) in which they are considered.[3] In particular at the outset NUM(1) = 1 and NUM(I) = 0 for $i > 1$, which indicates that initially no nodes except the root have been considered; NUM(I) = t means that $k_i$ has been considered as the tth node and potentially belongs to a maximal connected set of nodes; NUM(I) = $-1$ indicates that $k_i$ either does not belong to a maximal connected set of nodes or already has been printed, and in either case it can be considered *finished*.

In the program three stacks A, Z, PRINT are declared by

> **DCL** (A(N), AN(N), ZLO(N), ZUP(N), PRINTADR(N), PRINTNUM(N))
> **FIXED BIN**;

Each element (A(I), AN(I)) of A defines the address and number of a node. Initially except for A(1) = AN(1) = 1 (i.e., except for the root of the graph with numbering 1), A is empty. Each element (ZLO(I), ZUP(I)) of Z indicates that several of the nodes with numbering ZLO(I), ZLO(I) + 1, . . . , ZUP(I) constitute a connected set of nodes. Z is initially empty except for ZLO(1) = ZUP(1) = 0. Each element (PRINTADR(I), PRINTNUM(I)) gives the address and numbering of a node that has already been determined to belong to a connected set of nodes. The values of nodes given by PRINTADR(I) are printed, as soon as all nodes of a maximal connected set of nodes have been found. The stack PRINT is initially empty. A variable NU is used for numbering the nodes; initially NU = 1. The maximal connected set of nodes is obtained by performing the following process *Produce* beginning with the graph stored as described and the initial description of the stacks A, Z, PRINT and the variable NU.

*Produce:* If A is empty, then all maximal connected sets of nodes would already have been printed and the program is finished. Otherwise let (ak, nk) be the address and numbering of a node k defined by the first element in the stack A, and let (zl, zu) be the first value in the stack Z. In performing the algorithm, if $zl \leqslant zu$ for every pair (zl, zu) of Z and if we come to a pair (zl, zu) in stack Z before we come to a pair (zl', zu'), then it is always true that $zl \geqslant zu'$. If k has a successor k' that is not yet finished (let its numbering be nk'), then the procedure *Forward* is performed; otherwise the procedure *Back* is performed.

*Forward:* The edge from k to k' is removed. Now there are two cases:

*Case 1:* nk' = 0; therefore k' has not yet been considered. The value of NU is increased by 1, k' is numbered with NU, and the address of k' along with the numbering NU is added to stack A. Then the process Produce is repeated.

---

[3] Notice that this order in general does not correspond to the order of the nodes in input.

*Case 2:*   nk' > 0. If nk' > zu (meaning a new potential connected set of nodes has been discovered), then (nk', nk) is added to stack Z. Otherwise, in the value (zl, zu) at the top of stack Z, zl is replaced by nk' if nk' < zl and zu is replaced by nk if nk > zu (whereupon an increase in the set of connected nodes found thus far is printed); as long as zu' < zl, the second element (zl', zu') is combined with the first element (zl, zu) of Z to form a new element (min (zl, zl'), zu). Then the process Produce is repeated.

*Back:*   First, one of the three processes *Case 3*, *Case 4*, *Case 5* is performed; then a node is removed from stack A and the process Produce is repeated.

*Case 3:*   nk = zl. Then all nodes of a maximal connected set of nodes are determined; an appropriate message and all those nodes $\bar{k}$ in stack PRINT, whose numberings lie between zl and zu (zl $\leqslant$ n$\bar{k}$ $\leqslant$ zu), and also the node with address ak are printed out. Each printed node is marked as *finished* and the nodes printed from the stack PRINT are removed from the stack PRINT.

*Case 4:*   zl < nk $\leqslant$ zu. The pair (ak, nk) is added to the stack PRINT.

*Case 5:*   nk > zu. The node with address ak is marked as *finished*; it does not belong to any set of connected nodes.

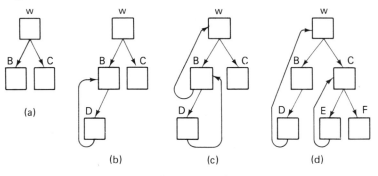

**Figure 4.1.3**

| A | Z | PRINT |
| --- | --- | --- |
| (αW, 1) | (0, 0) | Empty |
| (αW, 1), (αB, 2) | (0, 0) | Empty |
| (αW, 1), (αB, 2) | (0, 0), (1, 2) | Empty |
| (αW, 1), (αB, 2), (αD, 3) | (0, 0), (1, 2) | Empty |
| (αW, 1), (αB, 2), (αD, 3) | (0, 0), (1, 3) | Empty |
| (αW, 1), (αB, 2) | (0, 0), (1, 3) | (αD, 3) |
| (αW, 1) | (0, 0), (1, 3) | (αD, 3), (αB, 2) |
| (αW, 1), (αC, 4) | (0, 0), (1, 3) | (αD, 3), (αB, 2) |
| (αW, 1) | (0, 0), (1, 3) | (αD, 3), (αB, 2) |
| Empty | (0, 0) | Empty |

Resulting output: ωB, ωD, ωW

**Figure 4.1.4**

For a thorough understanding of the following program, work through the algorithm by hand first, using simple graphs such as those in Fig. 4.1.3 and then the graph in Fig. 4.1.1.

If the successors of nodes are considered from "left to right" and the described technique is applied to the graph in Fig. 4.1.3(c), then the stacks A, Z, PRINT, from the beginning to the end of the process Produce, are as shown in Fig. 4.1.4.

```
MAXCS: PROC OPTIONS (MAIN);
    DCL (N, M) FIXED BIN; GET LIST (N, M);
    BEGIN; DCL (D(N + M), R(N + M), NUM(N), A(N),AN(N),
               ZLO(N), ZUP(N), PRINTADR(N), PRINTNUM(N),
               I, J, K, NU, PA, PD, PZ, AUX, TI, AK, NK,
               AKS, NKS, ZL, ZU, ND, AD) FIXED BIN;
        /* FIRST THE GRAPH MUST BE CONSTRUCTED IN INDIRECT
           STANDARD FORM */
        J = N + 1;
        DO I = 1 TO N;
            GET LIST (AUX, D(I), TI);
            IF AUX ¬= 1 THEN DO; PUT LIST ('INVALID INPUT');
                                 STOP; END;
            IF TI = 0 THEN R(I) = 0;
                    ELSE R(I) = J;
            DO K = 1 TO TI;
                GET LIST (D(J));
                R(J), J = J + 1;
            END;
            R(J - 1) = 0;
        END;
        /* NOW SEVERAL PRELIMINARY STEPS */
        NUM = 0;
        A(1), AN(1), NU, NUM(1), PA, PZ = 1;
        ZLO(1), ZUP(1), PD = 0;
        /* THE ACTUAL PROGRAM CAN NOW BEGIN */
        PRODUCE: DO WHILE (PA ¬= 0);
                    AK = A(PA); NK = AN(PA);
                    ZL = ZLO(PZ); ZU = ZUP(PZ);
                    IF R(AK) = 0 THEN GOTO BACK;
                    DO WHILE (NUM(D(R(AK))) = -1);
                        R(AK) = R(R(AK));
                        IF R(AK) = 0 THEN GOTO BACK;
                    END;
                    /* SINCE INDIRECT STORAGE IS USED, THE
                       ADDRESS AKS OF THE SUCCESSOR OF A NODE
                       WITH ADDRESS AK IS GIVEN NOT BY R(AK) AS
                       USUAL BUT RATHER BY D(R(AK)) */
                    AKS = D(R(AK)); NKS = NUM(AKS);
                    /* AK AND AKS DEFINE THE ADDRESSES OF NODES
                       K AND SUCCESSOR K', NK AND NKS DEFINE THE
                       NUMBERING OF K AND K' */
        FORWARD: R(AK) = R(R(AK)); /* THE EDGE FROM K TO K'
                                      IS REMOVED */
```

```
IF NKS = 0 THEN DO;
   NU = NU + 1; NUM(AKS) = NU; PA = PA + 1;
   A(PA) = AKS; AN(PA) = NU; GOTO PRODUCE; END;
IF NKS > ZU THEN DO;
   PZ = PZ + 1; ZLO(PZ) = NKS; ZUP(PZ) = NK;
   GOTO PRODUCE; END;
IF NKS < ZL THEN DO;
   ZLO(PZ) = NKS;
   DO WHILE ((PZ > 0) & (ZLO(PZ) <= ZUP(PZ − 1)));
       IF ZLO(PZ) < ZLO(PZ − 1) THEN
           ZLO(PZ − 1) = ZLO(PZ);
       ZUP(PZ − 1) = ZUP(PZ); PZ = PZ − 1;
   END;  END;
IF NK > ZU THEN ZUP(PZ) = NK; GOTO PRODUCE;
BACK: IF NK = ZL THEN DO;
   PUT LIST ('A MAXIMAL CONNECTED SET IS');
   DO WHILE (PD ¬= 0);
       ND = PRINTNUM(PD);
       IF (ZL <= ND) & (ND <= ZU) THEN DO;
           AD = PRINTADR(PD);
           PUT LIST (AD, D(AD));
           NUM(AD) = −1; PD = PD − 1; END;
       ELSE GOTO ONE;
   END;
ONE: PUT LIST (AK, D(AK)); NUM(AK) = −1;
   PZ = PZ − 1; END;
ELSE IF (ZL < NK) & (NK <= ZU) THEN DO;
   PD = PD + 1; PRINTADR(PD) = AK;
   PRINTNUM(PD) = NK;        END;
ELSE IF NK > ZU THEN NUM(AK) = −1;
   PA = PA − 1;
END;
PUT LIST ('THERE ARE NO MORE CONNECTED SETS');
   END;
END;
```

**Definition 4.1.8** (Ordered Graph, List) Just as defined for trees, a graph $B = (K, R)$ of degree n is said to be *ordered* if for every successor $k'$ of a node k it is also specified whether $k'$ is the first, second, ..., nth successor of k. (If $n = 2$, B is a *binary graph*.) As with binary trees, in the standard form of a binary graph, two one-component pointer fields are used that give the first or *left* successor of a node and the second or *right* successor of a node. A *List* (capitalized to distinguish this "list structure" from the linear list introduced earlier) is an ordered rooted graph in which only the leaves have nonempty values and in which at least one pointer occurs. If W is the root of a List, then the successors of W define the *elements* of the List.

Figure 4.1.5 shows the graphical representation of two Lists. To obtain an ordered graph, think of the several paths leaving one node as being numbered from left to right.

In an ordered graph a root uniquely determines the nodes of the graph in preorder. For example, starting from $k_1$ the preorder of the nodes in the List of Fig.

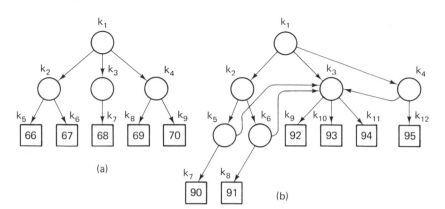

(a)

(b)

**Figure 4.1.5**

4.1.5(b) is $k_1, k_2, k_5, k_7, k_3, k_9, k_{10}, k_{11}, k_6, k_8, k_4, k_{12}$. The most common method for storing a List is based on the transformation of the List into a binary graph (corresponding to the transformation of an ordered tree into a binary tree) and the standard form of the resulting graph.

**Definition 4.1.9** (Rounding, Binary Form) A List $B = (K, R)$ is said to be *rounded* if every node with more than one successor does not have any leaf as a successor. Any List can be rounded: if a node has more than one successor (one of which is a leaf k), this node k is replaced by a new node $\bar{k}$ without a value that has a single successor k.

Let B be a List obtained by rounding a List $B'$. To represent the *binary form* of B or $B'$, memory locations with two one-component pointer fields are used. First, each node $k \in K$ is associated with a memory location $\xi k$ where $\delta \xi k = \omega k$, $\rho_1 \xi k = \rho_2 \xi k = 0$. To obtain a binary form of B, the process *Link* is applied to all nodes in a preorder beginning with a root W. All nodes except W are initially unmarked.

*Link:* Let k be a node with $n \geqslant 0$ successors $k_1, k_2, \ldots, k_n$. If $n = 0$, the process is finished. Otherwise let $z_1, z_2, \ldots, z_n$ be a sequence of memory locations where $z_i$ (for $i = 1, 2, \ldots, n$) is obtained as follows: if $k_i$ is unmarked, then let $z_i$ be the memory location $\xi k_i$ and mark $k_i$; if on the other hand $k_i$ is already marked, then let $z_i$ be an additional memory location whose first pointer field gives the address of the first successor of $k_i$. Then it is necessary to make sure that in both cases the first pointer field of k points to $z_1$ and the second pointer field of $z_j$ points to $z_{j+1}$ (for $j = 1, 2, \ldots, n - 1$).

If a rounded List B is an ordered tree, then the binary form of the List B is just exactly the standard form of the binary tree corresponding to the tree B.

Figure 4.1.6(a) shows the rounded List B that corresponds to the List $B'$ in Fig. 4.1.5(b). Figure 4.1.6(b) gives a binary form of B and therefore of $B'$. The binary form of a List can always be interpreted as the standard form of a *corresponding* binary

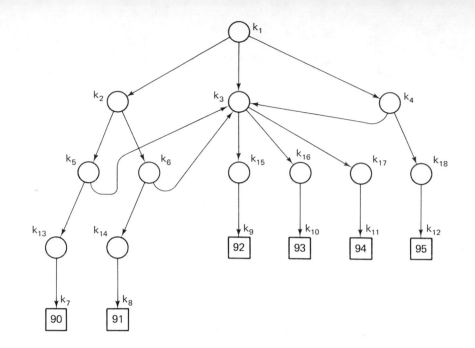

(a)

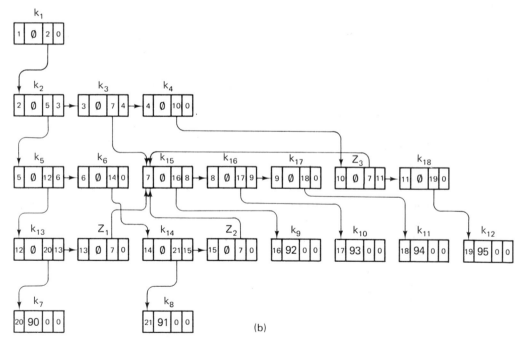

(b)

**Figure 4.1.6**

196

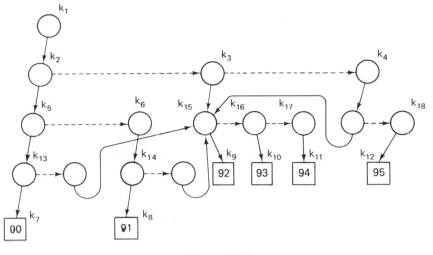

**Figure 4.1.7**

rooted graph, in which only the leaves have a nonempty value. Represented graphically in Fig. 4.1.7 is the binary rooted graph corresponding to the List in Fig. 4.1.6(a). The relation "first successor" is indicated with solid lines; the relation "second successor," with dashed lines.

If B is a List and B′ is a corresponding binary rooted graph, then the preorder of the leaves, starting from a root W, is the same for B and B′.

Since in the binary form of a List the pointer fields of all leaves have the value 0 and the data fields of all other nodes are empty, in actual practice in order to conserve memory space, memory locations are used that in some cases serve as two pointer fields and in other cases as a data field, and an indicator tells how the contents of a particular memory location should be interpreted. Or alternatively the data field of a nonterminal node may be used advantageously as a counter (see page 200).

**Example 4.1.4** Given is the binary form of a List B with positive whole-number leaves. We wish to develop a program segment that prints the values of the leaves of the List in preorder.

As declarations we use **DCL** (D(M), R1(M), R2(M), W) **FIXED BIN**;, where D, R1, R2 give the data fields and pointer fields for the binary form and W is the address of a root of the List.

If the given binary form of the List B is interpreted as standard form of the corresponding binary rooted graph B′, then the two program segments below are easy to follow.

In both programs the data fields of all nonterminal nodes have the value 0. We wish to visit the nodes of the binary rooted graph B′ in preorder and to mark each node as having been visited by replacing the value x of the data field by $-x - 1$.

In program segment A a stack S is used which gives the addresses of roots of sub-Lists which at the time have not yet been considered (similar to program B of Example 3.1.5).

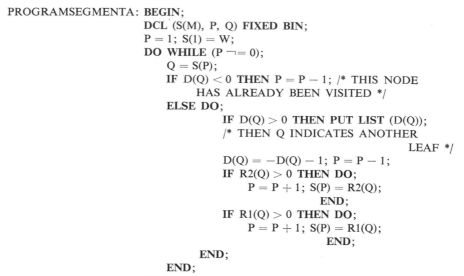

```
PROGRAMSEGMENTA: BEGIN;
                 DCL (S(M), P, Q) FIXED BIN;
                 P = 1; S(1) = W;
                 DO WHILE (P ¬= 0);
                     Q = S(P);
                     IF D(Q) < 0 THEN P = P − 1; /* THIS NODE
                         HAS ALREADY BEEN VISITED */
                     ELSE DO;
                             IF D(Q) > 0 THEN PUT LIST (D(Q));
                             /* THEN Q INDICATES ANOTHER
                                                        LEAF */
                             D(Q) = −D(Q) − 1; P = P − 1;
                             IF R2(Q) > 0 THEN DO;
                                 P = P + 1; S(P) = R2(Q);
                                         END;
                             IF R1(Q) > 0 THEN DO;
                                 P = P + 1; S(P) = R1(Q);
                                         END;
                         END;
                     END;
                 END;
```

In program segment B, in order to backtrack a path already taken, certain pointer fields are temporarily altered in such a way as to make possible this retracing. The stack S is "carried along in the pointer fields of the graph." If the nodes of a binary rooted graph are searched in preorder starting from a root W and if a node A has been reached, then there is a path $k_0, k_1, k_2, \ldots, k_n$ with $k_0 = W$, $k_n = A$ from W to A. In the binary graph, if $k_i$ points to $k_{i+1}$ (for $i = 1, 2, \ldots, n − 1$), then in program segment B it is provided that $k_i$ temporarily points back to $k_{i-1}$. If from out of A a further node C is visited, then A will also point to $k_{n-1}$, etc.

If later, however, we return again to A, then the pointer field of A in question is adjusted so that A again points to C.

In the following program three pointers P, PP, PS are used. Here P always gives the node k currently under consideration, PP gives the node from which k is reached (thus one of the predecessors of k), and PS gives the node from which k can be reached using some kind of backtracking (thus one of the successors of k).

```
PROGRAMSEGMENTB: BEGIN;
                 DCL (P, PP, PS, AUX) FIXED BIN;
                 P = W; PP = 0;
                 H: IF D(P) > 0 THEN DO; /* THEN ANOTHER
                                            LEAF IS FOUND */
                     PUT LIST (D(P)); D(P) = −D(P) − 1;
                         END;
```

```
        ELSE IF D(P) = 0 THEN DO;
          /* THIS NODE IS VISITED FOR THE FIRST
              TIME */
          D(P) = −1; IF (R1(P) > 0) & (D(R1(P)) > = 0)
        THEN DO;
                  PS = R1(P); R1(P) = −PP;
                  PP = P; P = PS; GOTO H;
              END;
                  /* −PP IS TAKEN AND THE POINTER
                      IS MARKED */
        IF R2(P) > 0 THEN DO;
        IF D(R2(P)) > = 0 THEN DO;
          PS = R2(P); R2(P) = −PP; PP = P;
          P = PS; GOTO H; END; END;
        /* OTHERWISE THE NODE HAS NO MORE
            UNMARKED SUCCESSORS */ END;
    ELSE IF D(P) = −1 THEN DO; /* THEN THIS
                  NODE HAS ALREADY BEEN VISITED */
        IF (R2(P) > 0) & (R2(P) ¬= PS) THEN DO;
        IF D(R2(P)) > = 0 THEN DO;
          PS = R2(P); R2(P) = −PP;
          PP = P; P = PS; GOTO H; END; END;
        /* OTHERWISE THE NODE HAS NO MORE
            NEW UNMARKED SUCCESSORS */ END;
    IF (R1(PP) ¬= 0) | (R2(PP) ¬= 0) THEN DO;
          /* THEN ONE OF THE NUMBERS R1(PP)
              OR R2(PP) MUST BE NEGATIVE */
        IF R1(PP) < 0 THEN DO;
          AUX = −R1(PP); R1(PP) = P; END;
                  ELSE DO;
                          AUX = −R2(PP);
                          R2(PP) = P;
                      END;
          PS = P; P = PP; PP = AUX; GOTO H; END;
          /* OTHERWISE THE ROOT IS CONSIDERED */
          R1(PP) = P;
  END;
```

Carefully work through program segment B using the binary form of the List in Fig. 4.1.6(b). The method used can of course also be used for searching trees without recursion, without stacks, and without inverse storage.

Heretofore, Lists have been considered as a special case of graphs. They may also be interpreted, however, as a generalization of linear lists or sequences by defining a *List* as a sequence of *elements*, where each element is either an *atom* (i.e., a leaf) or is itself a List.

Notice that Lists can be arbitrarily nested in one another; a List A, for example, can appear as an element in a List B and this again as an element of A, etc. The List in Fig. 4.1.5(b) is a sequence (with name $k_1$) of three elements, in which each element is a List with name $k_2$ or $k_3$ or $k_4$. The List with name $k_2$ is then a sequence of two elements; the two are again Lists with names $k_5$ and $k_6$. The List $k_5$ consists of two elements; the first is an atom with value 90, the second is the List with name $k_3$.

Parenthetical representation effectively expresses the construction of Lists from elements. For clarity, leaves may be emphasized by underlining and names of Lists that do not appear as elements of other Lists may be suppressed.

As a parenthetical representation of the List in Fig. 4.1.5(b) we have

$$k_1 [k_2 [k_5 [\underline{k_7}, k_3], k_6 [\underline{k_8}, k_3]], k_3 [\underline{k_9}, \underline{k_{10}}, \underline{k_{11}}], k_4 [k_3, \underline{k_{12}}]]$$

or

$$[[[\underline{k_7}, k_3], [\underline{k_8}, k_3]], k_3 [\underline{k_9}, \underline{k_{10}}, \underline{k_{11}}], [k_3, \underline{k_{12}}]].$$

If Lists are interpreted as a generalization of linear lists as suggested, then the stipulation that only leaves have nonempty values is meaningful since all other nodes are used simply as "names" of Lists.

From a small group of basic operations that are defined for Lists it is easy to construct powerful algorithms for manipulating Lists. For this, however, the reader is referred to the literature.

The binary form used for Lists facilitates the management of available memory space in a supply stack, allowing memory locations to be removed from the stack as they are needed and to be returned to the stack when they are no longer needed. Of course it is not so easy, as when using linear lists or trees, to determine when a memory location is no longer needed. If a memory location z points using a certain pointer field to a memory location z' and if this pointer field is changed, then if we are using linear lists or trees, z' can be considered as no longer needed. Using Lists, this is not possible since there can be other memory locations pointing to z' and thus z' would still be in use.

Consider the memory location $\sigma 7$ in Fig. 4.1.6(b) to which memory locations $\sigma 3, \sigma 10, \sigma 13$, and $\sigma 15$ point. Changing the pointer field of only one of these memory locations would not mean that $\sigma 7$ should be added to the supply stack.

Two techniques are suggested here for determining whether a memory location is still needed:

(1)  For each memory location z which does not correspond to a leaf a counter is carried along which indicates how many memory locations point to z. If this counter falls to 0, then memory location z can be added to the supply stack.

(2)  Memory locations are only put into the supply stack when no more free memory space is available. This can be done by first marking all memory locations in use, then adding the unmarked ones to the supply stack, and then removing the mark from all marked memory locations.

Technique 1 is particularly recommended and can be easily implemented using binary form since, in exactly those memory locations that need a counter, the data field can be used for that purpose. The programming may present some difficulty because unless care is taken in Lists that contain themselves, the counters will not drop to 0 if the memory locations of the List are no longer needed.

For technique 2 an efficient method is needed to be able to find and mark all memory locations of a List, as much as possible without using additional memory space for an auxiliary stack, since memory locations are not available for that purpose if technique 2 is employed. Such a method, however, has already been given in program segment B of Example 4.1.4.

*Remarks and References*

Many algorithms for solving problems in graph theory are found in Dörfler [1], Neumann [1]. As an alternative to *parenthetical representation*, Berztiss has introduced *star representation* {see Berztiss [1]; for the solution of problems mentioned, refer to Berztiss [2]}. The idea in program segment B in Example 4.1.4 originated with Schorr [1]. Among the first languages concerned with list processing are IPL V, LISP, and SLIP, which are described briefly in Bobrow [1]. A short book on list processing is J. M. Foster [1]; for LISP, see McCarthy [1]. A good survey of several systems of list processing and other aspects of data structures is found in D'Imperio [1].

## Exercises

**4.1.1**  Consider the graph B in Fig. 4.1.8:
(a)  Determine all roots of B.
(b)  Determine all leaves of B.
(c)  Determine all possible preorders of B starting with the node $k_4$.
(d)  Graphically represent a standard form of B.

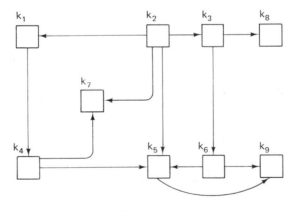

**Figure 4.1.8**

**4.1.2**  Consider the ordered graph B' obtained from B in Fig. 4.1.8 by arranging all successors of a node k as $k_{i_1}, k_{i_2}, \ldots, k_{i_t}$ so that $i_1 < i_2 < \cdots < i_t$.
(a)  Determine the preorder of the nodes of B' that can be reached from $k_4$.
(b)  Graphically represent the List B'' obtained by rounding B'.
(c)  Graphically represent a binary form of B''.

**4.1.3**   Write a program to store a graph with whole-number nodes, whose parenthetical representation is given as input, in standard form, with indirect allocation of the pointer fields. In the parenthetical representation each node of the graph occurs as a pair of numbers $(i, j)$ where $i > 0$ gives the numbering of a node and $j$ gives its value.

**4.1.4**   Write a program to store a List with whole-number leaves whose parenthetical representation is given as input, in binary form. In the parenthetical representation each node of the List occurs as a pair of numbers $(i, j)$. If $i > 0$, then we have a leaf with numbering $i$ and value $j$; if $i < 0$, then we have a node with numbering $i$ that is not a leaf. The List of Fig. 4.1.5(b), for example, is given by the parenthetical representation

$$k_1 \, [k_2 \, [k_5 \, [k_7, \, k_3 \, [k_9, \, k_{10}, \, k_{11}]], \, k_6 \, [k_8, \, k_3]], \, k_3, \, k_4 \, [k_3, \, k_{12}]],$$

i.e., the corresponding input is

$$(-1, 0)[(-2, 0)[(-5, 0)[(7, 90), (-3, 0)[(9, 92), (10, 93), (11, 94)]], (-6, 0)$$
$$[(8, 91), (-3, 0)]], (-3, 0), (-4, 0)[(-3, 0), (12, 95)]].$$

**4.1.5**   A List with whole-number leaves is given in binary form. Write a program that prints the List in parenthetical form, where each node, as in Exercise 4.1.4, is defined by a pair of numbers.

**4.1.6**   A supply of memory locations with two pointer fields is given as in Exercise 3.2.7. Define some procedures such as the following for manipulating Lists whose leaves have as values whole numbers $> 0$ and which are given in binary form:

(a)   CONSTRUCT: **PROCEDURE** (L1, L2) **FIXED BIN**;
produces a List with two elements, both of which are Lists, and for which the addresses of the roots are given by L1 and L2.

(b)   LIST: **PROCEDURE** (L) **FIXED BIN**;
produces a List with one element that is itself a List, namely the one given by L.

(c)   LEAF: **PROCEDURE** (N) **FIXED BIN**;
produces a List with one element having one leaf (atom) with value N.

(d)   COMB: **PROCEDURE** (L1, L2) **FIXED BIN**;
produces a List in which the elements of the List given by L2 are added to the elements of the List given by L1.

(e)   LENGTH: **PROCEDURE** (L) **FIXED BIN**;
yields the number of elements of the List L.

(f)   FIRST: **PROCEDURE** (L) **FIXED BIN**;
yields the first element of the List L.

(g)   REST: **PROCEDURE** (L) **FIXED BIN**;
yields a List consisting of L in which the first element of L is removed.

(h)   ATOM: **PROCEDURE** (L) **BIT**;
yields '1'B if L is not a List but rather an atom.

(i)   NULL: **PROCEDURE** (L) **BIT**;
yields '1'B if L is the empty List.

Then if, for example, we have

A = COMB(COMB(LEAF(4), LEAF(6)), LIST(COMB(LEAF(7), LEAF(9))));

then the List A has the parenthetical representation [4, 6, [7, 9]]; ATOM(FIRST(A)) = '1'B, LENGTH(A) = 3, REST(REST(A)) has the parenthetical representation [7, 9] and NULL(REST(REST(REST(A)))) = '1'B.

**4.1.7** Write a program (a) using recursion (b) without using recursion, to print the nodes of a given graph in preorder.

## Section 4.2    Multilinked Structures and Composite Inquiries

All data structures considered heretofore have been relatively simple in comparison with the general concept of a data structure that is a set of nodes with arbitrarily many arbitrary relations. Any more rigorous discussion of the manipulation of very general data structures is beyond the scope of this book. If an arbitrary data structure $B = (K, R)$ with $R = \{r_1, r_2, \ldots, r_m\}$ is given, however, each of the relations $r_i$ (for $1 \leqslant i \leqslant m$) can be classified as *linear* [in which case the data structure $(K, \{r_i\})$ is a linear list], as *hierarchical* [in which case the data structure $(K, \{r_i\})$ is a tree], or as *general* [and the data structure $(K, \{r_i\})$ is a graph]. Then the techniques mentioned throughout this book can be used for the manipulation of the individual relations as lists, trees, and graphs.

In Sec. 4.2 we round out the discussion of data structures by considering, in contrast to Sec. 4.1, not data structures with a single arbitrary complex relation but rather data structures with arbitrarily many simple relations.

**Definition 4.2.1** (m-Attribute File) A data structure $B = (K, R)$ is called an *m-attribute file* if $R$ consists of m equivalence relations $R = \{r_1, \ldots, r_m\}$. The relations of such a data structure are called *attributes*. Every equivalence class A of every relation $r_s$ is associated with a *value* v(A). If k is a node in the equivalence class $r_s(k)$, then the value $v(r_s(k))$ associated with $r_s(k)$ is called the *value* of attribute $r_s$ *for* the node k.

**Example 4.2.1** (Three-Attribute File) Let $B = (K, R)$ be a data structure representing the books in a bookstore. Each node k describes a book: $\omega_1 k$ is the subject area, $\omega_2 k$ is the language in which the book is printed, $\omega_3 k$ is the publisher, and $\omega_4 k$ is an identifying number. R consists of three equivalence relations $R = \{S, L, P\}$, where books in the same subject area are put into an equivalence class using S; those in the same language, using L; and those from the same publisher, using P so that, for example,

S = {(k, k') | k and k' are books of K in the same subject area}.

The values of the attributes S, L, P define the possible subject areas, languages, and publishers.

For this example, we shall assume

$$\{v(S(k))\,|\,k \in K\} = \{CSC, MAT, PHY, CHE\} = \{\omega_1 k\,|\,k \in K\}$$

$$\{v(L(k))\,|\,k \in K\} = \{ENG, GER, FRE, RUS\} = \{\omega_2 k\,|\,k \in K\}$$

$$\{v(P(k))\,|\,k \in K\} = \{PH, TEU, SPR, DOV, WIL\} = \{\omega_3 k\,|\,k \in K\},$$

although in an actual application each of the attributes would have many more values.

A node k with $\omega k = (CSC, ENG, PH, 7038)$ might for example describe a Computer SCience book in the ENGlish language, published by Prentice-Hall having an international standard book number 7038. Accordingly $v(S(k)) = CSC$, $v(P(k)) = PH$, etc.

Using the attribute file described here, it may be desirable to make an *inquiry*[4] to determine, for example, all those books in the subject area CSC either in the language GER or in one of the languages ENG or RUS but excluding those published by SPR; i.e., we are interested in any book k with

$$v(S(k)) = CSC \wedge (v(L(k)) = GER \vee ((v(L(k)) = ENG \vee v(L(k)) = $$
$$RUS) \wedge \neg\, v(P(k)) = SPR))$$

or written more simply [and using the usual priorities for not ($\neg$), and ($\wedge$), or ($\vee$)]

$$S = CSC \wedge (L = GER \vee (L = ENG \vee L = RUS) \wedge \neg\, P = SPR)$$

**Definition 4.2.2** (Inquiry Problem) Let $B = (K, R)$ with $R = \{r_1, r_2, \ldots, r_m\}$ be an m-attribute file and let $r_{s,1}, r_{s,2}, \ldots, r_{s,t_s}$ (for $1 \leqslant s \leqslant m$) denote the $t_s$ values of the attribute $r_s$. The variable $\langle INQ \rangle$ in the following Backus system defines the set of *inquiries*.

$$\langle INQ \rangle \quad ::= \langle Term \rangle\,|\,\langle Term \rangle \vee \langle INQ \rangle$$

$$\langle Term \rangle \quad ::= \langle Fact \rangle\,|\,\langle Fact \rangle \wedge \langle Term \rangle\,|\,\langle Fact \rangle \wedge \neg \langle Term \rangle$$

$$\langle Fact \rangle \quad ::= \langle EQ \rangle\,|\,(\langle INQ \rangle)$$

$$\langle EQ \rangle \quad ::= r_1 = r_{1,1}\,|\,r_1 = r_{1,2}\,|\cdots|\,r_1 = r_{1,t_1}\,|$$
$$\qquad\qquad r_2 = r_{2,1}\,|\,r_2 = r_{2,2}\,|\cdots|\,r_2 = r_{2,t_2}\,|$$
$$\qquad\qquad \cdot$$
$$\qquad\qquad \cdot$$
$$\qquad\qquad \cdot$$
$$\qquad\qquad r_m = r_{m,1}\,|\,r_m = r_{m,2}\,|\cdots|\,r_m = r_{m,t_m}$$

The *inquiry problem* is to determine for each inquiry all nodes $k \in K$ that satisfy the conditions defined by the inquiry.

---

[4]Notice that this is a generalization of the search problem presented in Def. 2.7.1.

**Example 4.2.2** The Backus system corresponding to the three-attribute file of Example 4.2.1 is

$$\langle \text{INQ} \rangle \quad ::= \langle \text{Term} \rangle \, | \, \text{Term} \rangle \vee \langle \text{INQ} \rangle$$

$$\langle \text{Term} \rangle \quad ::= \langle \text{Fact} \rangle \, | \, \langle \text{Fact} \rangle \wedge \langle \text{Term} \rangle \, | \, \langle \text{Fact} \rangle \wedge \neg \langle \text{Term} \rangle$$

$$\langle \text{Fact} \rangle \quad ::= \langle \text{EQ} \rangle \, | \, (\langle \text{INQ} \rangle)$$

$$\langle \text{EQ} \rangle \quad ::= S = CSC \, | \, S = MAT \, | \, S = PHY \, | \, S = CHE \, |$$
$$\qquad\qquad L = GER \, | \, L = ENG \, | \, L = FRE \, | \, L = RUS \, |$$
$$\qquad\qquad P = TEU \, | \, P = DOV \, | \, P = SPR \, | \, P = PH \, | \, P = WIL$$

and typical inquiries are therefore

(a)   $S = CSC \wedge (L = GER \vee (L = ENG \vee L = RUS) \wedge \neg P = SPR)$

(b)   $S = MAT \wedge P = TEU \vee S = CSC \wedge L = ENG \vee P = DOV \wedge L = RUS$

(c)   $(S = MAT \wedge P = TEU) \vee (S = CSC \wedge L = ENG) \vee (P = DOV \wedge L = RUS)$

(d)   $S = MAT \wedge (P = TEU \vee S = CSC) \wedge ((L = ENG \vee P = DOV) \wedge L = RUS)$

(e)   $S = MAT \wedge S = CSC \wedge P = TEU$

where, for example, b and c are equivalent but d is different from them. Further, e describes an empty set since books are requested that simultaneously belong to the subject areas CSC and MAT and, for the concept we are using for equivalence classes, a book cannot belong at the same time to different equivalence classes (relative to one relation).

Later in this section three techniques will be described for solving the inquiry problem and several extensions of the inquiry problem will be mentioned.

**Definition 4.2.3** (Sequential Search of an m-Attribute File) The nodes of the m-attribute file are stored in any way. To solve an inquiry problem they are examined successively to see if they fulfill the required conditions.

This method corresponds to the sequential search in Def. 2.7.2. The sequential search is recommended for linear lists only in the rarest cases since other more efficient techniques are known for linear lists. The available search techniques are not always applicable to m-attribute files, however, so sometimes the sequential search remains the best solution. This is the case particularly if several inquiries are being made simultaneously (since regardless of the number of inquiries each node must be examined only once) or if the inquiries are not well-suited for more specialized solution techniques.

**Definition 4.2.4** Let $F_A$ and $F_B$ be two sorted sequences of addresses of nodes, which together comprise all the nodes of a certain set of nodes K that have property

A or B.[5] To construct sorted sequences $F_{A \vee B}$, $F_{A \wedge B}$, $F_{A \wedge \neg B}$ of addresses consisting of the addresses of exactly those nodes of K that have the property $A \vee B$, $A \wedge B$, or $A \wedge \neg B$, it suffices to go through the two sequences $F_A$ and $F_B$ a single time, as with a merging process, and choose the appropriate nodes.

The significance of *multilinked structures* and *inverted list structures* is that for a given m-attribute file each set of nodes determined by a particular value of a certain attribute can be directly obtained and the compound attributes specified in an inquiry can be interpreted as combinations of properties. The techniques described above can be used for processing such inquiries.

**Definition 4.2.5** (Searching Multilinked Structures) Let $B = (K, R)$, $R = \{r_1, r_2, \ldots, r_m\}$, be an m-attribute file. For multilinking, the nodes are numbered arbitrarily as $k_1, k_2, \ldots, k_n$ and each node $k \in K$ is associated with a memory location having m pointer fields. The group of memory locations corresponding in this way to the n nodes is called the *data table*. Each node $k_i$, for each attribute $r_s$, points to an additional node with the same attribute value; i.e., $k_i$ points using the sth pointer field to that node $k_j$ with the smallest $j > i$ for which $v(r_s(k_i)) = v(r_s(k_j))$. If there is no such node $k_j$, then for the sth pointer field of $k_i$, $\rho_s k_i = 0$. For each value X of every attribute $r_s$ there is an additional memory location in the *attribute table* that points to that node $k_i$ in the data table with smallest i for which $v(r_s(k_i)) = X$.

If an m-attribute file is stored using multilinking, then the addresses of all nodes whose sth attribute has a certain value can be determined directly: in the data table they are chained, using the sth pointer field, and the address of the first node in the chain can be found in the attribute table.

**Example 4.2.3** Figure 4.2.1 shows the multilinked storage of 15 nodes $k_1, k_2, \ldots, k_{15}$ of the three-attribute file from Example 4.2.1.

For the inquiry $S = CSC \wedge (L = GER \vee (L = RUS \vee L = ENG) \wedge \neg P = SPR)$ the following addresses arise using Fig. 4.2.1 and Def. 4.2.4:

| | |
|---|---|
| $L = RUS$: | 75 |
| $L = ENG$: | 62,63,68,71,74; therefore, |
| $L = RUS \vee L = ENG$: | 62,63,68,71,74,75 |
| $P = SPR$: | 68,69,71; therefore, |
| $(L = RUS \vee L = ENG) \wedge \neg P = SPR$: | 62,63,74,75 |
| $L = GER$: | 61,64,65,66,67,69,70, 72, 73; therefore, |
| $L = GER \vee (L = RUS \vee L = ENG) \wedge \neg P = SPR$: | 61,62,63,64,65,66,67, 69,70,72,73,74,75 |
| $S = CSC$: | 61,65,66,68,69,70, 75; therefore, |
| $S = CSC \wedge (L = GER \vee (L = RUS \vee L = ENG)$ $\wedge \neg P = SPR)$: | 61,65,66,69,70,75 |

---

[5]In the following, property X always means that a certain attribute has the value X, though there may be other properties.

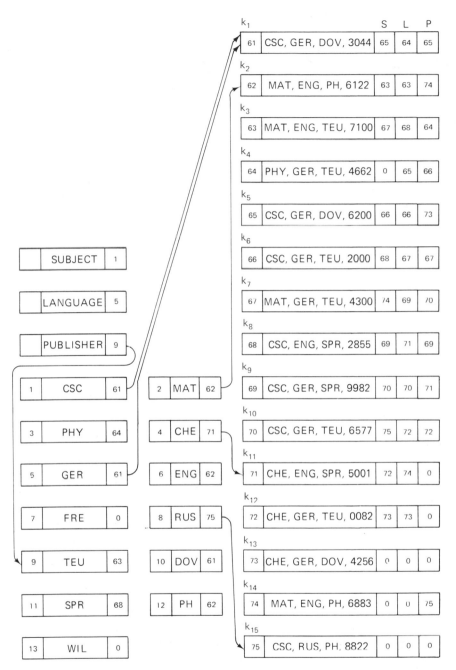

**Figure 4.2.1**

207

For large m-attribute files[6] it is not possible to place the whole data table in the fast storage of a computer. Rather it is usually necessary to store the table (or part of it) in a secondary storage device such as magnetic tape. Then multilinking requires too much effort, however, since to follow through the chain it may be necessary to read several blocks of data from the secondary storage device. An alternative to the use of multilinking is the *inverted list*.

**Definition 4.2.6** (Searching Inverted Lists) Let $B = (K, R)$, $R = \{r_1, r_2, \ldots, r_m\}$, be an m-attribute file. In an *inverted list* again the nodes are stored in a *data table* but now the memory locations need not have pointer fields. For every attribute $r_s$ and every value X of the attribute $r_s$ there is a *list of addresses* that gives the addresses of all nodes k with $v(r_s(k)) = X$. The lists of addresses are stored and an *attribute table* (similar to that used for multilinked structures) is designed so that every memory location in the attribute table now points to the beginning of a list of addresses.

In this way, inquiries can be handled just as with multilinked structures; however, a secondary storage can be used for the data table, and even for the lists of addresses, without significant loss of efficiency.

Figure 4.2.2 shows an inverted list of the three-attribute file of Fig. 4.2.1. The lists of addresses are linked in memory.

**Example 4.2.4** Let there be given a three-attribute file for books as in Example 4.2.1, stored using an inverted list. We shall design a program segment that will print out the appropriate books for any inquiry.

The declarations for m books and the four subject areas, four languages, and five publishers described in Example 4.2.1 are **DCL** (S(M), L(M), P(M), NU(M)) **CHAR** (K); and **DCL** (D(O: M1), R(0: M1), ZG(13)) **FIXED BIN**;. Here S(I), L(I), P(I), and NU(I) represent a memory location in the data table and give the subject area, language, publisher, and number for a book; D and R serve for the linked storage of the lists of addresses considered first and later generated, and the array ZG represents the attribute table consisting of 13 start pointers for the 13 address sequences corresponding to the attribute values being considered. The following numbering is used:

$$S = CSC \ldots 1, S = MAT \ldots 2, S = PHY \ldots 3, S = CHE \ldots 4,$$

$$L = GER \ldots 5, L = ENG \ldots 6, L = FRE \ldots 7, L = RUS \ldots 8,$$

$$P = TEU \ldots 9, P = DOV \ldots 10, P = SPR \ldots 11, P = PH \ldots . 12,$$

$$P = WIL \ldots 13$$

The first memory locations not used for address sequences are stored linked as a supply stack with start pointer AF. The variable BOUNDARY indicates that every D(I), R(I) with $I \leqslant$ BOUNDARY belongs to the original list of addresses, and every D(I), R(I) with $I >$ BOUNDARY belongs only to a temporarily built list of addresses.

---

[6] In just such files the use of faster techniques is particularly necessary.

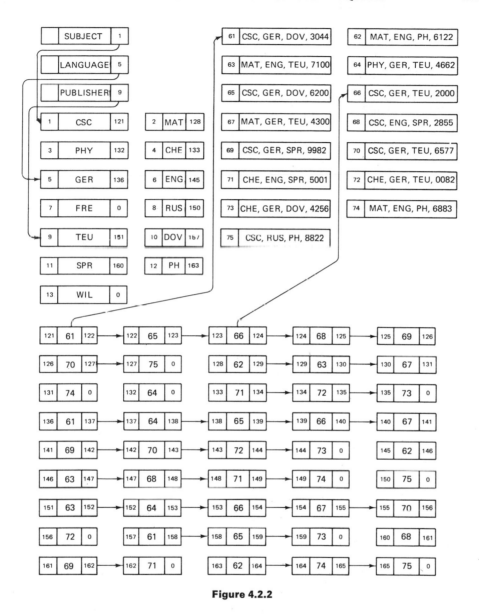

**Figure 4.2.2**

D(0) containing the number 999999999 (larger than any address possibly occurring) serves as a stopper, and R(0) is used to avoid exceptional cases.

We can assume that the inquiry is submitted in a modified form, namely,

(a)    Parenthesis-free, so that the operators $\vee$, $\wedge$, $\wedge\neg$ occur after the operands rather then between operands; see Def. 2.2.4.

(b) The inquiries S = CSC, S = MAT, ... are replaced by their numbering selected above.

(c) The operators $\vee$, $\wedge$, $\wedge\neg$ are replaced by $-1$, $-2$, $-3$, and the number 0 indicates that the end of the inquiry has been reached.

For example, the inquiry

$$S = CSC \wedge (L = GER \vee (L = ENG \vee L = RUS) \wedge\neg P = SPR)$$

corresponds to the modified inquiry

$$1, 5, 6, 8, -1, 11, -3, -1, -2, 0.$$

For simplicity in the following program segment, input consists of inquiries that are already modified as just described. Notice that the transformation of inquiries into modified inquiries can be accomplished with a Backus pair $P = (B, \bar{B})$, using $P(\langle I \rangle, \langle MI \rangle)$, where B consists of the productions

$$\langle I \rangle \quad ::= \langle INQ \rangle$$

$$\langle INQ \rangle \quad ::= \langle Term \rangle | \langle Term \rangle \vee \langle INQ \rangle$$

$$\langle Term \rangle \quad ::= \langle Fact \rangle | \langle Fact \rangle \wedge \langle Term \rangle | \langle Fact \rangle \wedge \neg \langle Term \rangle$$

$$\langle Fact \rangle \quad ::= \langle EQ \rangle | (\langle INQ \rangle)$$

$$\langle EQ \rangle \quad ::= S = CSC | S = MAT | S = PHY | S = CHE | L = GER |$$

$$\qquad\qquad L = ENG | L = FRE | L = RUS | P = TEU | P = DOV |$$

$$\qquad\qquad P = SPR | P = PH | P = WIL$$

and $\bar{B}$ consists of the productions

$$\langle MI \rangle \quad ::= \langle INQ \rangle \, 0$$

$$\langle INQ \rangle \quad ::= \langle Term \rangle | \langle Term \rangle \langle INQ \rangle -1,$$

$$\langle Term \rangle \quad ::= \langle Fact \rangle | \langle Fact \rangle \langle Term \rangle -2, | \langle Fact \rangle \langle Term \rangle -3,$$

$$\langle Fact \rangle \quad ::= \langle EQ \rangle | \langle INQ \rangle$$

$$\langle EQ \rangle \quad ::= 1, | 2, | 3, | 4, | 5, | 6, | 7, | 8, | 9, | 10, | 11, | 12, | 13,$$

For processing a given (modified) inquiry, a stack A is used that contains the current first addresses of the lists of addresses. If the next number of the input is $n > 0$, then n indicates an address list whose first address is added to A; if the next number in the input is $n < 0$, then n is one of the operations $\vee$, $\wedge$, $\wedge\neg$ and from the two lists of addresses determined by the top nodes of A, a new address list is produced whose first address replaces the two top addresses in A. (This is done using the procedure "OR" if $n = -1$, "AND" if $n = -2$, and "ANDNOT" if $n = -3$.) If the next number of the input is $n = 0$, then all books whose addresses occur in the address list determined by the top node of A are printed.

```
INQUIRY: PROC OPTIONS (MAIN);
   DCL (A(100), P, IP, N) FIXED BIN;
   OR: PROCEDURE (P1, P2) RETURNS (FIXED BIN);
   /* A(P1) AND A(P2) GIVE THE FIRST ADDRESSES OF TWO
      SORTED ADDRESS LISTS A1 and A2 THAT ARE MERGED INTO
      ONE LIST C. ADDRESSES OCCURRING MORE THAN ONCE
      ARE INCLUDED ONLY ONCE. THE VALUE OF THE PROCEDURE
      IS THE FIRST ADDRESS OF THE LIST C STORED AS A CHAIN */
   DCL (P1, P2, QA, QE, Q1, Q2) FIXED BIN;
   QA = AF; QE = 0;
   /* AF IS THE START POINTER OF THE SUPPLY STACK; QA AND QE
      ARE START AND END POINTERS FOR C */
   Q1 = A(P1); Q2 = A(P2);
   DO WHILE ((D(Q2) ¬= 999999999) | (D(Q1) < D(Q2)));
      IF D(Q1) < D(Q2) THEN DO;
         IF D(Q1) ¬= D(QE) THEN DO;
            /* IF D(Q1) = D(QE) THEN D(Q1) ALREADY OCCURS
               IN C. OTHERWISE D(Q1) IS TAKEN IN THE LIST C */
            D(AF) = D(Q1); R(QE) = AF; QE = AF; AF = R(AF);
            R(QE) = 0; END;
         IF (R(Q1) = 0) & (A(P1) > BOUNDARY) THEN DO;
            /* THEN THE END OF THE LIST A1 IS REACHED;
               A1 WAS ONLY A TEMPORARY LIST AND ALL MEMORY
               LOCATIONS ARE ADDED TO THE SUPPLY STACK OF
               AVAILABLE SPACE */
            R(Q1) = AF; AF = A(P1); Q1 = 0; END;
                              ELSE Q1 = R(Q1);
                  END;
            ELSE DO;
               IF D(Q2) ¬= D(QE) THEN DO;
                  D(AF) = D(Q2); R(QE) = AF; QE = AF;
                  AF = R(AF); R(QE) = 0;
                                    END;
               IF (R(Q2) = 0) & (A(P2) > BOUNDARY) THEN DO;
                  R(Q2) = AF; AF = A(P2); Q2 = 0; END;
                           ELSE Q2 = R(Q2);
                     END;
      END;
   IF QE = 0 THEN RETURN (0); ELSE RETURN (QA);
   END OR;
   AND: PROCEDURE (P1, P2) RETURNS (FIXED BIN);
   DCL (P1, P2, QA, QE, Q1, Q2) FIXED BIN;
   QA = AF; QE = 0; Q1 = A(P1); Q2 = A(P2);
   DO WHILE ((D(Q2) ¬= D(Q1)) | (D(Q2) ¬= 999999999));
      IF D(Q2) < D(Q1) THEN DO;
         IF (R(Q2) = 0) & (A(P2) > BOUNDARY) THEN DO;
            R(Q2) = AF; AF = A(P2); Q2 = 0; END;
                        ELSE Q2 = R(Q2);
                     END;
      ELSE DO;
         IF D(Q2) = D(Q1) THEN DO;
            D(AF) = D(Q1); R(QE) = AF; QE = AF; AF = R(AF);
            R(QE) = 0; END;
```

```
        IF (R(Q1) = 0) & (A(P1) > BOUNDARY) THEN DO;
          R(Q1) = AF; AF = A(P1); Q1 = 0; END;
                        ELSE Q1 = R(Q1);
              END;
    END;
    IF QE = 0 THEN RETURN (0); ELSE RETURN (QA);
    END AND;
    ANDNOT: PROCEDURE (P1, P2) RETURNS (FIXED BIN);
                /* ANALOGOUS TO "OR" AND "AND" */
    PRINT: PROCEDURE (P);
          DCL (P, Q, T) FIXED BIN;
          Q = A(P);
          DO WHILE (Q ¬= 0);
                T = D(Q); PUT LIST (S(T), L(T), P(T), NU(T));
                Q = R(Q);
          END;
    END PRINT;
    P = 0; GET LIST (N);
    DO WHILE (N ¬= 0);
        IF N > 0 THEN DO;
            P = P + 1; A(P) = ZG(N); PUT LIST (A(P));
                    END;
        ELSE IF N = −1 THEN DO;
            A(P − 1) = OR (P − 1, P); P = P − 1;
                        END;
        ELSE IF N = −2 THEN DO
            A(P − 1) = AND (P − 1, P); P = P − 1;
                        END;
        ELSE IF N = −3 THEN DO;
            A(P − 1) = ANDNOT (P − 1, P); P = P − 1;
                        END;
        GET LIST (N);
    END;
    CALL PRINT (P);
END;
```

Work through the program for the input 1, 5, 6, 8, −1, 11, −3, −1, −2, 0 from Fig. 4.2.2 with AF = 166 and BOUNDARY = 165.

In the procedure "AND," both sequences are processed completely to the end even though we could stop when the end of one sequence is reached. This is done in order to be able to add all memory locations no longer in use to the supply stack but it could be avoided with appropriate programming.

If the data table contains n entries, if there are at most m nodes for each attribute, and if an inquiry contains at most t operations, then to process the inquiry using an inverted list at most $2m + 3m + \cdots + (t − 1)m \approx t^2m/2$ comparisons are necessary since, for the ith operation, address lists with a total of at most $(i + 1)m$ elements must be searched. To process an inquiry with a sequential search, $\approx tn$ comparisons are required. The inverted list is therefore to be preferred if $tm < 2n$; otherwise it should be used only with discretion.

Since the use of an inverted list is more desirable for shorter address lists, we often look for ways to shorten the address lists. One way to reduce the length of the address sequences drastically is to introduce new attributes by using combinations of existing attributes. Consider, for example, the three-attribute file from Example 4.2.1. If we allow only inquiries in which two attributes are connected by the operator $\wedge$, i.e. inquiries such as

$$((P = SPR \wedge L = GER) \wedge \neg (S = CSC \wedge L = ENG)) \vee (S = MAT \wedge P = DOV)$$

then for every pair $(x, y)$ of attribute values, the (shortest) address list of all nodes with attribute value $x$ and attribute value $y$ can be produced.

Increased efficiency in dealing with inverted lists is also possible (a) by appropriately rewriting the given inquiry and (b) in the case of address lists of very different lengths, instead of the "merging technique" described in Def. 4.2.4, by using a "check technique": if, for example, attribute A occurs "seldom" but attributes B and C occur "frequently," then it is practical to rewrite the inquiry $A \wedge (B \vee C)$ as $(A \wedge B) \vee (A \wedge C)$. Then to determine $A \wedge B$ it is not necessary to go through both address lists but only the shortest and then for each address in this list to check to see if the node given by the address also satisfies condition B.[7]

As an alternative to the sequential search and to the use of an inverted list, the *block-by-block* search is sometimes suggested. The set of nodes K of the m-attribute file is divided into subsets or *blocks* $B_1, B_2, \ldots, B_m$ in such a way that for any inquiry A many blocks $B_i$ can immediately be excluded and only the remaining blocks are searched sequentially.

In actual applications, the inquiry problem described in this section often occurs in a significantly more general and complex form. Several important variations are mentioned.

(1)   Besides the combinations $A \vee B$, $A \wedge B$, $A \wedge \neg B$ of conditions A and B, some other combinations such as $A \vee \neg B$ and $\neg A \wedge \neg B$ are allowed.

(2)   An attribute can have many values so the attribute table and the inquiries can become quite extensive. If, for example, an attribute S (salary) is given with values $0, 1, 2, 3, \ldots, 8000$, then an inquiry for all persons with a salary between 2000 and 3000 would require a thousand operands:

$$S = 2000 \vee S = 2001 \vee S = 2002 \vee \cdots \vee S = 2999 \vee S = 3000.$$

A frequently chosen remedy in such a situation consists of creating a new attribute SR (salary range) to combine persons whose salaries differ only in the ones or tens place. (Of course, by doing this, inquiries of certain types are difficult or impossible: an inquiry to determine all persons with a salary between 2550 and 2650 would not be possible.)

---

[7]This technique is usually not practical if the data table is stored in a secondary storage device.

(3)  Operators other than $\vee$, $\wedge$, $\neg$ may be allowed in the inquiries, such as the relational operators $>$, $<$, $\geqslant$, $\leqslant$ or a special operator N to determine the number of elements of a set. For example, using $S \geqslant 2000 \wedge S \leqslant 2500$ we describe all persons with a salary between 2000 and 2500, while $N(S \geqslant 2000 \wedge S \leqslant 2500)$ determines the number of such persons.

(4)  The data structure under discussion need not be an m-attribute file. If, for example, in an m-attribute file there is an attribute subject area with values CSC and MAT, then every node must be classified as either CSC or MAT, although one classification with two approaches might be just as useful.

(5)  The data structure under discussion can hardly be considered static. In general, it must be taken into account that the collection of nodes and values of attributes can change in the course of time.

### Remarks and References

Among the books on information retrieval, Knuth [2] and Lefkovitz [1], [2] are strongly suggested. A data structure that is completely dependent on the allowed inquiries is proposed in Wong [1].

### Exercises

**4.2.1**  Write a program segment to define the procedure "ANDNOT" in Example 4.2.4.

**4.2.2**  As input there is given a number n followed by n quadruples (S, L, P, NU), each of which describes a book, as in Example 4.2.1, by a subject area S, a language L, a publisher P, and a number NU. Write a program to store the data structure with three relations S, L, P, using (a) linked allocation and (b) an inverted list. The program should also print out the stored data table, the attribute table, and in case b also the address lists.

**4.2.3**  From the program segment for Exercise 4.2.2 and the program in Example 4.2.4, produce a complete program system to store a small file of books that allows inquiries of the type described in Example 4.2.4 and gives a response to such inquiries.

### Remarks on the Exercises

Many additional problems and hints to the solution of exercises can be found in Gruenberger [1] and Maurer [2]. The method of solving Exercise 2.1.4 corresponds exactly to the technique used in Quicksort. Permutations using stacks as in Exercise 2.2.2 are studied in Knuth [1]. The suggestion for generating random numbers in Exercise 2.4.4 is derived from Maurer [2] where it is discussed in detail. In Exercise 3.4.7 it turns out that for a normal eight by eight chessboard a knight's tour can be found without backtracking. Exercise 4.1.6 is actually more complicated if we try to carry out the management of available space described at the end of Sec. 4.1 by using a supply stack.

# Index of Symbols

*Standard Symbols*

| | | | |
|---|---|---|---|
| $=$ | equal | $\div$ | integer division |
| $\neq$ | not equal | $/$ | division |
| $<$ | less than | $\wedge$ | logical and |
| $\leqslant$ | less than or equal | $\vee$ | logical or |
| $>$ | greater than | $\neg$ | logical not |
| $\geqslant$ | greater than or equal | $\uparrow$ | exponentiation |
| $\approx$ | approximately equal | $\sqrt{\phantom{x}}$ | square root |
| $+$ | addition | $!$ | factorial symbol |
| $-$ | subtraction | | $n! = n \times (n - 1) \times \cdots \times$ |
| $\times$ | product | | $2 \times 1$ |

*Set Symbols*

| | | | |
|---|---|---|---|
| $\{\ \}$ | set parentheses | $\subset$ | proper subset of |
| $\|$ | set definition symbol | $\supseteq$ | contains |
| $\in$ | is an element of | $\supset$ | properly contains |
| $\notin$ | is not an element of | $\cup$ | set union |
| $\varnothing$ | empty set | $\cap$ | set intersection |
| $\subseteq$ | subset of | | |

*Backus Symbols*

| | | | |
|---|---|---|---|
| $\langle\ \rangle$ | Backus parentheses | $\xrightarrow{*}$ | one (or more) substitution |
| $::=$ | definition symbol | | steps |
| $\|$ | alternative symbol | $\Sigma$ | terminal alphabet |
| $\longrightarrow$ | one substitution step | | |

215

*Greek Alphabet*

| | |
|---|---|
| $\alpha$ | address of a memory location (Sec. 1.3) |
| $\beta$ | load factor (Sec. 2.4) |
| $\gamma$ | an auxiliary value (Sec. 2.7) position information for a node (Sec. 3.3) |
| $\delta$ | data field of a memory location (Sec. 1.3) |
| $\epsilon$ | distance (Sec. 3.3) |
| $\lambda$ | length of a branch to a node (Sec. 3.1) |
| $\mu$ | an auxiliary value (Sec. 2.6, 3.3) |
| $\nu$ | level number of a node (Sec. 3.1) |
| $\pi$ | position in a sequence (Sec. 1.1) |
| $\rho$ | pointer field of a memory location (Sec. 1.3) |
| $\sigma$ | memory location with a given address (Sec. 1.3) |
| $\tau$ | indicator (Sec. 1.3) |
| $\omega$ | value of a node (Sec. 1.2) |
| $\xi$ | memory location for a node (Sec. 1.3) |

# Bibliography

ADELSON-VELSKII, G. M. [1]; LANDIS, E. M.: "Ein Algorithmus zur Informationsorganisation" (Russian). *Doklady Akad. Nauk SSSR* **146** (1962) 263–266.

AHO, A. V. [1]; ULLMAN, J. D. [2]: *The Theory of Parsing, Translation and Compiling.* Vol. I: *Parsing.* Prentice-Hall, Englewood Cliffs, N.J., 1972.

AHO, A. V. [2]; ULLMAN, J. D. [3]: *The Theory of Parsing, Translation and Compiling.* Vol. II: *Compiling.* Prentice-Hall, Englewood Cliffs, N.J., 1973.

BACKUS, J. W. [1]: "The Syntax and Semantics of the Proposed International Algebraic Language of the Zurich ACM-GAMM Conf. ICIP," Paris (1959).

BAYER, R. [1]: "Symmetric Binary B-Trees." *Acta Informatica* **1** (1972) 290–306.

BELL, J. R. [1]; KAMAN, C. H.: "Linear Quotient Hash Codes." *C. ACM* **13**, No. 11 (1970) 675–677.

BERZTISS, A. T. [1]: *Data Structures.* Academic Press, New York, N.Y., 1971.

BERZTISS, A. T. [2]: "A Backtrack Procedure for Isomorphism of Directed Graphs." *J. ACM* **20**, No. 3 (1973) 365–377.

BLUM, M. [1]; *et al.*: "Time Bounds for Selection." *J. Comp. System Science* **7**, No. 4 (1973) 448–461.

BOBROW, D. G. [1]; RAPHAEL, B.: "A Comparison of List-Processing Computer Languages." *C. ACM* **7** (1964) 231–240.

BRUNO, J. [1]; COFFMAN, E. G., Jr.: "Nearly Optimal Binary Search Trees." *Proc. of the IFIP Congress* **71** (1972) 99–103.

CRANE, C. A. [1]: "Linear Lists and Priority Queues as Balanced Binary Trees." Stanford University Ph.D. Thesis, 1972.

d'IMPERIO, M. [1]: *Data Structures and their Representation in Storage.* Oxford—New York—Toronto—Sydney, 1969. Annual Review in Automatic Programming 5.

217

DOMSCHKE, W. [1]: *Kürzeste Wege in Graphen: Algorithmen, Verfahrensvergleiche*. Meisenheim/Glan, 1972. Mathematical Systems in Economics 2.

DÖRFLER, W. [1]; MÜHLBACHER, J.: *Graphentheorie für Informatiker*. Berlin, 1973. Samml. Göschen Bd. 6016.

ELSON, M. [1]: *Data Structures*. Science Research Associates, Chicago, Ill., 1975.

FORD, L. R. [1]; JOHNSON, S. M.: "A Tournament Problem." *Amer. Math. Month.* **66** (1959) 387–389.

FOSTER, C. C. [1]: "Information Storage and Retrieval Using AVL Trees." *Proc. ACM 30 Nat. Conf.* (1965) 192–205.

FOSTER, J. M. [1]: *Listenverarbeitung*. Munich, 1970.

GINSBURG, S. [1]: *The Mathematical Theory of Context-Free Languages*. McGraw-Hill, New York, N.Y., 1966.

GRUENBERGER, F. [1]; JAFFRAY, J.: *Problems for Computer Solution*. Wiley, New York, N.Y., 1966.

HARARY, F. [1]: *Graph Theory*. Addison Wesley, Reading, Mass., 1969.

HARRISON, M. C. [1]: *Data Structures and Programming*. Scott, Foresman, and Co., Glenview, Ill., 1973.

HEISING, W. P. [1]: "A Note on Random Addressing Techniques." *IBM Systems J.* (1963) 112–116.

HELLER, J. [1]; SCHNEIDERMAN, B. [2]: "A Graph Theoretic Model of Data Structures." *ACM SIGIR Forum* **7**, No. 4 (1972) 36–44.

HERMES, H. [1]: *Aufzählbarkeit, Entscheidbarkeit, Berechenbarkeit*. Berlin—Göttingen—Heidelberg, 1961.

HOARE, C. A. R. [1]: "Quicksort." *Computer J.* **5** (1962) 10–15.

HU, T. C. [1]; TUCKER, A. C.: "Optimal Computer Search Trees and Variable-Length Alphabetic Codes." *SIAM J. Appl. Math.* **21**, No. 4 (1971) 514–532.

HUFFMANN, D. [1]: "A Method for the Construction of Minimum Redundancy Codes." *Proc. IRE* **40** (1952) 1098–1101.

*IBM System/360 PL/I Language Reference Manual* (GC28-8201-3).

KANDZIA, P. [1]; LANGMAACK, H.: *Informatik: Programmierung*. Stuttgart, 1973. Teubner Studienbücher Informatik, Leitfäden der angewandten Mathematik und Mechanik Bd. 18.

KNOTT, G. D. [1]: "A Balanced Tree Storage and Retrieval Algorithm." *Proc. Info. Stor. and Retr.* (1971), U. of Indiana, Bloomington, Ind.

KNUTH, D. E. [1]: *The Art of Computer Programming*. Vol. I: *Fundamental Algorithms*. Addison-Wesley, Reading, Mass., 1967.

KNUTH, D. E. [2]: *The Art of Computer Programming*. Vol. III: *Sorting and Searching*. Addison-Wesley, Reading, Mass., 1973.

KOLESAR, P. J. [1]: "A Branch and Bound Algorithm for the Knapsack Problem." *Management Science* **13**, No. 9 (1967) 723–735.

KRAL, J. [1]: "Some Properties of the Scatter Storage Technique with Linear Probing." *Computer J.* **14**, No. 2 (1971) 145–149.

KRIEGEL, H. P. [1]: "Formale Übersetzungen." Diplomarbeit Univ. Karlsruhe, Institut für Angewandte Informatik und Formale Beschreibungsverfahren (1973).

LANDAUER, W. I. [1]: "The Balanced Tree and its Utilization in Information Retrieval." *IEEE Trans.* **EC 12** (1963) 863–871.

LEFKOVITZ, D. [1]: *Data Management for On-Line Systems.* Hayden Book Co., Rochelle Park, N.J., 1974.

LEFKOVITZ, D. [2]: *File Structures for On-Line Systems.* Hayden Book Co., New York, N.Y., 1969.

LEWIS, T. G. [1]; Smith M. Z.: Applying Data Structures. Houghton Mifflin Co., Boston, Mass., 1976.

LUM, V. Y. [1]: "Multi-Attribute Retrieval with Combined Indexes." *C. ACM* **13**, No. 11 (1970) 660–665.

LUM, V. Y. [2]; YUEN, P. S. T.; DODD, M.: "Key-to-Address Transform Techniques: A Performance Study." *C. ACM* **14**, No. 4 (1971) 228–239.

MARTIN, W. A. [1]: "Sorting." *ACM Computing Surveys* **3**, No. 4 (1971) 147–173.

MARTIN, W. A. [2]; NESS, D. N.: "Optimizing Binary Trees Grown with a Sorting Algorithm." *C. ACM* **15**, No. 2 (1972) 88–93.

MAURER, H. [1]: *Theoretische Grundlagen der Programmiersprachen.* Mannheim, 1969. BI-Hochschultaschenbücher Bd. 404/404a.

MAURER, H. [2]; WILLIAMS, M. R.: *Programming Problems and Techniques.* Prentice-Hall, Englewood Cliffs, N.J., 1972.

McCARTHY, J.; [1] *et al.*: *LISP 1.5 Programmers Manual.* MIT Press, Cambridge, Mass., 1962.

NEUHOLD, E. J. [1]; LAWSON, H. W.: *The PL/I Machine: An Introduction to Programming.* Addison-Wesley, Reading, Mass., 1971.

NEUMANN, K. [1]: *Graphentheorie.* Hauser Verlag, Munich, 1975.

NIEVERGELT, J. [1]; REINGOLD, E. M.: "Binary Search Trees of Bounded Balance." *SIAM J. Computing* **2**, No. 1 (1973) 33–43.

NOLTEMEIER, H. [1]: *Datenstrukturen und höhere Programmiertechniken.* Berlin, 1972. Samml. Göschen Bd. 5012.

PERLIS, A. J. [1]; THORNTON, C.: "Symbol Manipulation by Threaded Lists." *C. ACM* **3** (1960) 195–204.

PRICE, C. E. [1]: "Table Lookup Techniques." *ACM Computing Surveys* **3**, No. 2 (1971) 49–65.

RIVEST, R. L. [1]: "On Self-Organizing Sequential Search Heuristics," 15th Annual Symp. on Switching and Automata Theory, New Orleans (1974) 122–126.

SCHNEIDERMAN, B. [1]: "Bibliography on Data Base Structures." *ACM SIGIR Forum* **8**, No. 2 (1973) 15–22.

SCHORR, H. [1]; WAITE, W. M.: "An Efficient Machine-Independent Procedure for Garbage Collection in Various List Structures." *C. ACM* **10** (1967) 501–506.

SIX, H. W. [1]: "Verbesserung des m-Weg-Suchverfahrens." *Agnew. Informatik* **2** (1973) 79–83.

STANFEL, L. E. [1]: "Practical Aspects of Doubly Chained Trees for Retrieval." *J. ACM* **19**, No. 3 (1972) 425–436.

STONE, H. S. [1]; SIEWIOREK, D. P.: *Introduction to Computer Organization and Data Structures*. McGraw-Hill, New York, N.Y., 1975.

SUSSENGUTH, E. H. [1]: "Use of Tree Structures for Processing Files." *C. ACM* **6**, No. 5 (1963) 272–279.

ULLMAN, J. D. [1]: "The Design of Hashing Functions." Technical Report No. 85, Elec. Eng. Dept, Princeton Univ., Princeton, N.J., 1970.

VAN EMDEN, M. H. [1]: "Increasing the Efficiency of Quicksort." *C. ACM* **13**, No. 11 (1970) 693–694.

WEDEKIND, H. [1]: *Datenorganisation*. Berlin, 1970.

WEINBERG, F. (Ed.) [1]: *Einführung in die Methode Branch and Bound*. Berlin—Heidelberg—New York, 1968. Lecture Notes in Operations Research and Math. Economics No. 4.

WILLIAMS, J. W. J. [1]: "Heapsort." *C. ACM* **7**, No. 6 (1964) 349–358.

WONG, E. [1]; CHIANG, T. C.: "Canonical Structure in Attribute Based File Organization." *C. ACM* **14**, No. 9 (1971) 593–597.

# Index

# Index